Twentieth Century World History in Focus

Harry Mills
Head of History, Taita College, New Zealand

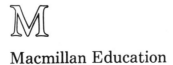

Macmillan Education

Contents

Note: References to (**T**) in the question mean that students should refer back to the text on the opposite **page**.

First published 1984
Reprinted 1985, 1986, 1987

Published by
MACMILLAN EDUCATION LTD
Houndmills, Basingstoke, Hampshire RG21 2XS
and London
Companies and representatives
throughout the world

Printed in Hong Kong

British Library Cataloguing in Publication Data
Mills, Harry
Twentieth century world history in focus.
1. History, Modern—20th century
I. Title
909.82   D421
ISBN 0-333-28662-6

1 THE ORIGINS OF THE FIRST WORLD WAR

The roots of the conflict

The birth of modern Germany

Until the 1860s Germany was little more than a loose collection of states. Then Prussia, the largest of these states, defeated her rival Austria and brought the North German states under Prussian control. France, her other rival, was then defeated in the Franco-Prussian War of 1870-71. Now the other German states joined with Prussia to form a united Germany. In the peace treaty that followed France was also forced to hand over two of her provinces, Alsace and Lorraine, to Germany.

The threat to Germany

Bismarck, the German Chancellor (Prime Minister) realised that the French would want revenge for their earlier defeat. He also thought that the other countries surrounding Germany would club together to try to destroy the strong new power.

Alliances

To stop this, Bismarck began to build up a network of *alliances* with the other European powers. He had two basic aims:
 (i) he wanted to gain friends (*allies*) for Germany
(ii) he wanted to *isolate* France from the other European powers and keep her powerless.

   Bismarck's success can be judged by looking at the most important of his alliances. In 1879 he signed a secret treaty (agreement) with Austria known as the Dual Alliance. Germany and Austria agreed to help each other if attacked by Russia. Three years later Italy signed the agreement and the Dual Alliance became the Triple Alliance. In 1887 Bismarck signed a secret alliance with Russia called the Reinsurance Treaty.

   As a result, all the mainland powers of Europe except France were tied to Germany in a network of alliances. France was isolated, friendless and therefore powerless.

(A) *France signs the peace treaty at the end of the Franco-Prussian War (1871)*

(B) *The strength of the European powers in 1900*

	Austria-Hungary	France	Germany	Great Britain	Italy	Russia
Population	45 015 000	38 641 333	56 367 176	41 605 323	32 450 000	132 960 000
Men in regular army	397 316	589 541	585 266	280 733	261 728	860 000
Annual iron & steel production (tons)	2 580 000	3 250 000	13 790 000	13 860 000	500 000	5 015 000
Annual value of foreign trade (£)	151 599 000	460 408 000	545 205 000	877 448 917	132 970 000	141 799 000
Merchant fleet (net tonnage)	313 698	1 037 720	1 941 645	9 304 108	945 000	633 820
1st class battleships		13	14	38	9	13
2nd class battleships	6	10		11	5	10
Points						
Ranking						

(Adapted from *Purnell's History of the Twentieth Century*)

Questions

1. Which country does the woman sitting down in the cartoon represent? (**A**)
2. Who are the soldiers surrounding her? What are they forcing her to do? (**A**)
3. What point is the cartoonist trying to make? (**A**)
4. What warning is Bismarck making to his emperor? (**C**)
5. Why was Bismarck so worried about France? (**T**)
6. With which European powers did Bismarck make alliances between 1879 and 1887? (**T**)
7. What was the purpose of these alliances? (**T**)
8. Copy out table (**B**) but do not put the figures in. Using the information from (**B**), indicate on a 1 to 6 scale where each power ranks according to population, size of army and so on. e.g. Russia has the largest population so it gets 1 point. Austria has the third largest population so give it 3 points. Fill in the blank columns to show each country's score. Now add up all the points for each country. Finally rank each power from strongest to weakest. The country with the least number of points will rank as the strongest power; the weakest power will have the most points. Compare and discuss your findings with the rest of the class.

(C) *Bismarck wrote to his emperor in 1872:*
'Our chief danger in the future begins at the moment when France once more appears to the [other countries] of Europe as a possible and [useful] ally.'
(Quoted in GORDON CRAIG, *Germany 1866–1945*)

5

Germany seeks to become a world power

The fall of Bismarck

In 1889 William II became Germany's new Kaiser (Emperor). He was a vain, boastful man, who had little time for Bismarck's moderate policies. William wanted Germany to become a respected *world power* with a large overseas *empire*.

First he forced Bismarck to resign. Then he appointed a number of reckless and foolish advisers. Disaster soon followed. In 1891 William decided not to renew Germany's Reinsurance Treaty with Russia. The way was now clear for an alliance between France and Russia.

In 1894 what Bismarck had always feared came true. In an alliance known as the Dual Entente, Russia promised to aid France if she was attacked by Germany. France's isolation had come to an end. Furthermore, five of Europe's great powers were split into two rival groups.

The German economy and colonial expansion

William had good cause to feel that Germany could become a leading world power. Germany's economy was growing at a fantastic rate and iron, steel, ships and engines were pouring out of her factories.

In the nineteenth century, both Britain and France had vast overseas empires and Germany was eager to do the same. A large empire would provide Germany with a market for her growing industries and the respect which the Kaiser so desperately wanted.

But most of the best land had already been taken. All that was left for Germany were a few small islands in the Pacific and some near-useless parts of Africa.

Naval expansion

Military might was a must for a world power. Germany already had the world's best army and in 1898 began to build a fleet of battleships to rival the British navy.

(A) *Some difficult terms*
An *empire* is a group of states or countries ruled over and owned by another country. The foreign territories that make up an empire are called *colonies*. The ruler of an empire is called an *emperor*. *Imperialism* is the policy or practice of building up an empire. An *imperialist* is a believer in or supporter of imperialism.

(B) *Major European colonies in 1914* (Map from JOHN HAMER, *The Twentieth Century*)

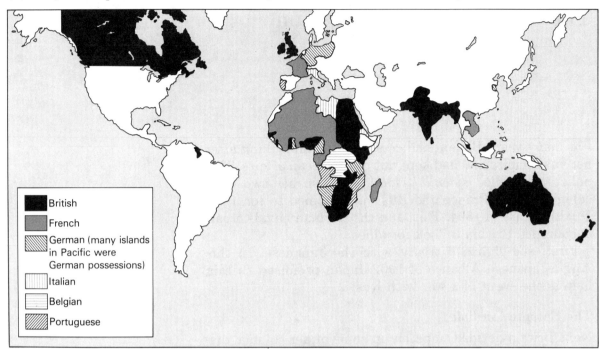

(C) *In 1898 Germany added the tiny Caroline Islands in the Pacific to its empire. This is how Von Bülow told the Kaiser about the new colony.*

'This [colonial] success will stimulate people and navy ... to follow your Majesty along the road which leads to world power, greatness and eternal glory.'

(D) *In 1897 Admiral Tirpitz, the secretary of state, sent a secret note to the Kaiser:*

'For Germany, the most dangerous enemy at the present time is England. It is also the enemy against which we most urgently require a [navy].'

(E) *In 1900 the German government publicly declared that:*

'For the protection of sea trade and colonies there is only one means – a strong battle fleet.'

(Extracts C, D and E quoted in F. FISCHER, *War of Illusions*)

Questions

1 In what areas of the world were most of Germany's colonies located? (**B**)
2 Draw a bar graph to show the sizes of the British, French and German empires. (**F**)
3 Using your own words, write a definition for each of the following terms: imperialism, imperialist, empire, colonies, emperor. (**A**)
4 What does Von Bülow's statement suggest was behind Germany's drive for colonies? (**C**)
5 Why did Admiral Tirpitz want a navy? Why do you think Tirpitz wanted this note kept secret from the British? (**D**)
6 What reason did the Germans publicly give for building a navy? (**E**)
7 Why do you think the official German government statement differed from Tirpitz's? (**D**) and (**E**)

(F) *The major colonial powers of Europe: 1914*

	Number of Colonial Territories
Britain	55
France	29
Germany	10
Netherlands	21

(Table from D. MACINTYRE, *The Great War*)

The end of splendid isolation

For many years Britain had concentrated on looking after her vast empire and had kept out of European affairs. This policy was called *splendid isolation*. Then her two chief colonial rivals, France and Russia, combined to form the Dual Entente in 1894. This, and the German naval threat, encouraged Britain to look for allies.

First, she signed a treaty with the Japanese. In this Anglo-Japanese Alliance of 1902 Japan promised Britain help in the event of a war with Russia.

The Entente Cordiale

Next Britain decided to patch up some of her colonial disputes with France. In 1904, an Entente Cordiale (friendly understanding) was signed. France said that Britain could have a free hand in Egypt. In return Britain said France could have a free hand in Morocco. The Entente Cordiale was not a military alliance. Yet Germany was furious and was determined to break it up. She therefore deliberately provoked a quarrel with France.

The first Moroccan crisis, 1905

In 1905 the German Kaiser paid a visit to the Moroccan port of Tangier. There he declared that Morocco should be independent of France. Germany calculated that in the crisis that was sure to follow, Britain would refuse to back up France. The entente would then collapse. But at the Algeciras conference, 1906, set up to solve the crisis, the opposite happened! Britain backed France, and Germany suffered a diplomatic defeat.

The Anglo-Russian Entente and Triple Entente

Germany's action also pushed Britain towards an understanding with Russia in the Anglo-Russian Entente of 1907. This meant Britain was now linked to both France and Russia, thereby creating the Triple Entente. Now Europe was divided into two great hostile camps, with the Triple Alliance on one side and the Triple Entente on the other.

(A) *'An uncertain embrace' – a German cartoonist's comment on the Entente Cordiale*

(B) *British cartoon of the Entente Cordiale – 'Let Germany be careful now'*

(C) *Europe: The alliance system*

The diagram represents the pattern of alliances and ententes at various dates between 1882 and 1907. Countries with alliances or ententes are joined together.

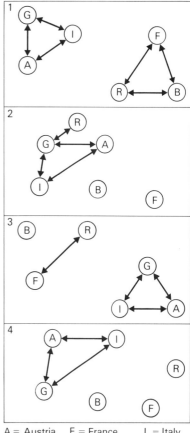

A = Austria   F = France   I = Italy
B = Britain   G = Germany   R = Russia

(Adapted from J.G. QUINN AND H.G. MAC-INTOSH, *European History 1789 to 1945*)

Questions

1 Compare the two cartoons on the Entente Cordiale. (**A**) and (**B**). What point is the German cartoonist making about the Entente Cordiale? (**A**)

2 Does the British cartoonist agree or disagree with the German cartoonist? Give reasons. (**B**)

3 Suggest reasons why the Germans were so upset by the Entente Cordiale. (**T**)

4 Which diagram in (**C**) represents the system of alliances in (a) 1882 (b) 1887 (c) 1894 (d) 1907? You may need to refer back to pages 4 and 6 to refresh your memory on the early alliances.

5 Copy and label the diagrams in their correct order into your book.

6 Talking point: Once the Triple Alliance was formed, a Triple Entente was bound to follow. Do you agree?

9

Trouble in the Balkans, 1908

The Balkans (south east Europe) was known as the powder keg of Europe. At any moment it seemed likely to explode into war. Three empires were in conflict there:

Turkey was struggling to hold on to her Balkan territories (see map (B)). As the Turkish Empire had weakened, various groups such as the Serbs, Greeks and Bulgars had revolted and set up their own separate countries.

Austria – Hungary   Like Turkey, Austria was an unstable *multinational* empire containing people of many different nationalities. Large numbers of Austria's Slav people wanted to break away and join up with fellow Slavs in Serbia (see the map). Austria therefore saw Serbia as a threat to her continued survival.

Russia was also vitally interested in the Balkans. It was essential to Russia that no possible enemy such as Austria ever gained control of the straits at Constantinople. Russia also supported Serbia and the other Balkan nationalists who wished to set up their own independent states. Indeed Russia saw herself as champion of the Slav people.

The Bosnian crisis

In 1908 a group of young officers seized power in Turkey. One of their aims was to rebuild the Turkish Empire. It seemed likely that they would try and reclaim the provinces of Bosnia and Herzegovina (see the map). These lands were part of the Turkish Empire but had been occupied by Austria since 1878.

To foil the Turks, the Austrians *annexed* (added) Bosnia and Herzegovina to their empire. Serbia was outraged, prepared for war and appealed to Russia for help. To fight the Austrians alone would be suicidal. Russia's answer was to call for an international conference to investigate the annexation. Austria, however, refused to attend. Then Germany came to Austria's aid and demanded that Russia accept the annexation. Russia had little choice but to back down. Her armies were no match for the German forces.

(A) *Some new terms*
A *nation* is a state or country. *Nationalism* is the name given to movements to form nations, often made up of the same race, language or religion. *Nationalists* are the people who support such movements.

(B) *The Balkans in 1909*

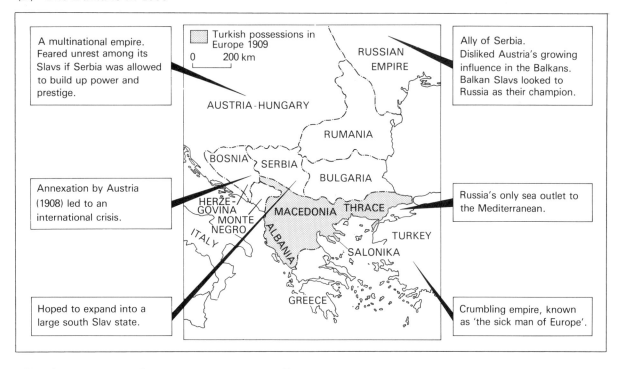

A multinational empire. Feared unrest among its Slavs if Serbia was allowed to build up power and prestige.

Turkish possessions in Europe 1909
0   200 km

RUSSIAN EMPIRE

Ally of Serbia. Disliked Austria's growing influence in the Balkans. Balkan Slavs looked to Russia as their champion.

AUSTRIA-HUNGARY

RUMANIA

Annexation by Austria (1908) led to an international crisis.

BOSNIA   SERBIA

BULGARIA

HERŽE-GOVINA   MACEDONIA   THRACE

Russia's only sea outlet to the Mediterranean.

MONTE NEGRO

ITALY   ALBANIA

TURKEY

SALONIKA

Hoped to expand into a large south Slav state.

GREECE

Crumbling empire, known as 'the sick man of Europe'.

(C) *An imaginary discussion among some Bosnians*

ILIĆ: 'We must free ourselves from Austrian rule. Only then will we be able to preserve our traditions, language and religion.'

POPOVIĆ: 'I agree. We could join up with our fellow Slavs in Serbia. I am sure Serbia would help us.'

GRABEŻ: 'That's easier said than done. Serbia is too weak to defeat Austria alone. Nevertheless there is always a chance that Russia will help her.'

OBILIĆ: 'I say be patient. It is only a matter of time until the Austrian Empire collapses. When that day comes we must be ready.'

Questions

1   Copy the map into your book. (**B**)
2   Serbia is an example of (a) a nationalist (b) a nation or (c) nationalism?
3   Ilić in (**C**) is an example of (a) a nation (b) a nationalist or (c) nationalism?
4   Why does Ilić want Serbia to break away from Austrian control? (**C**)
5   Why does Popović want to join up with Serbia? (**C**)
6   Talking point: Imagine Russia did help Serbia fight Austria as Grabeż is hoping. (**C**) Which power would come to Austria's aid? Why? How could this lead to a European war?
7   Talking point: Austria–Hungary was once described as 'a broken pot held together by a piece of wire'. What is meant by this statement?

The arms race

The naval race

Until the first Moroccan crisis few Britons worried about Germany's growing navy. It would take years for the Germans to catch up with the Royal Navy.

The Dreadnought

Britain's lead further increased when she launched the first 'Dreadnought' class battleship in 1906. Here was a ship with 11-inch armour-plating for protection which could also outgun and outrace any battleship afloat. These details show how the Dreadnought design compared with a battle-ship built only one year before:

HMS Dominion built 1905; 16 350 tons; length 457 feet; 4 twelve-inch guns, 4 nine-inch guns, 5 torpedo tubes; armour 9 inches thick; top speed 18.2 knots.

HMS Dreadnought built 1906; 17 900 tons; length 526 feet; 10 twelve-inch guns, 18 four-inch guns, 5 torpedo tubes; armour 11 inches thick; top speed 21.6 knots.

The Germans were horrified by this new threat. There was even talk that Britain might launch a surprise attack on the German fleet. The Anglo-Russian Entente of 1907 added to this fear. Britain was now allied with both France and Russia in the Triple Entente. The Germans complained that they were surrounded by hostile powers.

Yet *HMS Dreadnought* also made most of Britain's battleships obsolete. By building Dreadnoughts of their own the Germans began to quickly catch up with the British. Britain replied by speeding up her own shipbuilding programme. A full-scale naval race had developed.

The arms race

The naval race was part of a general arms race between all the big powers. The generals and admirals claimed that a large modern army and navy was the only way to keep the peace. No enemy, they said, would dare attack a nation which had strong armed forces to defend itself.

(A) HMS Dreadnought *1906*

(B) *The naval race*

| | Dreadnoughts | | Dreadnought battle-cruisers | |
	Great Britain	Germany	Great Britain	Germany
1906	1	—	—	—
1907	3	—	3	—
1908	2	4	—	—
1909	2	3	1	—
1910	3	1	1	2
1911	5	3	2	1
1912	3	2	1	2
1913	7	3	1	2
1914	3	1	—	—
total:	**29**	**17**	**9**	**7**

(C) *Spending on armaments 1872–1912*

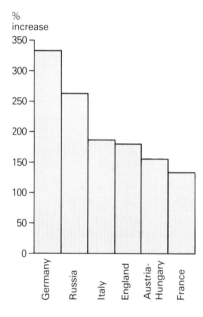

% increase

(D) *In 1909 the British newspaper the* Daily Mail *ran a series of reports on Germany. One report said*:
'Germany is deliberately preparing to destroy the British Empire. All of Europe is to be [Germanised]. We are all to be drilled and schooled and uniformed by [German] officials, and the Emperor William II is to rule us with a rod of iron. Britain alone stands in the way of Germany's [path to] world power and domination.'

(Quoted in J. REMAK, *The Origins of World War I*)

Questions

1. Give three reasons why *HMS Dreadnought* would be likely to win a naval battle against *HMS Dominion*. (**T**)
2. Who won the naval race between 1906 and 1914? Quote figures. (**B**)
3. What was the average percentage increase in arms spending among the great powers between 1872 and 1912? (**C**)
4. How could reports like (**D**) have helped speed up the arms race?
5. Talking point: A strong defence force is the best way to keep peace.

The second Moroccan crisis: the Agadir incident, 1911

At the Algeciras conference in 1906, the right of France to organise Moroccan affairs was officially recognised by Britain. For the next few years the situation remained unstable. Early in 1911 the Sultan of Morocco called for French help to crush a revolt by rebel tribesmen.

Gunboat diplomacy

Germany was certain this would be followed by a French takeover. So as soon as the French occupied Fez, the capital, Germany sent the gunboat *Panther* to the Moroccan port of Agadir. This show of force was followed up with a German demand for compensation in the form of the whole of the French Congo in Central Africa.

British reaction

The move, however, misfired and Britain became alarmed. Britain thought Germany was trying to acquire a naval base at Agadir. Here it seemed was yet another German attempt to destroy the Anglo-French Entente.

Lloyd George, the British Chancellor of the Exchequer, warned Germany that Britain would fight rather than see herself or her allies pushed around in this way. Britain's fleet was even prepared for war. In the end, Germany climbed down.

Results of the crisis

Yet the damage had been done. Britain was more than ever convinced Germany wanted to dominate Europe. Germany of course could not forget Lloyd George's threat. As far as she was concerned this was further proof that Germany was being encircled by a ring of vicious enemies. So Germany further expanded her navy. Britain did the same. As a result, Britain and France drew closer together.

In the Anglo-French Naval Convention of 1912 it was agreed that each of them would patrol certain areas of the surrounding seas. Britain would police the North Sea while France looked after the Mediterranean. The Anglo-French Entente was now virtually a military alliance.

(A) *A British cartoon on the Moroccan affair, from* Punch *2 August 1911*

GERMANY: "Donnerwetter! It's rock. I thought it was going to be paper."

(B) *A contemporary German cartoon on the Agadir crisis*

(C) *An historian comments*:
'The dispatch of the *Panther* to Agadir perfectly reveals the character of German policy, . . . They did not really want trading rights in Morocco, or compensation from France in Central Africa. They merely wanted everyone to go on being frightened of them.'

(L.C.B. SEAMAN, *From Vienna to Versailles*, 1955)

(D) *During the Moroccan crisis von Moltke, the German Chief of General Staff, wrote to his wife*:
'I am thoroughly fed up with this wretched Morocco affair . . . . If once again we crawl out of this affair with our tail between our legs, if we cannot pluck up the courage to take a [tough] line which we are prepared to enforce with the sword then I despair of the future of the German Empire. Then I shall quit. But before that I shall propose that we do away with the army and place our-selves under the protection of Japan; then we can concentrate on making money and become country bumpkins.'

(Quoted in F. FISCHER, *War of Illusions*)

Questions

Examine all of the sources carefully before answering the questions.

1   Which of the sources claims that the Germans only sent a gun boat to Morocco to scare the other powers?
2   Which of the sources blames the Germans for the crisis over Morocco?
3   Which of the sources suggests the Germans were being made to look fools over Morocco?
4   Which of the sources suggests that Germany was trying to break up the alliance between France and Britain?
5   Talking point: The Moroccan affair was one gigantic German blunder. Discuss.

More trouble in the Balkans

The Balkan Wars

Ever since the Bosnian disaster in 1908, Russia had tried to get the Balkan states to form an alliance. In this way Russia hoped to block an Austrian takeover of the Balkans. In 1912 Serbia, Greece, Bulgaria and Montenegro formed a group called the Balkan League.

The First Balkan War

In October 1912, the armies of the League took advantage of their newly combined strength to attack the Turks. They were so successful that they managed to drive Turkey almost completely out of Europe. Austria, looking on, was stunned. Five centuries of Turkish rule had suddenly come to an end. Worse still, Serbia had come out as the strongest Balkan state. What was Austria to do? The Austrian generals called for a quick war to crush Serbia once and for all. But the complicated system of alliances in Europe meant that other countries would soon have become involved as well. An attack on Serbia might therefore trigger off a general European war. And in 1912, none of the great powers – including Austria – wanted that.

So the great powers stepped in and forced a peace settlement on the Balkan states. At the peace conference Austria managed to defeat Serbia's plans to gain a coastline by having a new country, Albania, placed between Serbia and the Adriatic Sea (see map (C)). The rest of the conquered Turkish lands were shared out among the Balkan League.

The Second Balkan War

But within a month the Balkan League had fallen out over the spoils. Bulgaria quarrelled with Serbia and Greece. In June 1913, the Bulgarians began the Second Balkan War by attacking their former allies. They were, however, quickly defeated. In the peace settlement that followed, Bulgaria surrendered nearly all the lands she had won in the first war to Greece and Serbia.

> **Results of the Balkan Wars**
> 1 Even worse relations between Austria and Serbia.
> 2 Serbia was angry about Albania and being cut off from the sea.
> 3 Austria was bitter at the success of Serbia.
> 4 Serbia doubled in size and was keener than ever to control all the Slav people in the Austrian Empire.

THE BOILING POINT.

(A) *A cartoon about the Balkan crisis, from* Punch *2 October 1912*

(B) *The Balkans in 1912 (before the Balkan Wars)*

(C) *The Balkans in 1913 (after the Balkan Wars)*

Questions

1. Compare the two maps of the Balkans – before and after the Balkan Wars. (**B**) and (**C**)
   (a) What happened to the Turkish Empire?
   (b) Which Balkan state increased in size the most as a result of the wars?
   (c) What important geographical advantage apart from extra territory would Serbia have gained if she had been able to include Albania within her borders? (**C**)
2. Who are the people sitting on the lid of the pot? (**A**)
3. What point is the cartoonist making? (**A**)
4. Talking point: What trouble spots are there in the world around us similar to the Balkans? Could any of these trouble spots erupt into a world war? How?

Planning for victory

In the years before 1914, all the European powers made plans on what they would do if war did break out.

These plans went into great detail. They had to. Millions of men had to be called up to fight and organised into fighting units. Troops had to be provided with arms, clothing, food and other equipment. Then they had to be sent by railway to wherever they were to be stationed. Moreover, all of this had to be done within a few days.

The preparation of an army for war is called *mobilisation*. When one country mobilises the chances of war are increased because others usually follow. Nobody wants to risk giving an enemy a headstart in preparation for war. If the enemy wins the race to mobilise, there is a great risk of being caught off guard and of losing the war.

The Schlieffen plan

The German war plan was named after its designer Count Von Schlieffen. The Germans believed that a war with France must come. The French wanted revenge for their defeat by Germany in 1870–1. France was allied to Russia. Any future war would therefore be a war on two fronts, fought against both France and Russia at the same time.

But Schlieffen believed that the German army was not strong enough to fight on both sides of Europe at the same time. What could be done? Schlieffen's answer was simple. Germany would first crush France. Then the German army would move quickly to the East to fight the Russians.

But the plan had two giant flaws:

(i) there was no plan for a war with Russia only. Incredibly, a war with Russia meant Germany had to attack France first.

(ii) to defeat France quickly enough, Germany planned to bypass the French border forts and go through Belgium, catching the French by surprise. Belgium was a *neutral* country and her right to stay neutral was guaranteed by a treaty signed by Britain. By planning to invade France through Belgium, Germany was risking a war with Britain.

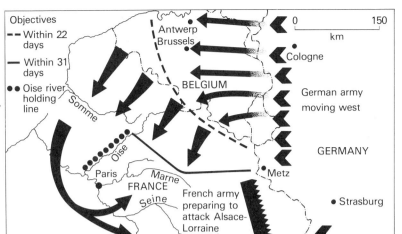

(A) *The Schlieffen plan*

(B) *To mobilise or prepare an army for war was a huge job. Here is a description of what mobilisation meant for the German army:* 'Once the mobilisation button was pushed the whole vast machinery for calling up, equipping and transporting two million men began turning automatically. Reservists went to designated depots, were issued uniforms, equipment and arms, formed into companies and companies into battalions, were joined by cavalry, cyclists, artillery, medical units, cook-wagons, blacksmith wagons, even postal wagons, moved according to prepared railway time-tables to concentration points near the frontier where they would be formed into divisions, divisions into corps and corps into armies ready to advance and fight. One army corps alone – out of the total of forty in the German forces – required 170 railway carriages for officers, 965 for infantry, 2960 for cavalry, 1915 for artillery, and supply wagons, 6010 in all, grouped in 140 trains, and an equal number again for their supplies.'

(B. TUCHMAN, *August 1914*, 1962)

(C) *Part of a British poster illustrating the Treaty of London, 1839, guaranteeing Belgian neutrality*

"BELGIUM . . . . SHALL FORM AN INDEPENDENT AND PERPETUALLY NEUTRAL STATE. IT SHALL BE BOUND TO OBSERVE SUCH NEUTRALITY TOWARDS ALL OTHER STATES."

These are the Seals and Signatures of the Six Nations who guaranteed Belgian Independence and Neutrality

GREAT BRITAIN - Palmerston
BELGIUM - Sylvain Van De Weyer
AUSTRIA - Senfft
FRANCE - H. Sebastiani
GERMANY - Bulow
RUSSIA - Pozzo Di Borgo

Questions

1. Why didn't the German armies attack France across the French–German frontier? (**A**) and (**T**)
2. Describe how the German armies planned to defeat the French forces. (**A**)
3. Do you think it was wrong for Germany to invade France through Belgium? Why or why not?
4. Why was it so difficult for the great powers to change their war plans at the last moment? (**B**)
5. Suggest why the generals had to plan out their mobilisation in great detail. (**B**)
6. Talking point: Imagine you were in command of the German army. Mobilisation has begun as in (**B**) and your troops are moving by railway towards the French frontier. At the last moment the emperor orders you to stop the attack on France and attack Russia instead. What problems would you face?

The outbreak of war

The crisis

On 28 June 1914, the Archduke Franz Ferdinand, heir to the Austrian throne, drove through the Bosnian capital, Sarajevo, in an open-top car. During that drive, he and his wife were murdered by a Bosnian Serb terrorist named Princip. Austria was outraged at the murder. It blamed the Serbian government. The time had come to teach the Serbs a lesson. Germany agreed and promised to support Austria in any action she took to punish Serbia. Germany was afraid that if the Austrian government missed this chance to squash Serbia, Austria's multi-racial empire would collapse. Then Germany would be without an ally. On 23 July Austria presented an *ultimatum* to Serbia which included 10 demands. The Serbs accepted all except one. But even this was not enough.

Timetable

28 July Austria declared war on Serbia. Serbia then appealed to Russia for help.

30 July Tsar Nicholas II ordered the Russian army to mobilise.

31 July Germany called on Russia to stop her war preparations.

1 Aug. When Russia did not reply, Germany declared war and began to mobilise. France, who was allied to Russia, now mobilised her army.

2 Aug. Germany presented an ultimatum to Belgium asking for a passage through Belgium.

3 Aug. Belgium rejected the ultimatum.

4 Aug. The German troops crossed the Belgian frontier. Under the terms of the Treaty of London, Britain had promised to guarantee Belgium's neutrality. Britain was also allied to both France and Russia. At 11.00 a.m. Britain sent an ultimatum to the Germans giving them twelve hours to withdraw from Belgium. Germany refused. At 11.00 p.m. Britain declared war on Germany. The First World War had begun.

(A) *How the Schlieffen plan pushed Europe into war*

One essential part of [the Schlieffen] plan was to go through Belgium. The other essential part which was equally important was that there could be no delay between mobilization and war because if there were delay then Russia would catch up and the Germans would get the two-front war after all. So the moment that the Germans decided on mobilization, they decided for war, or rather war followed of itself. The railway timetables . . . in the Schlieffen Plan . . . brought the troops not to their barracks but into Belgium and Northern France. The German mobilization plan actually laid down the first 40 days of the German invasion of France and none of it could be altered because if it did all the timetables would go wrong. Thus the decision for mobilization which the Germans [announced on 1 August] was a decision for a general European war.

(A.J.P. TAYLOR, *How Wars Begin*, 1979)

(B) *A cartoon showing British sympathies, from* Punch, *August 1914*

BRAVO, BELGIUM!

(C) *A British postcard of 1914*

HE WONT BE HAPPY TILL HE GETS IT

(D) *Stages of war, 1914*

Stage 1
Local War (Austria vs. Serbia)
– July 28

Stage 2
Continental War
Austria and Germany vs.
Russia and France
– Aug. 1–3

Stage 3
World War
Britain declares war
– Aug. 4

Questions

1. Explain how the German decision to mobilise was bound to lead to a general European war. (**A**)
2. Which country is represented by the small boy in the cartoon? (**B**)
3. Give two words to describe the attitude of the larger person. (**B**)
4. Explain why the larger person wanted to go through the gate. (**B**) and (**T**)
5. Explain why the boy might have good reason to expect some help against the larger person. (**B**) and (**T**)
6. What does the postcard suggest was the reason for Germany going to war in 1914? (**C**)
7. Talking point: Was there any stage when a world war might have been prevented? (**D**)

Summing up: what caused the First World War?

(A) *This viewpoint argues that there were four basic or fundamental causes for the First World War.*

1 Nationalism

One of the forces making for trouble was extreme nationalism. This was a very powerful emotion. People who fell under its spell were willing to take any action to help their own nation, regardless of its effect on others. To promote their nation's interests, they were even ready to start wars.

Nationalism inspired Bismarck's war with France and the German seizure of Alsace–Lorraine. Relations between France and Germany suffered badly as a result. French nationalists could not rest as long as other Frenchmen were under the rule of the Germans. They preached a war of revenge to regain the 'lost provinces'.

Nationalism also led to rivalries in the Balkan Peninsula. Russia stirred up the Slavs in order to extend its influence there. It also supported the claims of the little kingdom of Serbia, which dreamed of uniting all the south Slavs under its rule. These actions aroused the leaders of Austria–Hungary. They realised that their country would fall apart if the millions of Slav subjects broke away.

2 Imperialism

Imperialism (the building of overseas empires) also led to frequent quarrels among the powers. Disputes over colonies and commerce were a constant threat to peace during the late nineteenth and early twentieth centuries.

3 Militarism

Another threat to peace arose from the existence of large armies and navies. Leaders of the armed forces insisted that preparing for war was the only way to ensure peace. As long as a nation was strong, they said, its enemies would not dare to attack it. If a war did start, the nation would be able to defend itself successfully.

Nationalists, imperialists, and the makers of armaments supported these arguments. The result was an arms race. Each power kept building up its armed forces. Each was trying to have a bigger and deadlier war machine than its rivals.

4 The system of alliances

Nations also sought to increase their strength by gaining allies. Europe was crisscrossed by rival systems of military alliances. These alliances were dangerous because they increased suspicion and fear. Moreover, they meant that a war between two nations was likely to involve many others.

(Adapted from H. ZEBEL and S. SCHWARTZ, *Past to Present: A World History*, 1960)

Time line of events

1870–1	Franco-Prussian War
1879	Dual Alliance between Germany and Austria–Hungary
1882	Triple Alliance created with addition of Italy to Dual Alliance
1887	Reinsurance Treaty between Germany and Russia
1890	Bismarck resigns
1891	William II refuses to renew Reinsurance Treaty
1894	Dual Entente between Russia and France
1902	Anglo-Japanese Alliance
1904	Entente Cordiale Britain and France
1905–6	First Moroccan crisis
1906	*HMS Dreadnought* launched
1907	Triple Entente formed with signing of Anglo-Russian Entente
1908–9	Bosnian annexation crisis
1911	Second Moroccan crisis
1912	Anglo-French Naval Agreement
1912–3	First and Second Balkan Wars
1914	Outbreak of First World War

(B) *This is an imaginary discussion between a group of historians. They are debating which power or powers was responsible for the outbreak of war.*

Speaker 1: 'Germany was responsible for starting the First World War. It was Germany who seized Alsace and Lorraine in 1870. Germany started the naval race. German stupidity sparked off the first Moroccan crisis. This in turn led to the formation of the Triple Entente. While Germany did not start the Bosnian crisis in 1908, it did threaten Russia with war. Again, in 1911, it was Germany who blundered by sending a gunboat to Agadir. In the July crisis of 1914, Austria would never have declared war on Serbia, without German backing. Finally it was the German Schlieffen plan which pushed Europe into war.'

Speaker 2: 'That's hardly fair. The war was sparked off by the assassination of Archduke Ferdinand. Serbia must take much of the blame for this. After all it was Serbia who was stirring up trouble among the southern Slavs.'

Speaker 3: 'I agree. But Russia must share the blame with Serbia. Russia was also stirring up the Slavs, and Serbia would never have been as troublesome if she did not have Russian support. Furthermore, it was the Russian mobilisation in July, 1914, which caused the Germans to mobilise and declare war.'

Speaker 4: 'Yes, but Russia would never have mobilised if Austria had not declared war on Serbia. Remember, Austria was determined to crush Serbia once and for all. Therefore Austria must take the blame.'

Speaker 5: 'What about France? During the July crisis France never even bothered to try and stop the Russians from mobilising. And France's ambassador in Russia repeatedly urged the Russians to take a strong stand against Austria and Germany.'

Speaker 6: 'Britain also might have stopped the war. A strong warning to Germany in the early days of the July crisis, that England would fight alongside France and Russia in a war, might have made Germany see sense.'

Chart 1   The basic causes

Causes	Ranking (1−4)	Reasons
Nationalism		
Imperialism		
Militarism		
Alliance System		

Chart 2   Whose fault was the war?

Countries	Blame (see key)	Ranking (1−6)	Reasons
Germany			
Serbia			
Russia			
Austria			
France			
Britain			

Key

S.B.	− Solely to blame
L.B.	− Large share of the blame
S.S.B.	− Small share of the blame
F.B.	− Free from blame

Activities

1 Read through (**A**) carefully. Then rank the basic causes from 1 to 4 using Chart 1. 1 will indicate the most important cause, 4 will be the least important cause. In the reasons column explain why you ranked them in the order you chose.

2 Complete Chart 2 using (**B**) and your own knowledge. In the blame column use the key provided. In the ranking column number 1 will indicate the country most to blame. 6 will indicate the country least to blame. In the reasons column explain why you ranked them in the order you chose.

3 Compare your rankings with the rest of the class.

An overview of the First World War 1914–18

World war

When war broke out in 1914 Europeans expected it to last only a few weeks. It lasted four years. Before it was over, every continent had become involved and it had truly become a world war.

Sides

On the one side were the British Commonwealth, France, Belgium, Russia and Serbia, who with Japan formed the Allies. They were later joined by Italy, Rumania and some other countries. On the other side, the 'Central Powers' of Germany and Austria–Hungary were soon joined by Turkey, and later by Bulgaria.

Total war

The Great War, as it became known, was also a *total war*. All able-bodied men were called up to fight. Women joined the labour force to replace men sent to battle.

Stalemate

The war was fought mainly in Europe. On the Western Front it was characterised by trench warfare. Both sides dug themselves into long lines of trenches. From there they launched attacks in an effort to break through the enemy lines.

In the end three factors helped break the deadlock in favour of the Allies:

1 By 1917 the Allied naval blockade of Germany had cut off the flow of food and supplies to Germany.
2 The entry of the USA into the war in April 1917 greatly strengthened the Allied side.
3 The effective use of a new weapon – the tank – enabled the Allies to break through the German lines in 1918.

(A) *This poster shows the type of propaganda put out by both sides during the First World War. It created much bitterness and hatred against the enemy.*

RED CROSS OR IRON CROSS?

WOUNDED AND A PRISONER
OUR SOLDIER CRIES FOR WATER.
THE GERMAN "SISTER"
POURS IT ON THE GROUND BEFORE HIS EYES.
THERE IS NO WOMAN IN BRITAIN
WHO WOULD DO IT.
THERE IS NO WOMAN IN BRITAIN
WHO WILL FORGET IT.

(B) *Trench warfare: a dugout of the 105th Howitzer Battery, 4th Brigade, Australian Field Artillery during the Third Battle of Ypres, 27 August 1917*

(C) *Losses per day in the First World War compared with those in past wars*

		Losses per day
Napoleonic War	1790–1815	233
Crimean War	1854–1856	1075
American Civil War	1861–1865	518
Franco-Prussian War	1870–1871	876
Boer War	1899–1902	10
Russo-Japanese War	1904–1905	292
Balkan War	1912–1913	1941
World War I	1914–1918	5509

(Purnell's History of the Twentieth Century, 1968)

(D)   Effects of the Great War

- Some 10 million men were killed in direct action.
- The direct economic losses alone were over $180 billion.
- The Austrian and Turkish Empires were broken up and replaced by a number of smaller states.
- All the defeated countries were ruined while the victors, apart from the USA, were half bankrupt. The Allies therefore wanted revenge on Germany.

The peace settlement

Peacemaking

In January 1919, Wilson and representatives of twenty-seven other victorious nations met in Paris to draw up a peace treaty to deal with the losers of the First World War: Germany, Austria, Hungary, Bulgaria and Turkey.

Great Britain, France and the USA were the most powerful Allies at the conference. The French prime minister, Clemenceau, wanted a tough treaty. Great Britain led by Lloyd George also wanted to 'make Germany pay'. The USA, represented by Wilson, wanted a more lenient treaty in which Wilson's Fourteen Points for peace would be included. All three countries had to compromise in some way in order to agree.

The Treaty of Versailles

The Treaty of Versailles, which dealt with Germany, was eventually signed in June 1919. Under its terms Germany was forced:

(1) to pay war debts or *reparations* of £6.6 million to go towards the cost of the war ($3.3 billion).

(2) to disarm. The German army was reduced to 100 000 men and forbidden to have tanks. Only a small navy of six battleships and no submarines was allowed. No air force at all was permitted. Moreover no troops were to be allowed into the Rhineland.

(3) to agree never to unite with Austria.

(4) to sign a statement saying that Germany alone was guilty of starting the First World War.

(5) to give 13½ per cent of her territory, with seven million of her people, to neighbouring countries. Germany's losses included:
(a) the loss of Alsace and Lorraine to France.
(b) the loss of 17 800 square miles to the new state of Poland. East Prussia was split off from the rest of Germany by a strip of land called the Polish Corridor and Danzig was made into a 'free city'.
(c) the loss of land to Belgium and Denmark.
(d) all her overseas colonies.

The League of Nations

The Treaty of Versailles also set out the Covenant (constitution) of the League of Nations.

(A) *Germany's territorial losses in Europe by the 1919 Treaty of Versailles*

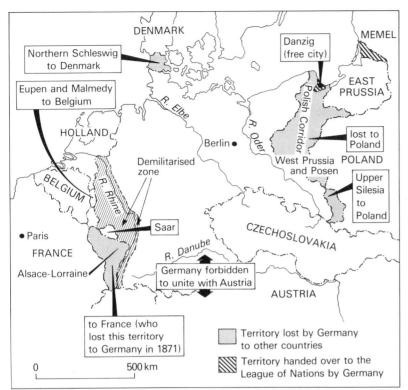

(B) *War deaths 1914–18*

Russia	1 750 000
Germany	1 750 000
France	1 500 000
Austria-Hungary	1 250 000
Great Britain	900 000
Italy	600 000
Turkey	300 000
USA	114 000
Bulgaria	100 000
Serbia	50 000
Rumania	30 000

(C) *French losses:*
1875 sq. miles of forest laid waste
8000 sq. miles of agricultural land laid waste

Buildings destroyed:
1500 schools
1200 churches
377 public buildings
1000 industrial plants
246 000 other buildings

(Purnell's History of the Twentieth Century)

(D) *The cost of war British Government spending* £7 852 000 000

Taxation
1914: 6p in £1
1922: 30p in £1

(E) *At an English election meeting in 1918 Sir Eric Geddes, a top English politician, promised:*

'If I am returned [to office] Germany is going to pay ... and I personally have no doubt that we will get everything that you can squeeze out of a lemon and a bit more.'

Questions

1 Draw up a chart setting out the key points of the Treaty of Versailles, in your notebook. (**T**)
2 What is a demilitarised zone? Why should one be set up around the river Rhine? (**A**)
3 Suggest why Germany was forbidden to unite with Austria. (**A**) and (**T**)
4 What evidence can you find to explain why France was much more eager than the USA to get revenge on Germany? (**B**) and (**C**)
5 Is there a *geographical* reason why France was more concerned than Great Britain about leaving Germany with a strong army? Which country would be more troubled by a strong navy? (**A**) and (**T**)
6 How much did taxation increase in Great Britain as a result of the First World War? Why did taxation have to increase? (**D**)
7 What was Sir Eric Geddes promising to do to the Germans if he was returned to power? (**E**)
8 Why was this sort of promise so appealing to the British public in 1918? (**E**)
9 Talking point: What makes a good peace treaty? Is it a tough treaty which leaves the beaten enemy so weak that she can never fight again? Or is it a lenient treaty that leaves her so contented that she never wants to make war again?

How harsh was the Treaty of Versailles?

Historians still argue over whether the Treaty of Versailles was too tough on the Germans. In this exercise we will look at both sides of the argument. Then you will be able to make up your own mind.

But first, examine resources **(A)**–**(C)**. Then answer questions 1–6. Do not read **(D)** until you have completed the answers to these. (While doing this keep your summary of the terms of the treaty in front of you.)

(A) *German reactions to the treaty*
  (i) Speaking at the National Assembly, Herr Schneidermann made a violent attack on the peace treaty describing it as a murderous proposal:
  'The Allies are driving the knife into the living body of the German people.... The proposed Peace means the miserable enslavement of children.'
  (ii) The *Berliner Tageblatt* says the terms mean the end of Germany as a great power.... The military terms are impossible.
  (iii) The *Bourse Courier* sums up the terms as 'intolerable'.

  ((i)–(iii) quoted in *Christchurch Press*, 1919)

> VENGEANCE!
> GERMAN NATION!
>
> Today in the Hall of Mirrors a disgraceful treaty is being signed. Never forget it. There will be vengeance for the shame of 1919.

  (iv) *Deutsche Zeitung*, 28 June 1919

  (Quoted in R.C.J. STONE, *The Drift to War*)

(B) *What aspects of the treaty upset the Germans most?*
(1) The Germans complained bitterly that the territorial losses (13½ per cent of her territory and about 7 million subjects) were far too harsh. In particular they resented the losses to Poland in the east and that Germany was split in two by the Polish Corridor.
(2) The Germans complained that the Allies were trying to bankrupt Germany with their high reparation claims. As proof they noted that John Keynes, the leader of the British financial experts sent to Versailles, had resigned in protest at the high demands for German reparations. (*Note*: Keynes resigned in 1919, but the final reparation figure was not set until 1921.)
(3) The terms were worked out in secret and forced upon the Germans.
(4) All Germany's colonies were taken from her but the Allies kept theirs.
(5) Germans hated having to accept the blame for the war.
(6) Above all, Germans hated having to disarm without any guarantee that their Allied neighbours would do likewise.

Questions

Examine resources (**A**)–(**C**) carefully before you start these questions. Do not read (**D**) until you have completed questions 1 to 6.

1   What word or words best describes for you, the reaction of the Germans to the terms of the treaty?
    a) annoyed   b) hurt   c) bitter   d) pleased
    (**A**)–(**C**)

2   Find the ONE sentence in resources (**A**) (i–iv) which implies the treaty will cause the Germans to rise up and fight another war.

3   Why should the *Deutsche Zeitung*, a German newspaper, put (**A** iv) on its front page on 28 June 1919?

4   At what occasion do you see black mourning bands worn? Why do you think the *Deutsche Zeitung* newspaper surrounded (**A** iv) with a black mourning band?

5   In your opinion, which aspects of the treaty seem to have been unduly harsh on the Germans? (**B**)

6   Based on the evidence you have so far read and the arguments put forward in (**C**), do you think the Treaty of Versailles was too tough on the Germans?

7   Now read (**D**) carefully. Has it caused you to change your opinion about the harshness of the treaty in any way? If so, how?

8   Select one of the following statements which best sums up your opinion of the Treaty of Versailles. If you don't agree with any of them, write your own statement. Give reasons for your choice.
    a)   The Treaty of Versailles was a harsh treaty. The Germans were treated unfairly and became bitter and resentful.
    b)   The treaty was fair. The Germans paid for a war they caused. They had no reason to complain.
    c)   The treaty may have been fair but it still left the Germans feeling bitter and humiliated.

(C)   *An historian's opinion of the treaty*

'Germany was not allowed to be represented at the Peace Conference. She had no say. She was forced to sign the treaty (including a clause saying she was guilty of starting the war). Countries such as France were determined to have revenge. The reparations were too tough. Here was the basis for another War.'

(TERESA LAWRENCE, *Notes on European History*, 1967)

(D)   *Another opinion*

The Germans had no right to grumble.

(1)   Look at the peace treaty the Germans forced on the Russians in 1918, the Treaty of Brest-Litovsk. By it Russia lost:
    a)   54 percent of her industry
    b)   34 percent of her population
    c)   89 percent of the coal mines
    d)   and, as the loser, she was fined 6 billion marks.

(2)   The treaty did not weaken Germany anywhere near as much as the Germans complained – Germany was still a large country with plenty of resources. By 1925 German steel production was twice that of Britain.

(3)   During the First World War the German finance minister had made it plain that, if the Germans won, the Allies would be made to pay for the cost of the war.

(4)   War guilt – most historians today believe Germany was most to blame for starting the First World War.

The other peace treaties

- Treaty of St Germain 1919 – with defeated Austria
- Treaty of Neuilly 1919 – with defeated Bulgaria
- Treaty of Sèvres 1920 – with defeated Turkey
- Treaty of Trianon 1920 – with defeated Hungary

Austria–Hungary

Austria – Hungary was carved up into four new nations: Austria, Hungary, Czechoslovakia and Yugoslavia. Both Austria and Hungary were reduced to tiny states. Like Germany they also had to pay reparations.

In the treaties the peacemakers tried to follow the principle of *self-determination*, i.e., that all races of people should be able to rule themselves. Yet in the Balkans, for example, the races were too mixed up to be neatly divided into separate nations. Czechoslovakia and Yugoslavia were therefore a mixture of different races.

Bulgaria

Like Austria and Hungary, Bulgaria was forced to surrender territory, pay reparations and limit her army.

The Turkish Empire

This was broken up. Some of its former territories were given their independence. Those in the Middle East were placed under British and French control.

The Russian Empire

At the same time as the Paris peace conference, the Russians were caught up in bloody civil war. They therefore did not attend and as a result, lost part of their empire. Four new nations (Finland, Estonia, Latvia and Lithuania) were formed. Russia also lost large chunks of territory to Poland, Czechoslovakia and Rumania.

Poland and Italy

Poland was set up as a *buffer state* between the old enemies Germany and Russia. Italy, as a reward for joining the Allies, was given part of Austria.

Questions
1 Trace maps (**A**) and (**B**).
2 On map (**A**) shade in, using different colours a) the Allies b) the Central Powers c) neutral countries.
3 On map (**B**) shade in, using different colours a) the new states b) the states with additional land in Europe since 1914 c) the states reduced in size since 1914.
4 How might the new nations in central Europe have acted as a barrier to stop the Germans expanding eastwards? (**B**)
5 Talking point: As a result of the peace treaties a number of subject peoples were given their independence. Do you think this would encourage more peace in Europe? Give reasons for your answer.

(A) *Europe in 1914*

(B) *Europe in 1920*

Italy: a troubled nation

Problems

In 1900 Italy was a poor troubled nation. The country was split into a rich industrial north and a poverty-stricken agricultural south. Few workers trusted their employers and strikes were frequent. Moreover, few Italians had much faith in their parliament. Weak leaders, crooked politicians and frequent changes of government were common events. A running quarrel between the Catholic church and the Italian government made matters worse. Some politicians thought a large overseas empire might be the answer to Italy's problems. But even here Italy had little luck.

The First World War

When war broke out in 1914 Italy decided to stay out of the war and remain *neutral*. But promises of territory won Italy over to the Allied side in 1915. Though on the winning side, the war went badly and there was a massive increase in the cost of living. When Italians received less territory than promised, they felt cheated.

D'Annunzio occupies Fiume

One Italian patriot named D'Annunzio was so angry at the peace settlement that he formed his own private army. He then seized the Yugoslav port of Fiume and claimed it for Italy. When the Italian government expelled D'Annunzio's men, it was accused of being unpatriotic and cowardly.

Economic and social discontent

The war was also followed by high unemployment, high prices, riots and strikes. Weak government followed weak government, adding to the general chaos. In 1919 peasants began to seize land from their landlords. In the towns workers took over factories in an effort to push up wages. Meanwhile extremists within the largest political party, the Socialists, frightened the rich and the middle classes with talk of revolution. In this revolutionary climate Italians began to look for a strong man.

(A) *Wealth per person in 1900, in various European countries*

England	6600 francs
France	5560 francs
Germany	2840 francs
Austria-Hungary	1960 francs
Italy	1600 francs

(*Journal des Economists*, 1906; quoted in C. WALSH, *A Documentary History of Europe 1846–1900*)

(B) *Living conditions in the slums of Naples in southern Italy*

(C) *Italy: annual emigration*
Numbers in thousands

1910	651.5
1911	533.8
1912	711.4
1913	872.6
1914	479.2
1915	146.0
1916	142.4
1917	46.5
1918	28.3
1919	253.2
1920	614.6

(B.R. MITCHELL, *European Historical Statistics 1750—1970*, 1975)

(D) *What did the people want from the government?*
'The shopkeeper wanted to be sure that when he opened in the morning, nobody would break his windows or walk off with the best of his stock. The lawyer who lived in the suburbs wanted to be sure that the trams would run every morning. Women wanted to be able to walk unmolested through the streets and know that their children would be safe on their way to school. Peasants wanted to know, at least in general terms, what the price of wheat would be at the end of the farming year. Land and property owners wanted something done about rents, which were lagging behind incomes; and tenants wanted something done about their wages, which were lagging behind prices. A policy, a direction, the strong man with the steady hand – this is what the average Italian wanted.'

(R. MACGREGOR-HASTIE, *The Day of the Lion*, 1963)

Questions

1 What sort of life did most of the people in the photograph appear to have lived? (**B**)

2 How did Italians rank in wealth compared to their European neighbours? (**A**)

3 How many Italians left Italy to live overseas between 1910 and 1914? (**C**)

4 How would these figures provide support for the idea that Italy was a relatively poor country? (**A**) and (**C**)

5 What does Macgregor-Hastie claim that the people wanted from their government? (**D**)

6 Why do you think the average Italian thought that his wants could best be solved by a strong man? (**D**) and (**T**)

7 Talking point: 'The soldiers won the war only for the politicians to lose the peace.' What do you think the Italians meant by this statement?

Mussolini and the rise of Fascism

The strong man many Italians were looking for turned out to be Benito Mussolini.

Fascism

In 1919 Mussolini founded a *Fascist* movement from a group of discontented war veterans and unemployed toughs. He called for an enlarged Italy, attacked the rich and called for a better deal for the workers. Above all Mussolini wanted power.

The Fascists were organised into a private army known as the Blackshirts. Mussolini realised that one way to win support was to play on the fears of the middle and upper classes who were afraid of a communist revolution. He therefore put the Fascists forward as the keepers of law and order. The Fascists broke up strikes and factory sit-ins. This won them the support of the propertied classes. By 1921 the Fascist party had 250 000 members.

Another tactic was simply to create as much chaos as possible and so undermine the government. Between 1920 and 1922 the Fascists murdered some 3000 opponents. In this task they were actually aided by the government. Like the Fascists many government leaders hated the Socialists and communists. They were only too happy for the Fascists to beat up their opponents. Even the police were encouraged to turn a blind eye to Fascist violence. But eventually this backfired. By late 1922 Mussolini had enough confidence to take on the government itself.

The march on Rome

On 24 October Mussolini declared that if Italy was not given a Fascist-style government then the Fascists would take Rome – by force. On 27 October Fascist squads occupied public buildings in Italy. At the same time three columns of Fascists began to march on Rome.

If King Victor Emmanuel had wanted to, he could have stopped Mussolini. The armed forces were willing to fight and they could easily have crushed Mussolini. But instead the king invited Mussolini to form a government.

(A) *A Fascist propaganda poster comparing the Bolshevism of 1919 with Fascism in 1923*

1919 –Bolscevismo–   1923 –Fascismo–

(B) *Mussolini founded Fascism. Here are some of his ideas:*

- The state is supreme. Everyone – rich and poor alike should band together to make the nation great.
- A strong state needs a strong leader (dictator).
- Democracies are weak and unworkable.
- Communism is the enemy of Fascism. Communists stir up trouble between workers and employers whereas Fascism appeals to all classes.
- It is the duty of a nation to acquire an empire. Racially superior people will conquer the weaker races. The strong will always triumph over the weak.

Questions

1 Which of the following statements would you expect Fascists to support?
  (a) People should be free to criticise the government
  (b) An elected parliament is the best government system
  (c) Some races of people are better than others
  (d) Workers and bosses should work together for the good of the country
  (e) All men are equal
  (f) A great nation needs a strong army.
2 What message is this Fascist poster trying to get across to the Italian people? (**A**)
3 Draw up two lists. In one, list those qualities which suggest Mussolini would make a good prime minister. In the other, list qualities suggesting Mussolini would make a bad prime minister. (**C**) Compare your lists with your classmates.
4 Talking point: 'You cannot have a king without subjects, or a leader without those willing to be led' (Ignazio Silone). What does Silone mean? Why were Italians willing to be led by a man such as Mussolini?

(C) *Mussolini's personality: extracts from a 1919 security police report*

'Benito Mussolini has a strong physique, though suffering from venereal disease. His robust constitution allows him to work long hours. He is a womaniser... He is emotional and impulsive and this enables him to speak effectively and convincingly, though he is by no means a skilful orator. He is basically sentimental... He spends freely and cares little for personal wealth... He is thoughtful and quick-witted, a shrewd judge of character in others... He develops violent likes and dislikes, is capable of self-sacrifice for his friends and tenacity in his hatreds. He is a bold organiser and personally brave, makes quick decisions, but is less firm in his beliefs and aims. He is most ambitious... He wants to lead and dominate. ...Mussolini's political ideas are changeable...'

(Quoted in R.N.L. ABSOLOM, *Mussolini and the Rise of Italian Fascism*)

(D) *Mussolini – Italy's strong man*

The growth of dictatorship

As soon as Mussolini became prime minister, he began to work towards establishing a dictatorship. He took the title of *Duce* (Leader). At the same time Mussolini had to continue working with the other political parties.

The Acerbo Law

In 1923 Mussolini had a new electoral law drafted. The party that won the most votes in the election would automatically get two-thirds of the seats in the lower house of parliament. In the 1924 elections the Fascists won easily.

One Socialist leader, Matteotti, attacked the way the Fascists had used terror tactics in the election campaign. He was later found stabbed to death. In protest most opposition MPs withdrew from parliament and demanded Mussolini's resignation. Mussolini's reply was to seize opposition newspapers and censor the press. Soon afterwards all opposing political parties were outlawed.

End of parliamentary rule

In December 1925 Mussolini became head of state, responsible only to the king and not to parliament. A month later parliament passed a law allowing Mussolini to rule by *decree*, i.e. without the approval of parliament. Over 100 000 decree laws were eventually to be made by Mussolini. In 1927, a secret police force (OVRA) was set up to hunt down Mussolini's enemies. Soon it was arresting over 20 000 political offenders a year. By 1928 parliament had become a total farce. A list of MPs, selected by a Fascist Grand Council which Mussolini had appointed, was to be offered to the electors. Either they accepted or rejected the lot. In 1929 the first such parliament was elected and Mussolini's dictatorship was complete.

Besides terror, Mussolini used propaganda to hold on to power. The press was state-controlled. Newspapers, radios and films hammered the idea that Fascism was the best system of government. Mussolini was a superb public speaker and knew how to speak a language that the people understood.

(A) *A contemporary cartoon on the Matteotti murder, from an underground newspaper*

(D) *Mussolini speaking in Rome*

(B) *His popularity with the people*
'At rallies the crowds would chant "Duce, Duce, Duce, we are yours to the end".'

(C) *The 1924 elections described by an anti-Fascist candidate, E. Lussu, in a book published in Britain in 1926:*
'Very few Opposition candidates were allowed to address public meetings, and many were even banned from their constituencies under threat of death. Others had to abstain from showing themselves in public for fear of compromising the electors. The Fascists threatened reprisals, and organized a special system of control to enable them to recognize the voting papers of suspected individuals. Once more the country was in the grip of terrorism. A Socialist candidate named Piccinini was killed for having disobeyed the order to keep away from his constituency.'

Questions
1 How does Lussu's evidence help explain the large victory won by the Fascists in the 1924 elections? (**C**)
2 What point is this cartoon trying to get across to the people? (**A**)
3 What techniques did Mussolini use to capture the attention of his audience? (**D**)
4 Talking point. Here are two opinions of Mussolini.
   (a) 'God has put his finger on the Duce. He is Italy's greatest son, the rightful heir to Caesar.'
   (b) 'He is a rabbit; a phenomenal rabbit; he roars. Observers who do not know him, mistake him for a lion.'
   Find out as much as you can about Mussolini and then decide which you think is the more accurate description. Compare your evidence with your classmates.

Fascism in action I

The corporate state

Much of the first part of Mussolini's rule was spent in solving Italy's economic problems. Mussolini allowed private business to continue, but he brought economic life under his control by making employers and workers join *corporations*. The aim of the corporations was to cut out the bitter class warfare between owners and workers that had previously troubled Italy. Strikes were declared illegal and trade unions were banned. Disputes were settled by the government, which acted like an umpire.

In 1939 representatives of the various corporations replaced parliament.

Economic achievements

Mussolini wanted to turn Italy into a prosperous self-supporting nation. To encourage Italians to grow their own wheat instead of importing much of it, Mussolini launched the 'battle for grain' in 1926. By 1935 wheat imports were down 75 percent and by 1939 wheat production had doubled. To bring more land into use, the Pontine Marshes were drained, reclaiming 3 million acres of land. Communications greatly improved: huge highways were built and mainline railways were electrified.

In order to help reduce unemployment huge building projects were introduced. Sports stadiums, schools, blocks of flats and even new towns were put up. They all helped to make Mussolini and Fascism look very impressive.

Underlying problems

But there were also many failures. Mussolini's 'battle of births', to increase the population by a third, fell well short of its target. The drive to make Italy self-sufficient in oil failed miserably while the lot of thousands of poor farmers with little land hardly changed. In fact the standard of living of most workers and peasants declined and unemployment remained high. This was a great problem. There were no social services and the government gave very little help to those who were out of work.

(A) *Consumption per head of popular foodstuffs*

	1922–9	1930–8
Wine	123	101
Wheat	100	91
Tobacco	99	81

(D. MACK SMITH, *Italy*, 1969)

(B) *Mussolini (fourth from left, in the haystack) helping in the battle for grain'*

(D) *The Fascist party emblem*

This ancient Roman symbol was used by the Fascist party of Italy as its emblem. The Fascist party used the bundle of rods to stress the idea of strength through unity. Each rod, on its own, was weak. Held together, they were strong. The axehead represents the state which ensures justice for all and punishes any group that weakens the state.

(C) *Steel output (annual production in million tons)*

	1900	1918	1930	1940
Italy	0.1	0.3	0.5	1.0
USA	10.4	45.2	41.4	60.8 (World leader)
Germany	6.6	15.0	11.5	19.0 (European leader)
Belgium	0.7	—	3.4	1.9
France	1.6	1.8	9.4	4.4

(R. WOLFSON, *Years of Change*, 1978)

Questions

1. Why did the Italian Fascist party adopt the ancient Roman symbol as its emblem? (**D**)
2. How many times did Italian steel production multiply between 1918 and 1940? (**C**)
3. How did Italy's progress compare with other European countries? (**C**)
4. Describe the trend in the consumption of popular foodstuffs between 1922–9 and 1930–8. (**A**)
5. What do these figures suggest was happening to the Italian standard of living under Mussolini? (**A**)
6. Why did Mussolini join in the work of bringing in the wheat? (**B**)
7. Talking point: Under Mussolini wages declined and unemployment remained high. How did these help defeat Mussolini's 'battle of the births'?

Fascism in action II

Settlement with the church

One of Mussolini's greatest successes was to end the dispute with the Catholic church which had lasted since 1870. In the Lateran Treaties of 1929 Mussolini recognised Catholicism as the only state religion in Italy. The Italian government also accepted the Pope's right to rule over the tiny Vatican city in Rome. In return Mussolini won the support of many Catholics and made himself respectable in the eyes of many overseas nations.

Sport

Recreation and sport were used to promote Fascism. When Italians won at international sport they were proving the superiority of Fascism.

Education and leisure

Gradually schools were placed under Fascist control. Education was designed to make Italians tough, warlike and disciplined. Outside school, Fascist youth organisations carried on the work of preparation for a disciplined military life. Similar bodies were set up for adults.

Racism

Racial minorities inside Italy such as the Germans, Slavs and French were cruelly persecuted. Mussolini never hated the Jews as Hitler did but in 1938 he began to copy some of the German racial laws. Marriages between Italians and Italian Jews were banned; Jews could not become journalists, teachers, lawyers or members of the Fascist party.

Foreign policy

Mussolini's aims in foreign policy were 'to make Italy great, respected and feared'. Mussolini wanted to revive the days when Rome was the centre of a large and powerful empire. Italians were always being urged to be warlike and prepare for battle. But this was mostly little more than talk. Very little actually happened until the invasion of Abyssinia in 1935 (see p. 76).

(A) *A company of Balillas in the Italian Youth Movement being reviewed by Mussolini*

(B) *Extracts from the compulsory reader issued for eight-year-olds in 1936*

'The eyes of the Duce are on every one of you. No one can say what is the meaning of that look on his face. It is an eagle opening its wings and rising into space. It is a flame that searches out your heart to light there a fire. Who can resist that burning eye, darting out its arrows? But do not be afraid; for you those arrows will change into rays of joy.

A child, who, even while not refusing to obey, asks "Why?," is like a bayonet made of milk. . . . "You must obey because you must," said Mussolini, when explaining the reasons for obedience.

How can we ever forget that fascist boy who, when near to death, asked that he might put on his uniform and that his savings should go to the [Fascist] party?'

(Quoted in D. MACK SMITH, *Italy*)

(C) *A page from an Italian school book*

BENITO MUSSOLINI ama molto i bambini. I bimbi d'Italia amano molto il Duce.

VIVA IL DUCE!

Saluto al Duce:

A noi!

(From HILL AND FELL, *Mussolini and the Fascist Era*, 1969)

(D) *Mussolini is always right*

Fascist slogans

- Believe! Obey! Fight!
- He who has steel has bread!
- Nothing has ever been won in history without bloodshed!
- Better to live one day like a lion than a hundred years like a sheep!
- War is to the male what childbearing is to the female!
- A minute on the battlefield is worth a lifetime of peace!

(Quoted in *Purnell's History of the Twentieth Century*)

Questions

1 What message is this poster trying to get across to Italian school children? (**C**)
2 What does this photograph tell us about the aims of the Italian Youth Movement? (**A**)
3 What sort of ideas did Fascist education try to instil in children? (**B**)
4 What do most of these slogans have in common? Which slogan best expresses the central idea behind Italian Fascism? (**D**)
5 If you had been an Italian at that time do you think you would have become a member of the Fascist party? Why or why not?
6 Why did Mussolini agree to recognise Catholicism as the state religion of Italy? (**T**)
7 Talking point: A totalitarian state is a one party state usually run by a dictator. All opposition is outlawed and the economy is controlled by the government. Education and the news media are used to teach the people the beliefs of the government. Was Italy a totalitarian state? Explain.

The birth of the Weimar Republic

The German revolution

When the First World War ended in 1918 Germany was in chaos. People were starving. The army and navy had mutinied and there was widespread unrest. As a result the Kaiser was forced to give up his throne. To quieten the discontent the new government did away with the monarchy altogether and instead turned Germany into a *republic*.

The Weimar Republic

This new government became known as the Weimar Republic. Under a new constitution Germany became one of the most democratic countries in the world. For the first time all Germans had a say in their government.

Unfortunately the new republic got off to a bad start. Germany was nearly bankrupt and millions of Germans were out of work. Furthermore, many Germans refused to accept that the German army had been defeated in battle. Instead German generals spread the lie that the army had been 'stabbed in the back' by the politicians.

Versailles treaty

Germans were also horrified at the terms of the Versailles peace treaty (see pp. 26, 28). Few accepted the term saying that Germany was guilty of starting the First World War. Even fewer accepted the terms that stripped Germany of much territory and forced her to disarm. Many Germans never forgave the politicians who signed the peace treaty. For them, the Weimar Republic was run by traitors.

Revolts – the Kapp Putsch

Attempts by communists and supporters of royal rule to overthrow the government further weakened the republic. The communists wanted a Russian-style government. In 1919 there were communist revolts in Berlin and Bavaria. They were crushed by the armed squads of ex-soldiers.

In 1920 Dr Wolfgang Kapp led a right-wing *putsch* or revolt. Kapp's supporters hoped to restore the Kaiser. Only a general strike caused the revolt to collapse.

(A) *The scene in a Berlin street, June 1919*

(B) *Towards the end of the First World War (2 October 1918) Hindenburg, the German commander-in-chief sent this letter to the German Chancellor [prime minister]*

'The Supreme Command [holds] to its demand made on Sunday September 29 for the immediate despatch of the Peace offer to our enemies.

Owing to the breakdown on the [Greek] front, which makes necessary a weakening of our reserves in the West, and because of the impossibility of making good our very heavy losses in the battles of the last few days, there no longer exists any prospect, according to human calculation, of forcing peace upon our enemies. The enemy is regularly bringing new and fresh reserves into action. The German army still holds fast and repulses all attacks with success. But the position gets worse every day, and may force the Supreme Command to make serious decisions.

In these circumstances, it is [essential] to stop fighting in order to spare the German people and its allies further useless sacrifices. Every day costs thousands of brave soldiers' lives.'

(Quoted in J. WHEELER-BENNETT, *Hindenburg the Wooden Titan*)

(C) *After the war the German parliament set up a Commission of Inquiry, into the war. Field-Marshal von Hindenburg told the commission:*

'that the army and the military chiefs had always done their best. The German people and the political parties, however, had deserted the men fighting at the front, and, in the words of a British general, "stabbed the army in the back".'

(Quoted in H. VOGT, *The Burden of Guilt*)

Questions

1. List the reasons why Hindenburg wanted to stop fighting in late 1918. (**B**)
2. When the war was over Hindenburg came up with a new set of reasons for losing the war. List these. Suggest why he might have changed his mind. (**C**)
3. How do you think Germans would have reacted to the news that they had to disarm under the terms of the Versailles settlement? (**T**)
4. Talking point: The Allied governments were happy to see the Kaiser replaced by a democratic republic (a government led by an elected president). How might they have helped to get it off to a better start?

Reparations and inflation

Economic collapse

During its first four years the Weimar Republic was in deep economic trouble. Most Germans blamed the high cost of *reparations* (war debts). In fact between 1921 and 1923 hardly any reparations were paid. The real cause was the failure of the German government to tax the rich heavily enough. Between 1919 and 1923 the government spent four times as much as it collected in taxes. As a result it was unable to balance its budget and keep up its reparations payments. To solve the shortage of money the government simply printed more money. The result was runaway inflation.

The invasion of the Ruhr

To force Germany to pay its reparations, France invaded and occupied the Ruhr in 1923. In reply the German workers went on strike. Industrial production slumped and inflation got worse. Money became virtually worthless and it took a suitcase-full of banknotes to buy even a loaf of bread.

Political results

Most Germans blamed the government for the economic collapse. The middle class in particular suffered badly. Inflation made their savings worthless. Many turned against the whole idea of democratic government.

Revolts

Once again Germany seemed ripe for revolution. There were communist risings in Hamburg, Saxony and Thuringia. All were easily smashed by the army. Rebellion from the left was followed by rebellion from the right. In November there was a nationalist *putsch* in Munich similar to that earlier staged by Kapp (see p. 42). However the uprising was badly planned and easily crushed. Among those arrested was Adolf Hitler.

(A) *The occupation of Essen*

'Essen was occupied this afternoon by two divisions of French troops. At twenty minutes to two, the main body of the French forces came down the hill to the railway station and chief post office. . . .

Despite the machine guns, the swords, and slung rifles of the horizon-blue cavalry, who came cantering down the street behind the armoured cars, there were angry murmurs from the crowd – many took no trouble to hide the hatred in their hearts. No one thought of his neighbour. Everyone's face was set in the effort to preserve his control or had already lost it in some cry of grief or pain.

The French troops behaved with absolute correctness – there was no hectoring and no jesting. As on a ceremonial parade, these men passed silently through the equally silent lanes of human beings. . . . The silence was remarkable. Only the clattering of horses' hooves over the cobbles broke it. . . .'

(*The Times*, 12 January 1923)

(B) *A German view of passive resistance*

'The scene is any pit in the Ruhr district. The miners peacefully work the coal and pile it at the pit mouth. One day French troops appear at the mine. The German miners and labourers indignantly leave the spot. The French remain there, and with great difficulty and the assistance of foreign labourers whom they have brought with them, they clear the coal from the pit-head. This done, they move off again. Immediately the German workers and officials reappear and carry on the work in the mine, until once more coal is piled up, and the French come back again. The whole procedure is known as *national passive resistance*.'

(A. ROSENBURG, *A History of the German Republic*, 1936)

(C) *Boys play with a kite made of German banknotes*

(D) *The price of 1 egg (in marks)*

	1914	.09
July	1921	1.6
July	1922	7.
July	1923	5000
September	1923	4 000 000
November	1923	320 000 000 000

Questions

1. How did the Germans react to the occupation of Essen by the French? (**A**)
2. Explain why these boys were allowed to make their kites out of German banknotes. (**C**)
3. What was passive resistance? How did it work? (**B**)
4. Why would it be difficult to convert this table into a graph? (**D**)
5. By what percentage did the price of eggs increase between July and November 1923? (**D**)
6. What economic term describes the trend shown in the table? (**T**) and (**D**)
7. Talking point: Imagine saving hard all your life to buy a retirement cottage. You have nearly enough for a deposit when prices begin to rocket upwards. Within months prices have multiplied a thousand-fold and your savings have become worthless. How would you feel in such circumstances? What would your attitude be towards the government?

Economic recovery 1924–9

At the peak of the economic crisis in 1923 a new *Chancellor* (Prime Minister) named Gustav Stresemann took over. Stresemann called off the strike in the Ruhr and said Germany would pay her reparations. He then issued a new currency to replace the old worthless paper money.

The Dawes Report, 1924 and the Young Plan, 1929

His actions won for Stresemann the support of the US and British governments. In a scheme known as the Dawes Plan they agreed to make it easier for Germany to repay her war debts. The Americans also agreed to loan Germany vast sums of money to rebuild her economy and so pay off her war debts. At the same time the French agreed to withdraw their troops from the Ruhr.

In 1929 a new scheme called the Young Plan cut Germany's reparations by 75 percent. (See also pp. 66, 67.)

For the next six years Germany prospered. Industry and commerce made remarkable progress. In foreign affairs Stresemann's skilful *diplomacy* turned Germany into a respected and trusted nation.

Signs of weakness

In spite of the progress there were still a number of problems.

- Germany's economic prosperity depended on large American loans. If the USA cut off its loans the German economy was bound to crash (see p. 68).
- A large number of Germans remained unhappy with the parliamentary system. Weak leaders and frequent changes of government were common.
- Violence and political murders remained a feature of Weimar life. A number of political parties even had their own private armies. The courts were biased in their treatment of offenders. Left wing offenders were punished harshly while the right wing got away with light sentences. Most of the judges were sympathetic to revolutionaries like Kapp who wanted to restore the Kaiser.

(A) *Production of manufactured goods, 1920–9 (100 = average level of production, 1925–9)*

(Adapted from *Purnell's History of the Twentieth Century*)

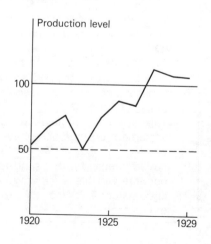

(B) *The National Socialists march on the 'German Day' in Halle, March 1924*
(*Süddeutscher Verlag*)

(C) *In November 1928 Stresemann issued a warning*:
'The economic position is only flourishing on the surface. Germany is in fact dancing on a volcano. If the short term credits are called in a large section of our economy would collapse.'
(Quoted in A.J. RYDER, *Twentieth Century Germany*)

Questions
1   What caused the drop in production in 1923? (**A**) and (**T**)
2   By what percentage did the output of manufactured goods rise between 1924 and 1929? (**A**)
3   How did the Americans contribute towards this increase in output? (**T**)
4   Why were private armies like the one shown in (**B**) a threat to the continued survival of the Weimar Republic?
5   What weakness in the German economy is Stresemann pointing to? (**C**)

The early years of National Socialism

Adolf Hitler

Hitler was born in 1889 and in 1914 volunteered for the German army. Germany's defeat came as a great shock. Like many other German *nationalists*, Hitler believed that the German army had been 'stabbed in the back' by the politicians.

The Nazi party

After the war Hitler joined the small right-wing German Workers party. In 1920 the party was renamed the National Socialist German Workers or Nazi party. In 1921 Hitler became party leader. He wanted to overthrow the republic and make Germany great again. As a speaker Hitler was superb. Crowds flocked to his meetings and party membership grew rapidly. To help gain power, Hitler built up his own private army, the SA or Stormtroopers.

The Munich Putsch

In 1923 Hitler decided that the time was right to seize power. Germany was suffering from runaway inflation and thousands of Germans were hungry (see p. 44). So he and his followers tried to overthrow the Bavarian state government in Munich. It was a miserable failure. A few shots ended what was known as the Beer Hall *Putsch*.

Mein Kampf

Hitler was arrested and sent to prison. While there, he wrote *Mein Kampf* (My Struggle). In his book, Hitler attacked the Treaty of Versailles. He attacked the Weimar Republic. He attacked democracy. Jews and communists were blamed for all the evils of the world. On the other hand pure bred Germans were said to be members of the Aryan master race who would one day rule the world.

After his release from prison, Hitler decided to try and gain power by lawful means rather than by revolution. But this proved difficult. Times were now prosperous and it was hard to attract supporters to any radical party. In the 1928 elections the Nazis won only 2.6 percent of the votes.

(A) *Some of the twenty-five points of National Socialism taken from the 1925 party programme*

1. We demand the union of all Germans ... to form a Great Germany.
2. We demand ... the abolition of the Peace Treaty of Versailles.
3. We demand land and territory for the nourishment of our people and for settling our surplus population.
4. None but members of the nation may be members of the State. None but those of German blood ... may be members of the nation. No Jew, therefore, may be a member of the nation.
6. The right of voting is to be enjoyed by citizens of the State alone ... all official appointments ... shall be granted to citizens of the state alone.
8. All further non-German immigration must be prevented.
11. We demand the abolition of incomes unearned by work.
14. We demand that there shall be profit-sharing in the great industries.
15. We demand a generous development of provision for old age.
18. We demand ruthless war against all whose activities injure the common interest. Common criminals against the nation – money lenders, profiteers etc. – must be punished with death.
19. We demand the education of specially gifted children of poor parents at the expense of the State.
25. That all these points may be realised, we demand the creation of a strong central government in the Reich.

(Quoted in EDWARDS, *Hilter and Germany 1919–39*)

(B) *Nazi election results 1924–8*

	% votes cast	Nazi seats in the Reichstag	Total seats in the Reichstag
May 1924	6.5	32	472
Dec 1924	3.0	14	493
May 1928	2.6	12	491

(C) *A Nazi party artist's impression of Hitler launching the Munich Revolt*

Questions

1. List the points which
   a) are anti-Jewish
   b) might appeal to those with strong *nationalist* (patriotic) feelings
   c) might appeal to those who were poor or came from working-class backgrounds in the National Socalists' party programme. (**A**)
2. Is the artist
   a) sympathetic
   b) neutral, or c) hostile towards Hitler? (**C**) Give reasons.
3. Why was Nazi support stronger in May 1924 than in May 1928? (**B**) and (**T**)
4. Roy Pascal wrote 'no serious historian writing before 1929 would have given more than a passing [mention] to the National Socialist [Nazi] party'. What evidence can you put forward to support this view?

Hitler gains power

Economic depression

In October 1929 the American stock market crashed and the USA slid into depression (see p. 68). Germany soon followed. Banks and businesses were forced to close. The number of unemployed shot up from 650 000 in 1928 to over 5½ million in 1932. Industrial output dropped by 30 percent over the same period. As the depression deepened, Germans lost whatever faith they had had in the Weimar Republic.

Nazis increase support

Here was Hitler's chance. Large numbers of Germans now seemed to want to believe Hitler's claims that the foreigners, the Jews and the communists were to blame for Germany's ills. The Nazi private army, the SA, was used to break up opposition meetings. In the September 1930 elections the Nazis became the second largest party in the Reichstag.

Further success

In April 1932 Hitler challenged the respected wartime leader, Hindenburg, in the presidential elections. He lost, but polled 13 000 000 to Hindenburg's 19 000 000. In the July 1932 elections the Nazis became the largest political party, winning 37 percent of the votes. This meant no government could rule unless it had Nazi support. Hitler was offered cabinet posts in return for his support. But he refused to accept any plan that did not give the Nazis control of the government. President Hindenburg refused this because he was afraid that any government led by Hitler would soon turn into a one-party dictatorship. So another election was held in November. Although the Nazis lost some votes, they were still easily the largest party. Hitler promised President Hindenburg he would act lawfully if he were appointed to lead the government. So, on 30 January 1933, Hindenburg named Hitler as Chancellor.

(A) *Social Democratic party poster 1932, 'The Worker in the Reich of the Swastika' (on the left)*

(B) *Nazi election poster in Berlin 1932, 'We Want Work and Bread. Vote Hitler!' (on the right)*

(C) *Reichstag elections 1928–33; seats won by the major parties*

	PARTY	1928	1930	July 1932	Nov. 1932	Mar. 1933
Left wing parties	Communist	54	77	89	100	81
	Social Democratic	153	143	133	121	120
Centre parties	Democratic	25	20	4	2	5
	Bavarian Peoples	16	19	22	20	19
	Catholic Centre	62	68	75	70	74
	People's	45	30	7	11	2
Right wing parties	Nationalist	73	41	37	52	52
	National Socialist	12	107	230	196	288
	Total Seats	491	577	608	584	647

Questions

1 Who were the left-wing parties? How many seats did they win in 1928? How did the depression affect their total number of seats in the next three elections? **(C)**
2 How many seats did the Nazis win   a) in 1928   b) in the next three elections? **(C)**
3 By how many did Germany's unemployed increase between 1928 and 1933? **(D)**
4 What happened to the popularity of the Nazis as the number of unemployed rose? **(T)**
5 Which group of Germans is the Nazi election poster trying to win the support of? **(B)**
6 What does the Social Democratic poster claim will happen to the workers if they vote for Hitler? **(A)**
7 Talking point: 'Only the Great Depression put the wind into Hitler's sails' (A.J.P. Taylor). Do you agree?

(D) *Unemployment in Germany 1928–33*

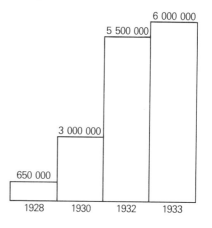

Hitler takes control

Hitler called an election for March 1933, then banned communist meetings and pushed the Nazi message across the radio.

Six days before the election, the Reichstag building went up in flames. Hitler blamed the fire on a communist plot. Here was just the excuse he needed to persuade President Hindenburg to sign an *emergency law*. Under this communist and socialist opponents were jailed without trial and opposition newspaper presses were smashed. A fair election was impossible.

In the March elections the Nazis won 44 percent of the vote. Though not a majority it was enough to convince the new Reichstag to pass an Enabling Law. This gave Hitler the power to pass any law he liked.

At once the Nazis set about bringing the whole of Germany under their control. Political enemies were arrested. All political parties except the Nazi party were dissolved and in July 1933 Germany became a one-party state.

The Night of the Long Knives

After 12 months of Hitler's rule there were rumbles of discontent amongst the SA (stormtroopers). Röhm, the SA chief was upset that Hitler would not let him unite the regular army with the SA under his control. Hitler however realised that if Röhm ran the regular army as well as the SA he would be a powerful threat. The army generals were also opposed to Röhm's plans. They made it clear that unless Hitler crushed Röhm and the SA, they would stop Hitler's succession to the presidency when Hindenburg died.

So, in the early hours of 30 June 1934, 'The Night of the Long Knives', Röhm and other SA leaders were rounded up and shot. The army leaders were delighted. When President Hindenburg died a month later, Hitler combined the offices of Chancellor and President and called himself *Fuehrer* (leader). The army also swore an oath of personal loyalty to Hitler. Hitler's rise to power was complete after only eighteen months.

(A) *Law against the new establishment of parties, 14 July 1933*

Article 1: The National Socialist German Workers' Party [is] the only political party in Germany.
Article 2: Whosoever undertakes to maintain the organizational structure of another political party or to form a new political party will be punished, unless a heavier penalty is prescribed under some other regulation, with penal servitude of up to three years or with imprisonment of from six months to three years.

(Quoted in CRANFIELD *et al.*, *Select Documents*)

(B) *Oath taken by members of the armed forces, 2 August 1934*
'I swear before God this sacred oath that I will render unconditional obedience to the Führer of the German Reich and People, Adolf Hitler, Supreme Commander of the Armed Forces, and that I shall be prepared as a brave soldier to stake my life at any time for this oath.'

(Quoted in CRANFIELD *et al.*, *Select Documents*)

(C) *English cartoonist Low, on The Night of the Long Knives*

THEY SALUTE WITH BOTH HANDS NOW.

(*London Express*, 3 July 1934)

(D) *1933 election poster, 'Our Last Hope: Hitler'*

Questions

1. According to the Nazi poster, why should the Germans vote for Hitler? (**D**)
2. What was the effect of this law? (**A**)
3. Who have their arms raised in the cartoon? (**C**) and (**T**)
4. Who are lying on the ground in the bottom right? (**C**)
5. Which group is in the top right? (**C**)
6. Explain what is meant by the caption. (**C**)
7. Why did Hitler have every soldier take this oath? (**B**)
8. Reread the text opposite and that on page 50. Then list the stages by which Hitler took power in Germany. (**T**)
9. Talking point: Hitler won power quite legally. The Reichstag voted him the powers that turned him into a dictator. What is your opinion?

The Reichstag fire – who was guilty?

Four weeks after Hitler became Chancellor, the Reichstag (the German parliament) was set on fire. Hitler blamed the communists and declared *a state of emergency*. This gave the Nazis power to imprison and wipe out many of their enemies.

A young Dutch communist named Van der Lubbe was caught inside the burning Reichstag. Soon after, four communist leaders were arrested. In the trial that followed the prosecution failed to prove any link between Lubbe and the other defendants. As a result only Lubbe was found guilty and executed. The other four were set free.

What really happened?

Since then historians have argued over who was responsible for setting light to the Reichstag. Some historians think that Lubbe was only a Nazi pawn. They claim it was the Nazis who set fire to the Reichstag as an excuse to crush the communists. Others have argued that Lubbe was the sole arsonist.

In this exercise we shall look first at the evidence which suggests that Lubbe acted alone. Then we shall examine the evidence which suggests that the Nazis were involved.

Van der Lubbe as the sole arsonist

Motive Lubbe set fire to the Reichstag for political reasons. Until 1929 he had been a member of the Dutch communist party. In 1933 Lubbe belonged to a small, extreme left-wing group. When Hitler came to power he decided to visit Germany. There he discovered that the workers were being oppressed.

Van der Lubbe as the pawn of the Nazis

Motive The Nazis were looking for an excuse to crush the communists. Only three days before the fire, they had raided the headquarters of the German communist party.

(A) *The burning Reichstag*

(B) *Lubbe claimed sole responsibility in his statement to the police on 3 March 1933. Over and over he repeated this story:*
'As to the question whether I acted alone, I declare emphatically that this was the case. No one at all helped me, nor did I meet a single person in the Reichstag.'

(C) *Lubbe declared his motive in his statement to the police:*
'. . . In my opinion something absolutely had to be done in protest against this system [National Socialism]. Since the workers would do nothing, I had to do something by myself. I considered arson a suitable method. I did not wish to harm private people but something that belonged to the system itself. I decided on the Reichstag as the centre of the system.'

(D) *After the war many Nazis were placed on trial at Nuremberg as war criminals. At the trial General Halder, the Chief of the General Staff, said:*
'On the occasion of a luncheon on the Führer's birthday in 1943, the people round the Führer turned the conversation to the Reichstag building and its artistic value. I heard with my own ears how Göring broke into the conversation and shouted: "The only one who really knows the Reichstag is I, for I set fire to it."'

(E) *Göring was later questioned on these claims. He replied:*
'What the general says is not true. I should very much like to see him here, so that he can say it to my face. The whole thing is preposterous. Even had I started the fire, I would most certainly not have boasted about it . . . .'

(Extracts **B**–**E** quoted in F. TOBIAS, *The Reichstag Fire*, 1963)

(F) *A recent investigation into the technical aspects of the fire was carried out by experts:*
'It is established beyond any doubt that, given the brief time involved and the primitive means available to Lubbe, it would have been utterly impossible for any one man to set the building alight on this scale.'

(R. MANVELL AND H. FRANKEL, *The Hundred Days to Hitler*, 1974)

(G) *In 1940 ex-Nazi Hermann Rauschning described a conversation he had overheard:*
'Göring described how "the boys" had entered the Reichstag building by a subterranean passage from the President's Palace, and how they had only a few minutes at their disposal and were nearly discovered. He regretted that the "whole shack" had not burnt down. They had been so hurried that they could not "make a proper job of it".'

(Quoted in F. TOBIAS, *The Reichstag Fire*, 1963)

Questions

Van der Lubbe as the sole arsonist
1 Who did Lubbe claim set fire to the Reichstag? (**B**)
2 Lubbe never once changed his story. What importance do you attach to this?
3 What reasons did Lubbe give for burning the Reichstag? (**C**) Would you have believed Lubbe if you had been on the investigation at the time?

Van der Lubbe as the pawn of the Nazis
1 Why should the Nazis want to burn the Reichstag?
2 What does (**F**) suggest about the fire?
3 What do (**D**) and (**G**) have in common?
4 Does Göring's reply seem convincing? (**E**)

Summing up
After considering all the evidence, which of these verdicts would you support?
a) Van der Lubbe was the sole arsonist.
b) Van der Lubbe was used by the Nazis.
c) There is not enough evidence to prove the case either way.

Hitler's Germany I

Racialism

Hitler's ambition was to build a Nazi empire which he hoped would last for a thousand years. Germans, Hitler said, were members of a master race called the Aryans. The Aryans, Hitler claimed, would one day rule the world.

The youth

Hitler looked to the youth to become the future leaders of his empire. Children were encouraged to join an organisation in the Hitler Youth movement. Boys were trained to be brave and tough. Girls were trained to become mothers of pure-bred Aryan Nazis. By 1938 two-thirds of all German children belonged to the Hitler Youth movement. In 1939 membership was made compulsory.

Education

The Nazis controlled all education from kindergarten to university. All teachers who did not believe in Nazism were dismissed. Text books were rewritten to include Nazi ideas. Any books that did not fit in with Nazi thinking were destroyed.

Propaganda

All newspapers were controlled by the Nazis. German-made films preached Nazi ideas. Radio was used to great effect.

Hitler believed propaganda had to be limited to a few simple ideas and that these should be repeated over and over again. He felt this was the only way people would remember what was said. Most of his speeches therefore just repeated the same simple points and ideas. Giant rallies and parades were also staged to whip up support for Hitler.

Dr Goebbels was appointed Minister of Public Enlightenment and Propaganda. His job was to make people think like good Nazis and believe in all the Nazi aims. He also made sure people heard about all the things the party and Hitler supported.

(A) *A Nazi motto for youth: 'Fuehrer command, we follow.'*

(B) *Hitler with a group of German youth*

(C) *An extract from a child's early reading book*

ON APRIL 20

When the Führer has a birthday, that is also a special day for us. At home we place flowers behind his picture.

We also take some flowers with us to school. There we have a big, coloured picture of the Führer. It hangs in such a way that we all can see it. There are always flowers under it. We bring them from our garden or we pluck them on the way to school. On April 20 they have to be especially pretty: catkins, or primroses, or the first may lilies of the valley!

When school begins, we all stand up before the picture, we sing a song to the Führer. One boy makes a speech, and our teacher tells us some birthday stories. Then we greet the Führer with a *Sieg-Heil* (hail-victory).

Where will the Führer be this year when he celebrates his birthday? If I could be there! I would say: 'Dear Führer, remain always healthy!' Then I would give him the most beautiful flowers from my garden.

(Quoted in L. SNYDER, *The Dynamics of Nationalism*)

(D) *The purpose of education*
'The whole function of education is to create Nazis' (Dr Rust, Nazi Minister of Education).

(E) *A German song*

Mein Führer!

(Das Kind spricht:)

Ich kenne dich wohl und habe dich lieb
        wie Vater und Mutter.
Ich will dir immer gehorsam sein
        wie Vater und Mutter.
Und wenn ich groß bin, helfe ich dir
        wie Vater und Mutter,
Und freuen sollst du dich an mir
        wie Vater und Mutter!

(E) *English translation of the German song*

MY LEADER!

(The child speaks:)
I know you well and love you like Father and Mother. I want always to obey you like Father and Mother.
And when I am big I will help you like Father and Mother,
And you shall take pride in me like Father and Mother.

Questions
1 What effect does Hitler exert over these young Germans (**B**)?
2 What evidence is there in the photograph to suggest that this scene was especially staged for publicity purposes? (**B**)
3 Why were the Nazis so interested in the youth? (**A**)
4 Why did the Nazis take over control of education? (**D**)
5 What do the extract from the child's reader and the illustration from the book have in common? (**C**) and (**E**)
6 Why did Hitler repeat the same ideas over and over again in his broadcasts and speeches? (**T**)

Hitler's Germany II

The economy

Hitler's economic policy had three main aims:
- to cut unemployment and end the depression
- to rearm Germany and gear the economy for war
- to encourage the workers, businessmen and farmers to serve the needs of the state.

To revive the economy, Hitler adopted a policy of massive public spending. Unemployment was slashed and industrial output rocketed. Jobs were provided by employing men on public works such as *autobahns* (motorways). Large scale rearmament provided jobs in building weapons. The *conscription* of young people into the armed forces cut unemployment even further.

Extra jobs were created by Hitler's policy of *autarky* or economic self-sufficiency. Instead of importing essential raw materials like oil and rubber, Germany began to make her own.

Opposition

Those who opposed Hitler were rapidly silenced. The SS, formed in 1925 as Hitler's bodyguard, grew into a giant secret police force. The most feared branch of the SS was the Gestapo. People were arrested, imprisoned or shot without reason. Those imprisoned often ended up in concentration camps run by the SS.

Support

The numbers arrested by the Gestapo should not be exaggerated. Most Germans seemed to support Hitler once he was in power. For most workers life seemed better under the Nazis. The jobless had work and working conditions and holidays improved. On the other hand workers had few rights. Trade unions were abolished and strikes were made illegal. Firms were told what and how much to produce. Most of them benefited also from the huge public spending on housing, public works and rearmament. Workers and employers were made to join a new organisation – the *German Labour Front*.

(A) *A giant Nazi rally, 1935*

(B) *Victims of the police state*
'Death sentences for "political opposition": 1930–1932, 8; 1934–1939, 534. Number under "protective arrest" (Gestapo report, April 1939) 162 734.
Population of the six concentration camps, 1939: Dachau – 4000; Mauthausen – 1500; Sachsenhausen – 6500; Buchenwald – 5300; Flossenburg – 1600; Ravensbruck – 2500.

The last Socialist leaders still in Germany were arrested in June 1933. . . . Almost all Communist groups had been broken up by the Gestapo by early 1934.

In 1934, many Protestant clergymen broke away from the Nazi controlled "National Church" to form the Confessional Church. Martin Niemoller became its leader. In March 1935, over 700 Protestant clergy were arrested, and Niemoller was forbidden to speak anywhere in Germany. In 1937, the Pope accused Hitler of attacking Christianity. Some 800 Catholic and Protestant clergy were sent to concentration camps. In 1938, Niemoller was taken into "protective custody". He spent the last seven years of his life in the concentration camps of Sachsenhausen and Dachau.'

(T. EDWARDS, *Hitler and Germany*, 1972)

(C) *No freedom of speech*
'We have to put a stop to the idea that it is part of everybody's civil right to say whatever he pleases.'
(ADOLF HITLER)

(D) *Number of unemployed 1928–38 (in millions)*
(Based on figures in D. CHILDS, *Germany Since 1918*)

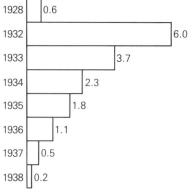

1928	0.6
1932	6.0
1933	3.7
1934	2.3
1935	1.8
1936	1.1
1937	0.5
1938	0.2

(E) *Hitler practising for a speech*

Questions

1. What was the effect of Hitler's policies on unemployment? (**D**) Quote figures.
2. Hitler was a superb public speaker. What sort of techniques did he use to work up his audiences? (**E**)
3. Compare Hitler's technique with Mussolini's (see p. 37). What do they have in common?
4. Why do you think Hitler felt this way? (**C**)
5. How many Germans were   a) under 'protective arrest' in 1939   b) in concentration camps in 1939? (**B**)
6. How did the Nazis silence opposition from the churches? (**B**)
7. How do you think Germans felt when attending giant rallies like the one in the photograph? (**A**)
8. Talking point: Do you think Hitler kept power chiefly   a) by using force and terror, or   b) because he enjoyed widespread support from the German people?

The persecution of the Jews

Hitler hated the Jews. They made up a mere one percent of the population, yet he blamed them for all Germany's troubles. Right from the start the Nazi party made anti-semitism (hatred of the Jews) a feature of its policy.

The first years of persecution

Once in power, Hitler ordered the first official boycott of Jewish shops, goods, doctors and lawyers. Germans were ordered not to do business with Jews. On 7 April 1933, 'public servants not of Aryan stock' i.e. those who were one-quarter or more Jewish, were dismissed. More than 2000 Jewish scientists and professors were fired. Similar acts barred Jews from the professions. Those who protested, or were simply a nuisance, were imprisoned.

The Nuremburg Laws

In September 1935 Hitler released the Nuremburg Laws.

The Reich Citizenship Act stated that no Jew could be a German citizen. He had no right to vote and he could not be appointed to any office of state. The Blood Protection Act forbade Germans to marry or have sex with Jews. Existing 'mixed' marriages were dissolved.

Towards the end of 1937 Jews were forced to sell their businesses.By now the majority of them had lost their jobs and had to live off their savings.

The pogrom of 9–10 November 1938

In early November 1938 a German official was assassinated by a Jew. This served as an excuse to unleash the Jewish pogrom (mob attack). On the night of 9–10 November Jewish synagogues and shops were destroyed. Over 90 Jews were murdered. 30 000 were imprisoned.

More Jews now left Germany than ever before. For those that remained, Hitler had other plans. In 1939 he told the Reichstag that if war came, it would result in 'the destruction of the Jewish race in Europe'. In the Second World War Hitler almost succeeded. Of Europe's ten million Jews, 6 000 000 were massacred.

(A) *In his book*, Mein Kampf, *Hitler wrote*:
'If, at the beginning and during the [First World] war, someone had only subjected about twelve or fifteen thousand of these Hebrew (Jewish) enemies of the people to poison gas – as was suffered by hundreds of thousands of our best workers from all walks of life and callings on the battlefield   then the sacrifice of millions at the front would not have been in vain.'

(Quoted in H. KRAUSNICK *et al.*, *Anatomy of the SS State*, 1968)

(B) *A German having his nose measured*

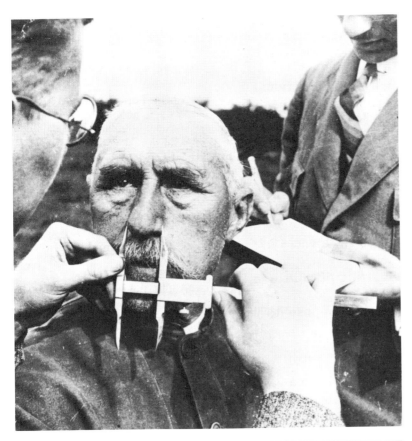

(C) 'The Eternal Jew'

(D) *Front page from the German newspaper, 'Der Stürmer'. Blood is pouring from innocent Germans into Jewish dishes. The bottom line reads, 'The Jews are our misfortune'.*

Questions

1   Describe Hitler's attitude towards the Jews. (**A**)
2   What happened to Jews who protested about being banned from the professions? (**T**)
3   If you saw a newspaper like this today, how would you react? (**D**)
4   What was the main aim behind the Nuremburg Laws? (**T**) Should Germans have been surprised at those laws?
5   Name three things that Jews are accused of being in this poster. (**C**)
6   Why do you think this German is having his nose measured? (**B**)
7   What do you think was the purpose behind the pogrom? (**T**)
8   What did Hitler plan to do with the Jews? (**T**)

The League of Nations

Towards the end of the First World War, President Wilson of the USA put forward a list of 14 points to bring about world peace. The last point called for the setting up of a world parliament where nations would meet together to settle arguments instead of going to war.

At the Paris peace conference an international body called the League of Nations was set up:

(1) If a member country was attacked, the rest of the League would treat the matter as an attack on themselves and go to the aid of their fellow members. This was called *collective security*.

(2) Member countries promised to seek to solve their problems by talking rather than fighting.

(3) If talks between nations broke down, they were to go before the League to settle their differences.

(4) If fighting broke out, the members would be asked to punish the guilty party by cutting off all trade. This was known as a *trade sanction*.

(5) If all else failed, the League could impose its will by force and apply a *military sanction*.

Other activities

Apart from peacekeeping, the League took on a vast range of other activities. These included organising *commissions* to deal with special jobs such as disarmament, health and *mandates*. A mandate was a former colony of Germany or of Turkey which had been confiscated. Under the mandate system, the Allies (e.g. Britain and France) took over the colonies and ruled them in trust for the League.

Successes

In the 1920s, the League was successful in solving a number of disputes between small nations. For instance, in 1925 when Greece invaded Bulgaria, the League ordered the Greeks to withdraw. The Bulgars were told not to oppose the Greeks. Both sides obeyed and peace was restored.

But the true test of the League was to come in the 1930s, when disputes arose involving the big powers.

Weaknesses of the League

- Three of the great powers were not members. To succeed, the League needed the support of all the great powers. The United States did not join the League even though it was their own President's brainchild. (Americans were afraid the League of Nations would tie them up in Europe's squabbles.) Because Germany was a defeated nation, it did not join until 1926. Russia, on the other hand, was in the middle of a civil war and was not invited to join.
- The League had no power to enforce its decisions. It had no police force or army of its own. Members were expected to provide troops when needed.
- The League could only use force in a dispute if all the members agreed.

(A) *'The Gap in the Bridge'*

THE GAP IN THE BRIDGE.

(*Punch*, 10 December 1919)

(B) *In 1920 at the First Assembly of the League of Nations, Lord Cecil, one of the League's strongest supporters, claimed:*
'By far the most powerful weapon at the command of the League of Nations is not the economic weapon or the military weapon or any other weapon of material force. By far the strongest weapon we have is the weapon of public opinion.'

(J. TERRAINE, *The Mighty Continent*, 1976)

(C) *A German view*
'In many aspects the League is heir and executor of the treaties of 1919. Out of these treaties, there have arisen ... many differences between the League and Germany.'
(G. Stresemann, foreign minister of Germany, two days after Germany joined the League in 1926)

(Quoted in R.C.J. STONE, *The Drift to War*)

(D) *A Russian view*
'The League is a robber's den to safeguard the unjust spoils of Versailles.'

(Lenin, Soviet leader)

(Quoted in R.C.J. STONE, *The Drift to War*)

Questions

1   In your own words, write down the five points that members of the League had to agree to when they joined the League. (**T**)
2   Which country's refusal to join at the start created serious problems? Why was this country so important to the success of the League? (**A**) and (**T**)
3   Germany and Russia were originally excluded. Germany joined in 1926, Russia in 1934. Which sources provide support for the idea that the League of Nations suffered from being associated with the hated Treaty of Versailles?
4   Why do you think Lenin thought the League was a robber's den? (**D**) You may need to refer back to the text on p. 30.
5   How could public opinion be a weapon for the League of Nations to use to stop war? (**B**)
6   Do you agree with Lord Cecil that public opinion can stop wars from breaking out or do the politicians and generals do what they like anyway?
7   Talking point: Under the constitution of the League of Nations every state was given one vote. New Zealand for example, with a population of under 1.3 million, had the same say as China with 500 million. Was this fair? How should votes be allocated in a world body?

The French search for security

At the conference of Versailles in 1919 the French had argued for a harsh treaty for Germany. They wanted revenge and a guarantee that Germany would never attack France in war again. (See p. 26).

On paper the Treaty of Versailles weakened Germany very considerably. The French however still worried that Germany would ignore the terms, rearm and once again threaten French interests. These fears increased when the other great powers began to lose interest in Europe. Great Britain was more concerned with her empire than France's worries and Russia also was still too involved with the effects of her own revolution.

French reactions

Left alone France aimed to protect herself in two ways:
(1) By keeping Germany weak
     One way of doing this was to make sure Germany paid the heavy reparations. In 1921 reparations were fixed at £6600 million to be paid back over 60 years. In 1923 however, Germany declared she could not afford to make any further payments. The French then decided to send an army to the industrial region of the Ruhr in Germany to force Germany to continue to pay the reparations. The French action was not very successful. The German workers went on strike in protest at the French army's occupation, the German government went bankrupt and the German mark soon became worthless.

     The French army did not withdraw from the Ruhr until 1925 when the Treaty of Locarno was signed. This treaty protected the boundary between France and Germany and was guaranteed by Italy and Britain. Together with the Dawes Plan which helped Germany to repay her war debts, it gave France more confidence in her own safety.
(2) By keeping a strong army and forming alliances

In the 1920s France signed a number of alliances with friendly countries including
• a military agreement with Belgium in 1920
• a military alliance with Poland in 1921
• a treaty with Czechoslovakia in 1924

(A) *France searches for security*

(C) *Hands off the Ruhr*

Hände weg vom Ruhrgebiet!

(B) *French security*

'What France wanted from Germany, after two damaging invasions in fifty years was above all, security. As M. Clemenceau (the French prime minister) told the peace conference in January 1919:

"If a new war should take place, Germany would not throw her forces upon Cuba or upon Honduras, but upon France; it would always be upon France."'

(J. TERRAINE, *The Mighty Continent*, 1976)

Questions

1   Why were the French so worried about a strong Germany? (**B**)
2   How did they intend keeping Germany in line? (**T**)
3   The Ruhr produced four-fifths of Germany's coal and iron. What evidence is there in (**C**) to show that the Ruhr was a valuable area?
4   How does the German cartoon picture the French? (**C**)
5   Examine the map. What does the pattern of alliances suggest was France's aim behind her system of alliances? (**A**)

The golden twenties?

The Locarno Pact, 1925

In 1925, a *pact* between Germany, France, Belgium, Great Britain and Italy was signed at Locarno. In it, Germany agreed to accept her western frontier with France and Belgium as final and settled.

Germany added to the goodwill she had created at Locarno by joining the League of Nations in 1926.

The Kellogg-Briand Pact, 1928

Briand, the French foreign minister, produced a plan that France and the USA should sign a pact to renounce war. Kellogg, the American secretary of state, was enthusiastic. Sixty-five countries signed, including the Japanese, Americans and Russians. Countries were allowed to fight only in self-defence.

The Young Plan, 1929

The total amount of reparations had been left unchanged by the Dawes Plan of 1924. In 1929 an international committee headed by an American banker, Owen Young, reduced Germany's reparations from £6.6 billion to £2 billion to be paid off by 1988. Not surprisingly, the plan was welcomed in Germany.

1924–9: An era of hope

Historians have sometimes called the period 1924–9 an era of hope; a time when Europe seemed to be settling most of its problems.

On the opposite page are a collection of jumbled pieces of evidence on the late 1920s. Some provide support for the argument that 1924–9 was a period of *real* hope! Other pieces of evidence support the opposite point of view. Sort them into two groups. Some irrelevant information has also been added in order to distract you. Be careful to leave this out!

Was 1924–9 a period of real hope?

(A) The Dawes and Young Plans settled Germany's reparation problems. Between 1924–9 Germany made the payments required by the Dawes Plan and expanded her economy.

(B) 1928, Kellogg Pact. 65 countries renounce war.

(C) France and Great Britain never agreed over what to do about Germany. France wanted to keep Germany weak by enforcing the Treaty of Versailles. Great Britain was not really interested in Europe, concentrating on her empire.

(D) The 1920s saw the revival of the Ku Klux Klan whose aim was white supremacy.

(E) At Locarno Germany never signed anything accepting her eastern frontiers with Poland and Czechoslovakia, as laid down in the Treaty of Versailles.

(F) 1925 Treaty of Locarno. Germany voluntarily accepted as settled, her western frontiers, as laid down at Versailles.

(G) The late 1920s were prosperous. Production, trade and personal incomes were rising.

(H) Anti-war feeling was very high in most countries in the late 1920s. In 1929 Remarque's anti-war novel *All Quiet on the Western Front* was a best-seller in several languages.

(I) 1928, Stalin launched the first five-year plan to make the USSR into a world industrial power.

(J) The Kellogg Pact made no provision for punishing any country which broke the agreement.

(K) 1926, Germany joined the League of Nations, and was given a permanent seat on the council with the other great powers.

(L) Germany borrowed abroad nearly three times as much as she paid in reparations. The USA lent money to Germany which enabled her to pay reparations to the European ex-allies, which enabled them to pay war debt payments to the USA and so the circle continued.

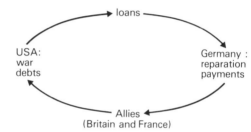

The world depression of the 1930s

The prosperity of the late 1920s was shattered by the great depression of the 1930s. Everywhere living standards fell, businesses closed and unemployment queues lengthened.

Causes of depression

To understand the causes of the depression we must go back to the First World War.

The European economies had collapsed under the strain of war and the USA had to come to the rescue with giant loans to the Allies. The Allies hoped to pay these back in two ways. First, by making Germany pay heavy *reparations*. Secondly, by exporting goods to the USA. But both ways proved difficult. The Germans could not pay their debts and the Americans had to help out with large loans. Most other European countries also had to borrow money from the USA in order to repay their first loans. The USA was thus more than ever the economic centre of the world.

End of the economic boom

In October 1929 the American *stock market* collapsed in what is called the Wall Street crash. Americans lost confidence and called in their loans to Europe. Forced to pay back these loans, a number of large European banks collapsed. Their customers panicked and tried to get their savings out, but found they had already lost their money.

These losses meant that people had little left to spend. Businesses were therefore not able to sell their goods and so had to cut production. Many firms had to close completely. The number of unemployed rose quickly to enormously high levels. The depression had well and truly set in.

As the world economy collapsed people felt threatened and insecure. They were ready to listen to any party or government who offered a solution.

(A) *The depression spreads to the rest of the world*

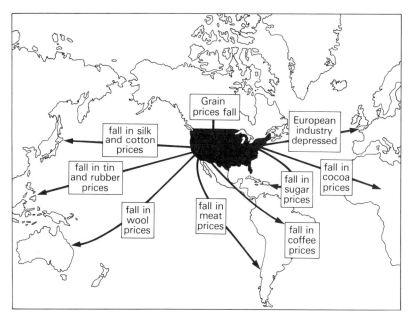

(B) *World dependence on the US economy*

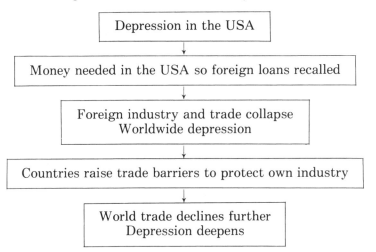

(C) *American overseas loans 1924–8 (in millions of dollars)*

to Canada	936
to Latin America	1421
to Europe	2815
to Asia and the Pacific	586
Total	5758*

*In this period the USA lent twice as much as Britain

(D) *Drop in world trade 1929–33*

	Value (millions US$)
1929	5352
1930	4857
1931	3529
1932	2134
1933	1788

(League of Nations, *World Economic Survey*, 1932–3)

Questions

1. What area of the world relied most on American loans between 1924 and 1928? (**C**)
2. What would be likely to happen to these countries if these money loans were withdrawn? Explain fully. (**C**) and (**T**)
3. Using your own words draw an illustrated flow diagram to show how the depression spread from the USA to the rest of the world. (**A**) and (**B**)
4. What was the volume of world trade in a) 1929 b) 1933? (**D**) Describe the trend in world trade between these two dates.
5. What caused the drop in world trade? (**B**) and (**T**)

Research

Try to find five people who remember the early 1930s. Interview them to find out what the depression meant to ordinary people. Then write a short account of what it was like.

The depression and Japan

The depression

Japan was hard hit by the depression. Export prices for her vital silk crop fell by 50 percent and by 1931 half her factories were lying idle. Among the people there was widespread unrest and this soon spread to the army.

For most of the army, the answer to depression was a strong government at home and expansion overseas.

The invasion of Manchuria

The ideal target overseas was China. Japan already owned industries in the northern province of Manchuria. There was also a Japanese army base near Port Arthur. So, in 1931, some Japanese troops deliberately blew up a section of the Japanese-owned railway near Mukden. They then blamed the Chinese for the explosion and used the excuse to invade Manchuria.

The League fails

China appealed to the League of Nations for help. But all the League could do was set up the Lytton Commission to investigate the incident. In the meantime the Japanese continued their invasion. By 1932 all of Manchuria was in Japanese hands and the region was renamed Manchukuo.

Eventually, after the commission had condemned Japan, the League ordered Japan to evacuate Manchuria. No other action was ever taken. No sanctions were imposed and no one was prepared to use force against Japan. In reply Japan simply withdrew from the League.

The League had failed its first real test. From 1932 to 1936 Japan expanded into northeast China. At the same time the army gained more and more power in the Japanese government. In 1937 Japan began a full scale war with China which lasted until 1945.

(A) *Some opinions on the effects of the Manchurian crisis on the League of Nations*

(i) 'Manchuria demonstrated that the League was toothless.'

(A.P. ADAMTHWAITE, *The Making of the Second World War*, 1977)

(ii) 'The failure of the League of Nations to stop aggression in Manchuria had grave consequences in Europe too . . . . The lesson was plain; there was no power in the world to stop a determined aggressor.'

(JOHN ROBOTTOM, *Modern China*, 1967)

(iii) In 1933 Dr Wellington Koo, China's representative to the League of Nations Assembly, warned: 'The absence of any effective action by the League (over Manchuria) had encouraged those who all along had been proclaiming the belief that might is right.'

(Quoted in A.P. ADAMTHWAITE, *The Making of the Second World War*)

(B) *Japanese invasion of China 1931-8*

Japan: problems
Depression
Unemployment
Strong militarist groups
Dissatisfaction with government
Falling markets

Manchuria: solutions
Coal
Iron ore
Bauxite
Timber
Living space
Markets

0   500 km

▦ Japanese territory before 1931
▨ Area seized in 1931
▧ Occupied by October 1938

(C) *'The Doormat'*

(D) *Japan's foreign trade 1919-37 (in million yen) – excluding trade with her colonies*

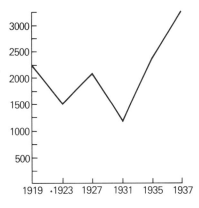

Questions

1 By approximately what percentage did Japan's trade drop between 1927 and 1931? (**D**) In what other period did Japan's trade fall off sharply?

2 Why was the takeover of Manchuria seen as the answer to Japan's economic problems? (**B**)

3 Who does the lady on the ground in the cartoon represent? Who does the soldier represent? (**C**)

4 Why do you think the cartoonist chose to caption his cartoon 'The Doormat'?

5 What point is the cartoonist trying to make about the Japanese invasion of Manchuria?

6 What do all three opinions in (**A**) have in common? Do you agree with them? Say why.

7 Talking point: There is only one rule between countries and that is might is right. No League of Nations could ever hope to change that. Do you agree?

The German depression and Hitler

The rise of Hitler

In the same way as it had hit Japan, the great depression
had flattened the German economy. Industry collapsed
and millions were unemployed. In desperation many
Germans turned to Adolf Hitler and the Nazis for leadership.

Hitler was strong and decisive. He offered explanations
of why things had gone wrong and was able to say what he
and the Nazis could do to improve the economy. People
turned to him because of this and by 1932 the Nazi party
became the strongest political party in Germany. By 1933
the Nazis were so strong that the German president appointed Hitler as Chancellor (prime minister). Within
eighteen months Hitler had the whole of Germany under
his personal control. (For a fuller picture of the rise of
Hitler and Hitler's domestic policies see pp. 50–61.)

Hitler's foreign policy

Through his foreign policy Hitler planned to:
- Make Germany great again by becoming the 'number
  one' power in Europe
- Overthrow the Treaty of Versailles and recover the
  lands lost during the First World War
- Unite all Germans in central Europe under his rule in an
  enlarged Germany
- Conquer land in the east to provide living space (*Lebensraum*). By subduing 'inferior' peoples such as the Poles
  and Russians, Hitler hoped that the Germans could
  prove to the world that they were indeed the master
  race. The east would also provide food and valuable raw
  materials for Germany.

(A) *In October 1936 Hitler sent the following memorandum to his right-hand man, Göring*
'I thus set the following task:
(1) The German army must be operational within four years.
(2) The German economy must be fit for war within four years.'

(B) *The Hossbach Memorandum*
On 5 November 1937, Hitler called a meeting of his military chiefs at which he outlined future plans. Hitler's personal *adjutant*, Colonel Hossbach, took detailed notes of what was said at the meeting:

(1) 'It is not a case of conquering space but of conquering agriculturally useful space. . . .
(2) German politics must reckon with its two hateful enemies, England and France. . . .
(3) The German questions can be solved only by way of force, and this is never without risk. . . .
(4) If the Führer is still living, then it will be his decision to solve the German space problem no later than 1943–45 . . . . For the improvement of our military position it must be our first aim . . . to conquer Czechoslovakia and Austria . . . in order to remove any threat from the flanks in case of a possible advance westwards. . . . Once Czechoslovakia is conquered then a neutral attitude by Poland could more easily be relied upon. . . . Military preparations with Russia must be countered by the speed of our operations.'

(Quoted in R.C.J. STONE, *The Drift to War*)

(C) *Quotations from* **Mein Kampf**, *1924*
'France is and will remain the . . . enemy of Germany.'

'Only two states remain to us as possible allies in Europe – England and Italy.'

'. . . when we speak of new territory in Europe today, we must think principally of Russia and the border states subject to her.'

'Germany – Austria must be restored to the great German Motherland.'

'Germany will either become a world power or will not continue to exist at all . . . to become a world power it needs that territorial magnitude which gives it the necessary importance today. . . . This colossal empire in the East is ripe for dissolution.'

'Only those with German blood can be citizens. No Jew can be a member of the race.'

Questions

1. In order to succeed, which points in the Nazi party programme would require Germany to enlarge her area? (**T**) (**A**) (**B**) and (**C**)
2. Read the quotations from *Mein Kampf* (My Struggle), a book Hitler wrote in 1924. (**C**)
   a) Who is Germany's enemy?
   b) Who are Germany's likely friends?
   c) Which country will Germany expand into? What direction will this be?
3. Can you suggest any reasons for Hitler's secret memorandum to Göring? (**A**)
4. In the Hossbach Memorandum:
   a) Who does Hitler now regard as his enemies?
   b) To what lengths will he go to achieve his aims?
   c) Which countries is he intending to take over?
   d) In what order is Hitler intending to invade the countries? (**B**)
5. Do you think Hitler's foreign policy was likely to lead to a war which would involve most of Europe? Give reasons.

Germany rearms

To make Germany great and powerful Hitler needed large armed forces. Yet under the Versailles treaty, Germany was forbidden to have an army of more than 100 000 men. The navy was not allowed any submarines and was limited to six battleships. No airforce at all was permitted.

Early moderation

For a time it even looked as though Hitler would accept this situation. In his early speeches, he talked of living in peace and friendship with his neighbours and of doing away with Germany's armed forces entirely.

Disarmament

Encouraged by Hitler's promises and by hopes of peace, the League of Nations organised a Disarmament Conference in 1932. Representatives of over 60 nations came to this to discuss ways in which their countries might disarm and so reduce the chances of war.

Unfortunately the conference did not achieve anything, largely because of German and French attitudes towards it. Germany wanted everyone to disarm to her own low level. She then argued that despite the Treaty of Versailles she should at least be allowed some of the weapons that other powers had. This German argument made France even more nervous. She still felt threatened by Germany and so suggested that all powers should be allowed conscripted armies for self defence. When France refused to co-operate, Hitler withdrew Germany from the conference and from the League of Nations as well.

After the failure of the conference, Germany began to rearm at great speed. In 1935 Hitler announced that Germany already had a new Luftwaffe (air force). He also announced that he was introducing conscription in order to increase the size of the German army to 500 000 men. Both these announcements confirmed that Hitler now felt powerful enough to challenge the Treaty of Versailles which had forbidden German armament.

(A) *Hitler speaks to the Reichstag on 17 May 1933 just after he became Chancellor:*
'Germany is at any time willing to undertake further [disarmament] ... if all other nations are ready ... to do the same.... Germany would also be perfectly ready to disband her entire military [forces] and destroy the small amount of arms remaining to her if the remaining countries will do the same thing with equal thoroughness.'
(Quoted in A.P. ADAMTHWAITE, *The Making of the Second World War*)

(B) *In October 1933 the London* Daily Mail *printed an interview with Hitler. It quoted Hitler as saying:*
'Almost all of us leaders of the National Socialist movement were actual combatants [fighters]. I have yet to meet the combatant who desires a renewal of the horrors of [the First World War].... Our youth [is] our sole hope for the future. Do you imagine that we are bringing it up only to be shot down on the battlefield?'
(Quoted in H. VOGT, *The Burden of Guilt*, 1965)

(D) *German military spending 1932–8 (in billions of marks)*

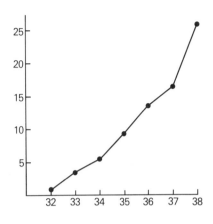

(C) *Military spending 1932–8* (as percentage of Gross National Product)

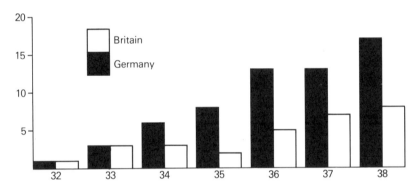

Questions

1 Why do you think politicians outside Germany were happy to hear speeches from Hitler such as (**A**) and (**B**)? Suggest why Hitler might have been keen in his early years as Chancellor to portray himself as a moderate politician to countries such as France and Britain.

2 What condition did Hitler place on Germany's disarming? Do you think this condition was ever likely to be met by the other countries? Why or why not? (**A**)

3 What percentages of a) Germany's b) Britain's GNP was spent by the military in 1932 and 1938? (GNP is a measure of a country's total wealth.) What pattern is shown by the figures? (**C**)

4 How many times did German military spending rise between 1932 and 1938? (**D**)

5 Do you think the Disarmament Conference set up by the League ever had a chance of success? (**T**) Why or why not?

6 Talking point: Was Hitler sincere in calling for disarmament or was he just trying to fool the foreign powers into a false sense of security?

The Abyssinian crisis

The Stresa Front

Germany's rearming soon alarmed the other European powers. In a move to check her, France, Italy and Britain met at Stresa in April 1935. Together they protested at German rearmament and at Hitler's breaking of the Treaty of Versailles. At the same time, they promised to safeguard the peace of Europe. But this anti-German 'Stresa Front' as it was known, lasted less than six months. When the Italians broke the peace themselves by making war on Abyssinia in late 1935, the Stresa Front fell apart.

The Abyssinian crisis

Ever since coming to power in 1922, Italy's leader, Mussolini, had talked of creating a large Italian overseas empire. Already there were three Italian colonies in North Africa – Libya, Eritrea and Somaliland (see map A). Weak and backward neighbouring Abyssinia was an easy target, and in 1935 Italian troops easily overran the country.

The League of Nations

Here was another test for the League, just like the invasion of Manchuria (see p. 70). This time not only was the aggressor condemned but economic sanctions were also passed. Ships were forbidden to carry arms to Italy or take goods away from Italy. But the sanctions proved useless. Above all, Italy's oil supplies were never cut off.

Hoare–Laval Pact

France and Britain could have stopped Italy by cutting off supplies with a naval blockade. But they had no wish to upset Mussolini. A move against Mussolini might have driven him into the arms of Hitler. Instead the foreign ministers of Britain and France, Hoare and Laval, secretly met in Paris and dreamed up a plan called the Hoare–Laval Pact, to give Italy most of Abyssinia. But when the pact was accidentally leaked to the press there was such a public outcry that the pact was dropped.

The end of the League

The results of the Abyssinian crisis were disastrous. Mussolini was annoyed by the sanctions and so looked increasingly towards Hitler for support. Hitler realised that the crisis proved that the League and the idea of collective security would not work. There was little now to discourage him from pursuing a more active foreign policy for Germany.

(A) *The Italian Empire in Africa*

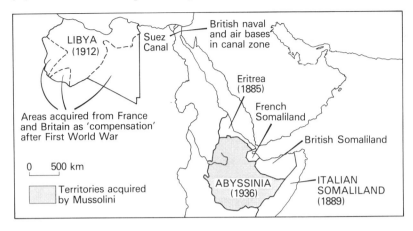

(B) *Haile Selassie protests to the League against the Italian invasion 1935–6*

'In October 1935, Italian troops invaded my territory . . . .

In that unequal struggle between a government commanding more than 42 000 000 inhabitants and having at its disposal financial, industrial and technical means which enabled it to create unlimited quantities of the most death-dealing weapons, and on the other hand, a small people of 12 000 000 inhabitants, without arms, without resources and having on its side only the justice of its cause and the promise of the League of Nations, what real assistance was given to Ethiopia by the fifty-two nations who had declared the Rome Government guilty of a breach of the covenant . . . ?

I assert that the problem submitted to the Assembly today is much wider than merely a question of settlement of Italian aggression; it is collective security, it is the very existence of the League.

Representatives of the world. What reply have I to take back to my people?'

(Quoted in *New York Times*, 1 July 1936)

(C) *Mussolini explains why Italy invaded Abyssinia*

'It is not only our Army that marches to its objective, 44 million Italians march with that Army, all united and alert. Let others try to commit the blackest injustice, taking away Italy's place in the sun. When, in 1915, Italy united her fate with the Allies, how many promises were made? To fight the common victory Italy brought her supreme contribution of 670 000 dead, 480 000 disabled and more than a million wounded. When we went to the table of that odious peace they gave us only the crumbs of the colonial booty.'

(Speech of Mussolini, 2 October 1935 (quoted in *Keesing's Contemporary Archives*, 1935)

(D) *Cartoon, by Low, on Mussolini's invasion of Abyssinia*

THE LEAGUE ? PAH! 'THE LEAGUE IS CONTEMPTIBLE!' THE LEAGUE CAN DO NOTHING!

Questions
1. What territories had Mussolini gained for Italy before Abyssinia? (**A**)
2. Which sentence in Mussolini's speech claims that all Italians supported the invasion of Abyssinia? (**C**)
3. Look again at the map. What are the 'crumbs of the colonial booty' referred to in Mussolini's speech? (**A**) and (**C**)
4. How does Mussolini justify his takeover of Abyssinia? (**C**)
5. What evidence does Haile Selassie use in his speech to show that the Abyssinians did not stand a chance in battle? (**B**)
6. What does he suggest will happen to the League of Nations if the Abyssinians do not receive its support? (**B**)

The reoccupation of the Rhineland

The Saar

Under the Treaty of Versailles the Saar, a rich coal-mining area, had been taken from Germany and placed under League of Nations control for 15 years. In 1935 a *plebiscite* or vote was taken among the people of the Saar. They were asked to choose between union with Germany, union with France or remaining under League control. Over 90 per cent voted to return to Germany. For Hitler this was a great boost. The unification of German-speaking peoples had begun.

The reoccupation of the Rhineland

In March 1936, while most eyes were still on Italy and Abyssinia, Hitler ordered his troops to occupy the Rhineland. It was a daring move. The invasion was a deliberate breach of the Treaties of Locarno and Versailles. (Under the Treaty of Versailles the Rhineland had to be kept free of troops and armaments.) Hitler's generals had advised against the move. They felt the French would resist and the German army was still too weak to fight back.

When the German troops moved into the Rhineland they had instructions to withdraw if they met any opposition. In fact the invasion went very smoothly and the German people living in the area welcomed the troops. Later, over 98% of them voted in favour of the German re-occupation.

The French do nothing

Hitler's gamble paid off. The French were unwilling to fight and the British would do nothing without the French. Neither country, in fact, was prepared to risk another full scale war with Germany. For Hitler the message was clear. France and Britain lacked both the nerve and the will to fight. As soon as the time was right he would make another bid for extra territory.

(A) *Article 42 of the Versailles treaty*

'Germany is forbidden to maintain or construct any fortifications either on the left bank of the Rhine, or on the right bank to the west of a line drawn 50 km. to the east.'

(B) *An American newspaper reporter, in Berlin, wrote in his diary*:

March 8 [1936]

'Hitler has got away with it. France is not marching.... No wonder the faces of Hitler and Goering and Blomberg ... were all smiles this noon.... Oh the stupidity (or is it a paralysis?) of the French. I learned today on absolute authority that the German troops who marched into the demilitarised zone of the Rhineland yesterday had strict orders to beat a hasty retreat if the French army opposed them in any way.'

(W. SHIRER, *Berlin Diary*, 1941)

(C) *Hitler speaks on the risk he ran*

'More than once, even during the war, I heard Hitler say: "The 48 hours after the march into the Rhineland were the most nerve-racking of my life." He always added: "If the French had then marched into the Rhineland, we would have had to withdraw with our tails between our legs, for the military resources at our disposal would have been wholly inadequate for even a moderate resistance."'

(PAUL SCHMIDT, *Hitler's Interpreter*, 1951)

(D) *The Rhineland*

(E) *A cartoon in* Punch, *March 1936*

The Goose-Step
'Goosey Goosey Gander,
Whither dost thou wander?'
'Only through the Rhineland,
Pray excuse my blunder!'

Questions

1. Why were German troops forbidden to reoccupy the Rhineland? (**A**)
2. Which area voted to return to Germany in 1935? (**D**) and (**T**)
3. What safeguards did Article 42 of the Versailles treaty provide for France? (**A**) and (**D**)
4. If you had been a German living in the Rhineland, how would you have reacted to Hitler's reoccupation? Give reasons. (**T**) and (**E**)
5. Name two ways in which the cartoonist represents Germany. (**E**)
6. In his drawing of the goose, how does the cartoonist show that Germany is breaking the Treaty of Versailles? (**E**)
7. Why is the goose shown trampling on a piece of paper? (**E**)
8. What excuse does the goose give for its actions? (**E**)
9. What would have happened if the French had resisted? (**B**)
10. Was Hitler ever worried about failing? (**C**)
11. Talking point: If the French had stopped Hitler in 1936, the Second World War would never have broken out. Do you agree?

Spain and the Axis

In 1936 civil war erupted in Spain between Republican and Nationalist groups. The Republicans were supported by the socialists and communists and other left-wing groups. The Nationalists were supported by the landowners, the church and the fascists.

Outside powers

At first the great powers agreed to stay out of the war and signed a *non-intervention* agreement. But then Hitler and Mussolini sent troops and arms to help the Nationalists. Russia next sent aid to help the Republicans. Britain and France still stayed out of the war.

The Spanish Civil War brought Hitler and Mussolini closer together and in 1936 they formed a Rome-Berlin Axis. A month later Germany signed an anti-Comintern (or anti-communist) pact with Japan to keep Russia in check. When Italy joined the pact in 1937, a Rome-Berlin-Tokyo Axis was formed.

Guernica – experiment or blunder?

The Spanish Civil War had many bloody battles but one incident in particular horrified the outside world. In September 1937, the town of Guernica in Spain was bombed out of existence by German planes.

Some people argue that Guernica was bombed as part of a German experiment to see what the effects would be of large-scale bombing on a civilian population.

Others claim that Guernica was a military blunder and that the killing of civilians was not deliberate.

Read both sides of the argument opposite and then answer the questions that follow.

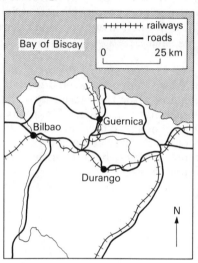

(A) *Guernica and its surroundings*

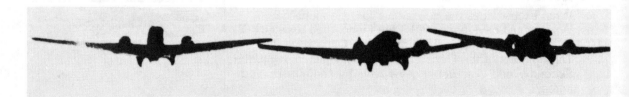

(B) *The bombers go in. This remarkable photograph was taken by a local priest just as the first wave of German bombers approached Guernica. If the Germans' target was the narrow bridge, as they claimed, why were the planes flying three abreast?*

Guernica was a military target

On 31 March 1937 the Nationalists had launched their attack against Northern Spain with support from the German Condor legion which was sent by Hitler to help General Franco.

As a result the Republican troops were forced back. Thousands of refugees fled to Guernica. Many considered that the Germans would not dare bomb Guernica, the ancient capital of the Basque people.

There was a danger that the Republicans would hole up in Guernica. It was in a possible defensible position surrounded by mountains. There the Republicans could have regrouped.

According to the German commander (Von Richthofen) the best way to stop this possibility arising was to destroy the key roads leading to Guernica. All the main roads joined there and passed across a bridge that led into the town. Therefore the military objectives were to destroy the bridge and roads leading into Guernica. (See map **A**.)

Questions

1 What military reasons were there for bombing the roads and bridge near Guernica?

2 Why might the Germans have bombed the town and the civilian population instead of the bridge?

3 According to the evidence, do you think the bombing of the town was   a) a deliberate attack designed to terrorise the townsfolk; or was it   b) an accidental by-product of an attack on the roads and bridge; or was it   c) part of a plan to destroy both the roads and bridge, and demoralise the townspeople? Explain your choice.

4 Talking point: 'In a war everything is a potential military target. If the bombing of civilians will reduce enemy morale, then civilians are military targets.' Do you agree?

The mission did not go according to plan. The bomb sights on the bombers were primitive. The target area was covered by smoke and dust. The bridge was missed and much of the town was destroyed.

Guernica was a German experiment

(1) Von Richthofen owned a book which argued that the best way to break an enemy's resistance was to stage air strikes behind the front line and against the civilian population.

(2) If the bombers were concerned with achieving accuracy and hitting the bridge, they should have flown lower. There were no enemy aircraft.

(3) The planes were equipped with incendiary or burning bombs. Yet the bridge was not wooden. When opposition to the use of these bombs was raised, it was brushed aside.

(4) 43 bombers and fighters carried 100 000 lbs of high-explosive shrapnel and incendiary bombs to knock out a stone bridge only 75 feet long and 30 feet wide.

(5) The bombers never hit the bridge, yet they managed to wipe out the town.

(6) We have photographic evidence that the bombers flew over the town three abreast. Yet the standard plan for bombing such a target would have been to fly over the bridge in single file – to achieve greater accuracy. (See (**B**).)

(7) German airmen stated that dust and smoke made it difficult to see the target and claimed high winds blew the bombs into the town. Yet citizens said there was little wind.

(8) Many years after the event former officers of the Condor legion admitted they did not know there were troops in Guernica.

(9) Von Richthofen himself did not regard the destruction of Guernica as a mistake. In a secret report he described the raid as most 'successful'.

Anschluss with Austria

Lebensraum

By 1938 the time had come for Hitler to put into practice his plan to add living space (*Lebensraum*) to Germany.

His first target was Austria. Hitler was Austrian by birth and 96 percent of Austrians were German-speaking. The problem was that under the Treaty of Versailles, Germany was forbidden to unite with Austria.

Back in 1934 a Nazi plot to take over Austria had failed. Then Mussolini had moved up troops to the Austrian border to block a German takeover. This time, however, there would be no opposition. Mussolini was now an ally.

Early moves

First Hitler ordered the Austrian Nazis to bomb public buildings and stage mass parades. Then he summoned Schuschnigg, the Austrian Chancellor, to Germany. For two hours Hitler ranted, raved and threatened the Austrian leader. Finally Schuschnigg agreed to give the Austrian Nazis more power. But on his return to Austria, Schuschnigg moved to outwit Hitler. On 8 March he ordered a *plebiscite* (vote) to be held. In it Austrians would decide whether they wanted to remain independent or unite with Germany. If Austrians voted to stay independent, as Schuschnigg was sure they would, then Hitler's claim that most Austrians wanted *Anschluss* or union with Germany would collapse.

Invasion plans

Hitler was furious at the move and ordered invasion plans to be drawn up. At the same time he forced the abandonment of the plebiscite. Schuschnigg was also made to resign and replaced by a pro-Nazi Austrian. The new leader asked Germany to send troops to restore order.

On 11 March German troops invaded Austria. Two days later Austria was made a province of Germany – part of the new Reich. A month later the Nazis claimed that 99 percent of the Austrian people had voted in favour of the *Anschluss* in a plebiscite held on 10 April.

(A) *Why appeasement?*

From late 1937 onwards it was clear that Hitler was set on taking over central Europe. International treaties such as Versailles and Locarno he treated as scraps of paper. Why then did Britain and France not step in and stop Hitler? Why instead did they adopt a policy of *appeasement* – of giving in to Hitler's demands?

There are several reasons:
- At the time it seemed better to give in to Hitler than run the risk of another terrible war like the First World War.
- Most Britons accepted that the Versailles settlement was unjust. It seemed only natural for Germany to take back territory that was rightfully hers. Once Germany had settled her grievances, people hoped that she would return to peaceful ways.
- Communist Russia was seen by some as the real *enemy*. For some, Germany was a possible ally against communism.
- The British armed forces were run down. By appeasement Britain could buy time to rearm.
- The British prime minister, Neville Chamberlain, thought Hitler was a reasonable man. With talk and patience, Chamberlain believed Hitler could be made to see reason.

(B) *When the Austrian Chancellor, Schuschnigg, was first called to Germany to hear Hitler's demands that the Austrian Nazis be given a larger say in the government of Austria, he was also told by Hitler:*

'Don't think for one moment that any one on earth is going to thwart my decisions. Italy? I see eye to eye with Mussolini.... England? ... And France? [she could have stopped Germany in the Rhineland] and then we would have had to retreat. But now it is too late for France.'

(Quoted in W.L. SHIRER, *The Rise and Fall of the Third Reich*)

(C) *When Hitler found out that Schuschnigg was trying to outwit him by calling a plebiscite, he issued this order:*

TOP SECRET

1. If other measures prove unsuccessful, I intend to invade Austria with armed forces to establish constitutional conditions and prevent further outrages against the pro-German population....

4. The forces of the Army and Airforce detailed for this operation must be ready for invasion on March 12, at the latest by 12.00 hours.

5. The behaviour of our troops must give the impression that we do not want to wage war against our Austrian brothers.... Therefore any provocation is to be avoided. If, however, resistance is offered, it must be broken ruthlessly by force of arms.

(Quoted in W.L. SHIRER, *Berlin Diary*, 1941)

Questions

1 What was appeasement? How did it help Hitler? (**A**) and (**T**)
2 List what you think were the three most important reasons for appeasing Hitler. Compare your choices with the rest of the class. (**A**)
3 Why did Hitler feel confident in making such demands from Schuschnigg? (**B**)
4 What did Hitler intend to do if Schuschnigg did not give into his demands? (**C**)
5 If you had been the British prime minister in 1938 would you have allowed Hitler to take over Austria? Explain. (**A**) (**B**) and (**T**)
6 Talking point: 'In war there are no winners, but all are losers' (Chamberlain, 1938). Do you agree? How did this sort of attitude encourage Hitler's territorial ambitions?

The Munich crisis

The Sudetenland

Hitler's next target was Czechoslovakia. Within the Sudeten area of Czechoslovakia there were over three million Germans. First Hitler instructed Henlein, the German Sudeten leader, to demand separation from Czechoslovakia. This, together with a few demonstrations and riots, would give Hitler the excuse he needed for a military takeover. In the meantime he ordered the German army to prepare to 'smash Czechoslovakia'.

The Munich Agreement

But as the unrest began to mount, Britain and France intervened. Britain was already convinced that Czechoslovakia would have to be sacrificed to save European peace. France, on the other hand, was tied by treaty to help Czechoslovakia if attacked. Nevertheless France was quite happy for Chamberlain, the British prime minister to work out a deal with Hitler.

So Chamberlain flew to Germany for talks with Hitler. Eventually after three meetings – and some heavy pressure behind the scenes upon the Czechs – agreement was reached. The Sudetenland was to be given to Germany. All the details were set out in the Munich Agreement signed by Hitler, Chamberlain, Mussolini and Daladier, the French premier. The Czechs, whose country was being carved up, were not even present. On 1 October 1938 German troops moved into the Sudetenland.

Peace?

On returning to Britain, Chamberlain was cheered for making peace. Hitler, he said, had promised 'to make no further demands'. Indeed he had signed an agreement with Hitler stating that 'Germany and Britain would never go to war with one another again'.

Yet the peace lasted little more than six months. In March 1939 German troops occupied most of what remained of Czechoslovakia. Hungary and Poland grabbed the rest.

(A) *Neville Chamberlain said, on his return from the Munich conference*:

'My good friends, this is the second time in our history that there has come back from Germany to Downing Street peace with honour.... I believe it is peace for our time.'

(B) *Winston Churchill's opinion of the Munich agreement, 5 October 1938*:

'We have suffered a total and unmitigated defeat. All is over.... I think you will find that in a period of time ... Czechoslovakia will be engulfed in the Nazi regime. We have passed an awful milestone in our history, when the whole equilibrium of Europe has been deranged.... And do not suppose that this is the end. This is only the beginning of the reckoning.'

(C) Should Hitler have been stopped at Munich?

Read this section, then answer the questions below.

Consequences of Munich
(1) When the Allies gave up the Sudetenland to Germany, they handed Germany 33 percent of Czechoslovakia's population, her main defences, and much of her industry – including the very large Skoda armament works.
(2) By giving up Czechoslovakia, the Allies sacrificed an ally, who could have been a great help if war broke out. The Czechs had:
  a)   45 divisions; Germany had 47
  b)   1582 aircraft; Germany had 2500
  c)   469 tanks; Germany had 720
  d)   2 000 000 trained men; Germany had 2 200 000.
(3) Hitler gained confidence. He had taken the Rhineland, Austria and now the Sudetenland and each time Great Britain and France had backed down. Small countries were giving up hope and losing the will to resist.
(4) Russia was upset. In 1938, she had been prepared to help stop the Germans. But in the end she lost faith in Britain and France, changed her foreign policy and, in 1939, made a *non-aggression* or friendship pact with the Germans.

An historian's judgement:
'As late as 1938 a firm ... stand in support of the Czech government would not have probably caused the kind of war that came a year later.... Germany was far from ready to fight a war on two fronts.... This weakness was realised by high-ranking German officers who [seemed ready] to attempt a *coup* [revolt] against Hitler if he pushed ahead with war.'

(G.A. CRAIG in (ed.) N.F. CANTOR, *Perspectives on the European Past*, 1971)

Other arguments:
(1) The Munich agreement gave the British and French public a chance to see whether Hitler would keep his word. When Hitler broke his word, he showed he could not be trusted. This made it easier for the politicians to change their policies and to get large increases in military spending.
(2) Britain and France gained valuable time to rearm and make preparations for war.
(3) Britain and France would have found it hard to justify going to war on behalf of Czechoslovakia since most Sudeten Germans supported Hitler and wished to join Germany. In any case, the majority of people in both Britain and France did not want to go to war.

Questions
1   How did Chamberlain and Churchill differ over Munich? (**A**) and (**B**) Suggest reasons for their differences.
2   Divide your page into two columns. On one, list briefly all the points in favour of the Munich settlement. On the other, list the points against the Munich settlement. (**C**)
3   Write a paragraph summing up your opinion of the Munich Agreement. Discuss your opinion in class with others.

Poland and the coming of war

Danzig

By early 1939 it was clear even to Chamberlain that Hitler had lied. On 24 November 1938, Hitler issued an order to his armed forces to prepare to occupy the Free State of Danzig.

Under the Treaty of Versailles, Danzig had been taken from Germany and placed under Polish control. A German occupation of Danzig was bound to lead to tension between Germany and Poland.

German relationship with Poland

In order to distract Poland, Hitler made several speeches designed to reassure Poland that Germany regarded her as a friend. In January 1939 the German foreign minister even gave a speech in Warsaw saying that 'Poland and Germany can look forward to the future with full confidence in the solid basis of their mutual relations'.

Preparation for the occupation of Danzig

Only two months later however, Hitler had clearly decided to go ahead with the invasion. He ordered that the army should be ready to go into operation at any time from 1 September 1939. At a meeting with army chiefs, Hitler confirmed his view that 'further successes can no longer be attained without the shedding of blood'.

Polish pledge

It was now only a question of when and where Hitler would strike next. Britain and France this time made their position clear. On 31 March 1939, they pledged to support Poland against a German attack.

The Nazi-Soviet pact

Then in August came a bombshell; Nazi Germany and communist Russia had signed a friendship or non-aggression pact. The once mortal enemies had promised not to make war on each other. In secret they also agreed to share out Poland between them after it had been conquered.

The coming of war

With the Nazi-Soviet pact signed, Hitler felt confident to move against Poland. On 1 September 1939 the German armies attacked. Two days later Britain and France stood by their promise to Poland and declared war on Germany. The Second World War had begun.

(A) *Axis aggression 1935–9*

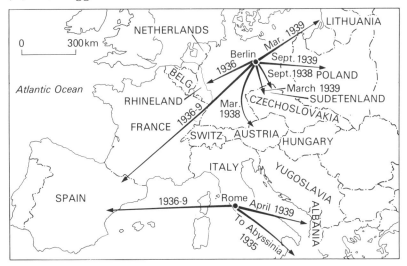

(B) *Cartoon from* Punch *5 April 1939*

AN OLD STORY RETOLD

Herr Hitler: 'It's all right; you know the proverb – "Barking dogs don't bite"?'
Signor Mussolini: 'Oh, yes, *I* know it, and *you* know it; but does the dog know it?'

(C) *'Wanted!' – a poster in the* Daily Mirror, *4 September, 1939*

Page 10   THE DAILY MIRROR   Monday, September 4, 1939.

WANTED!

FOR MURDER ... FOR KIDNAPPING ... FOR THEFT AND FOR ARSON

ADOLF HITLER

ALIAS

Adolf Schicklegruber,

~~Adolf~~ Hittler or Hidler

Last heard of in Berlin, September 3, 1939. Aged fifty, height 5ft. 8½in., dark hair, frequently brushes one lock over left forehead. Blue eyes. Sallow complexion, stout build, weighs about 11st. 3lb. Suffering from acute monomania, with periodic fits of melancholia Frequently bursts into tears when crossed. Harsh, guttural voice, and has a habit of raising right hand to shoulder level. DANGEROUS!

Can be recognised full face by habitual scowl. Rarely smiles. Talks rapidly, and when angered screams like a child.

Profile from a recent photograph. Black moustache. Jowl inclines to fatness. Wide nostrils. Deep-set, menacing eyes.

FOR MURDER Wanted for the murder of over a thousand of his fellow countrymen on the night of the Blood Bath, June 30, 1934. Wanted for the murder of countless political opponents in concentration camps.

He is indicted for the murder of Jews, Germans, Austrians, Czechs, Spaniards and Poles. He is now urgently wanted for homicide against citizens of the British Empire.

Hitler is a gunman who shoots to kill. He acts first and talks afterwards. No appeals to sentiment can move him. This gangster, surrounded by armed hoodlums, is a natural killer. The reward for his apprehension, dead or alive, is the peace of mankind.

FOR KIDNAPPING Wanted for the kidnapping of Dr. Kurt Schuschnigg, late Chancellor of Austria. Wanted for the kidnapping of Pastor Niemöller, a heroic martyr who was not afraid to put God before Hitler. Wanted for the attempted kidnapping of Dr. Benes, late President of Czechoslovakia. The kidnapping tendencies of this established criminal are marked and violent. The symptoms before an attempt are threats, blackmail and ultimatums. He offers his victims the alternatives of complete surrender or timeless incarceration in the horrors of concentration camps.

FOR THEFT Wanted for the larceny of eighty millions of Czech gold in March, 1939. Wanted for the armed robbery of material resources of the Czech State. Wanted for the stealing of Memelland. Wanted for robbing mankind of peace, of humanity, and for the attempted assault on civilisation itself. This dangerous lunatic masks his raids by spurious appeals to honour, to patriotism and to duty. At the moment when his protestations of peace and friendship are at their most vehement, he is most likely to commit his smash and grab.

His tactics are known and easily recognised. But Europe has already been wrecked and plundered by the depredations of this armed thug who smashes in without scruple.

FOR ARSON Wanted as the incendiary who started the Reichstag fire, on the night of February 27, 1933. This crime was the key point, and the starting signal for a series of outrages and brutalities that are unsurpassed in the records of criminal degenerates. As a direct and immediate result of this calculated act of arson, an innocent dupe, Van der Lubbe, was murdered in cold blood. But as an indirect outcome of this carefully-planned offence, Europe itself is ablaze. The fires that this man has kindled cannot be extinguished until he himself is apprehended—dead or alive!

THIS RECKLESS CRIMINAL IS WANTED—DEAD OR ALIVE

All the above information has been obtained from official sources and has been collated by CASSANDRA

Questions

1. Draw a time line. On it show all the acts of Axis aggression between 1935 and 1939. (**A**)
2. When did Hitler make plans to invade Danzig? On what date did he intend invading Poland? (**T**)
3. What point do you think the Punch cartoonist is making? What step had Britain taken in March 1939 to suggest the British 'dog' might bite if Germany trespassed on Polish land? (**B**)
4. For what purpose do you think (**C**) was published on the outbreak of war? Design a similar poster for Mussolini.
5. Write an essay showing how the major European Fascist powers carried out their policies of expansion in the 1930s. What was the result of these policies by the end of 1939?

An overview of the Second World War 1939–45

The Second World War was the most destructive and wide-ranging war in history. The fighting ranged across Europe, Asia, Africa and vast areas of the Pacific.

On one side Britain, France, the USSR, the USA and the 45 countries that fought alongside them were called the *Allies*. On the other side Germany, Italy, Japan and their supporters were the *Axis*.

Total war

As in the First World War whole societies were mobilised for total war. On the battlefield, new aircraft and tanks meant there would be no return to trench warfare. Factories and homes were exposed to saturation bombings – pushing the civilian death toll ever upwards.

Course

At first it looked as though Hitler would win. By mid-1941 all of mainland Europe, except Portugal and Switzerland, was in German hands.

But in June 1941 the Germans stupidly attacked Russia, despite their treaty of friendship. Hitler had underrated the Russians and by 1942 the Germans were overstretched and suffering enormous losses.

Then in December 1941, the Japanese attacked the American naval base of Pearl Harbour. The United States were now in the war. With America's huge resources the chances of an Allied defeat were now very small.

The end of the war

In 1942 and 1943 the Allies won a series of crucial victories. Then in June 1944 their troops landed in Normandy and crossed France, pushing the German troops back. One by one the countries of Western Europe were freed. In the east, the Russians were pushing towards Berlin.

On 7 May 1945, the Germans surrendered. Three months later, on 14 August the Japanese surrendered after atomic bombs had been dropped on Hiroshima and Nagasaki.

Consequences of the Second World War

- Hitler's, Mussolini's and Japan's empires were overthrown.
- Over 50 million men, women and children were killed. Among the dead were 6 million Jews murdered by the Nazis in the most atrocious crime in history.
- The USA and the USSR emerged from the war as the two giants – or super powers. Although Allies, they soon fell out over how the map of Europe was to be redrawn.

(A) *Allies–Axis involvement, showing when the main countries joined and left the war*

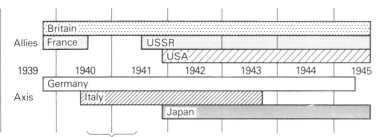

Britain alone against Germany and Italy

(B) *The costs of the Second World War*

Battle deaths	14 904 000
Battle wounded	25 218 000
Civilian deaths	38 573 000
Direct economic costs	$1 600 000 000 000

(R.E. DUPUY, *World War II: a Compact History*, 1969)

(C) *Allied war leaders*

Winston Churchill

Joseph Stalin

Franklin D. Roosevelt

(D) *Hiroshima 1945*

Russia in 1900

For 500 years Russia had been ruled by Tsars or emperors. In 1896 Nicholas II was crowned as Tsar. Like all the previous Tsars, Nicholas was an *autocrat* – a virtual dictator. He did not have to take advice from anyone. There was no parliament to voice the people's views and it was illegal to criticise the government. Police spies were everywhere and newspapers were *censored*.

The peasants

Eighty percent of Russians were poor and uneducated peasants who farmed the land. Until 1861 most peasants had been *serfs* living in virtual slavery with no land of their own. When they were freed in 1861 they were given some land which they had to repay the government for. Yet farming methods were too backward to earn enough money to pay off debts. With so many mouths to feed life for the peasants was a constant struggle.

The workers

By the time Nicholas II came to the throne, Russia had begun to develop her industry. One result of this was the growth of a working class. Life for the workers in the mines and factories was just as bad as for those on the land. Long hours, low wages, bad working conditions and terrible housing made life a misery. Sometimes the workers went on strike in protest but the Tsar's government would not listen to their demands.

The middle class and nobility

Beside the peasants and workers there was discontent among Russia's small middle class. This group included educated and professional people such as doctors, lawyers, teachers and engineers. Above all, they wanted a greater say in the way Russia was run.

The strongest supporters of the Tsar's autocratic rule came from the landowners and government officials, the *nobility*. They were afraid that under a different system they would lose their wealth and privileges.

(A) *Population of Russia in 1900*

(millions) people

Average life-expectancy: 32 years.

rural

500 000 villages of less than 200 people.

urban

(B) *The expansion of Russia 1584–1914*

0   1000 km

FINLAND
POLAND
•Moscow
RUSSIA
SIBERIA
AMUR
TURKESTAN

1584
Ivan IV (the Terrible)
1725
Peter I (the Great)
1914
Russian Empire
Lakes and inland seas

(C) *Russia is a huge country*:
(a) It is three times as big as the United States, 180 times as big as England and Wales.
(b) It takes a week in a train, travelling day and night, to cover the 4000 miles from Murmansk in the north to the border of Afghanistan in the south; and over a week to get from Moscow to the Pacific coast (this is the same distance as from the Equator to the Pole).
(c) When it is dawn over the eastern border it is dusk on the western one.
(d) It has frontiers with twelve countries; is washed by twelve seas from three oceans; and at one point is only thirty-six miles from the USA.
(e) In parts of southern Russia the climate is sub-tropical; the north is well within the Arctic Circle. There is a desert in Turkmenia where an egg can be boiled in the sand in summer; in northern Siberia the mercury freezes in the thermometer in winter, and it can be colder than at the North Pole.
(JOAN HASLER, *The Making of Russia*, 1969)

(D) *A breakdown of Russian society in 1900*

Nobles and Government Officials	1.5%
Priests	.5%
Middle Class	10.0%
Peasants	78.0%
Working Classes	10.0%

Questions
1 How many times larger was the Russian Empire in 1914 than in 1584? (**B**)
2 List as many reasons as you can why Russia was a difficult place to rule and protect. (**B**) and (**C**)
3 What was the population of Russia in 1900? (**A**)
4 What percentage a) were rural b) were urban dwellers? (**A**)
5 Why did such a high percentage of the population live in rural areas? (**A**), (**D**) and (**T**)
6 Draw a pie graph showing the make-up of Russian society. (**D**)
7 What figures in the graph suggest that Russia was an agricultural country with little industry? Explain. (**A**) and (**D**)
8 Talking point: As Russia expanded, it added many new racial groups to its population. What problems might this create?

91

Revolutionaries

Throughout the nineteenth century, discontent had grown among the Russian people. The cities were full of political groups who wanted to reform Russia.

(1) The largest group, the *liberals*, wanted to replace Tsarist rule with a democratic parliamentary government. The liberals hoped Nicholas would see the need for a parliament and so avoid a revolution.

Unfortunately for the liberals, Nicholas was unwilling to make political reforms. As a child he had watched Alexander II bleed to death from a terrorist bomb. For Nicholas this was all the thanks his grandfather received for being a great reformer.

An autocratic Tsar might have been able to save Russia from revolution if he had been an able and determined ruler. Nicholas, however, was a weak and indecisive character. After his marriage in 1895 his wife made sure he ruled Russia with an iron fist.

(2) The second group, the *Social Revolutionaries*, or SRs, believed that one day the peasants would rise up and seize all the land. To help this revolution along, the SRs would assassinate government leaders and encourage the peasants to rebel.

(3) The third group were the *Marxists*. They followed the writings of Karl Marx who said that revolution would come from the city workers. In 1898 the Marxists formed a political party called the Social Democrats. After a row in 1903 it split into two groups. One group led by Vladimir Lenin became known as the Bolsheviks (majority group). Lenin (whose real name was Ulyanov) was the son of a school inspector. When Lenin was 16, his elder brother was hanged for plotting to execute Tsar Alexander II. Soon afterwards Lenin began reading Karl Marx's writings and became a revolutionary. Lenin wanted the Social Democrats to remain a small handpicked party of dedicated revolutionaries. The other group, the Mensheviks (minority group), wanted a larger party which would include anyone who was sympathetic to Marxist ideas.

> The great difficulty facing all these opposition groups was that they were illegal. This meant they had to meet in secret and live in fear of arrest and imprisonment.

Marxism

Karl Marx (1818–83) was born in Germany, the son of a lawyer. Two of his books, *The Communist Manifesto* and *Capital*, are among the most famous works ever printed.

Capitalism

Marx argues that all history is a struggle between the haves and have-nots. In a free enterprise or capitalist society, the haves are the owners of all the wealth – the factories, machinery and natural resources. Because of this great wealth, the capitalists also control the government and run the country for their own benefit.

The have-nots are the workers, or *proletariat*, who sell their labour to the capitalists. The capitalists make huge profits by paying their workers miserable wages.

Socialism

Gradually however the workers will tire of being treated like scum. Eventually they will rise up and overthrow the capitalists in a violent revolution. Then they will take over the government and set up a *dictatorship of the proletariat*. This will be a period of rule by the workers' leaders, when all opposition will be crushed. During this time the state will take over privately-owned land, factories, banks etc. The wealth will now be owned by all the people instead of a few. With it the government will give everyone free education, good housing, etc. This stage is called *socialism*.

Communism

Under socialism the people will gradually learn to work together for the good of all. In time they will even stop being greedy and take just enough to meet their needs. At this stage, pure communism will be achieved.

(A) *Marx: From capitalism to communism*

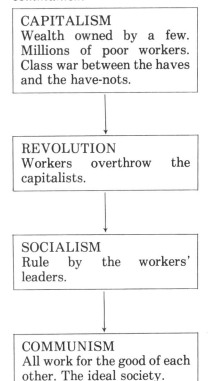

CAPITALISM
Wealth owned by a few. Millions of poor workers. Class war between the haves and the have-nots.

REVOLUTION
Workers overthrow the capitalists.

SOCIALISM
Rule by the workers' leaders.

COMMUNISM
All work for the good of each other. The ideal society.

Questions

1   Which of the three political groups in Russia at the start of the century might have co-operated with the Tsar? (**T**)
2   What are the main differences between the Social Revolutionaries and the Marxists? (**T**)
3   You have been asked to illustrate a Russian children's story-book on Karl Marx. Draw a series of four simple drawings or cartoons to explain his ideas. (**A**)
4   According to Marx what will happen when the workers refuse to accept their lot any more? (**A**)
5   Talking point: How likely did a revolution seem in Russia at the turn of the century? If you had been Tsar, what would you have done to reduce the chances of revolution?

The revolution of 1905

War with Japan

In 1904 Russia went to war with Japan. The Russians expected an easy victory but instead they were heavily defeated both on land and at sea. Discontented groups used this defeat to call for more reforms.

Bloody Sunday

In January 1905 a general strike broke out in the capital, St Petersburg. One of the workers' leaders, a priest called Father Gapon, decided to lead a march of workers to the Tsar's Winter Palace. There he hoped to present a petition to the Tsar. On Sunday 21 January some 150 000 marchers walked to the palace. They were unarmed and peaceful. They even carried pictures of the Tsar and sang hymns. But when they reached the Winter Palace, the Tsar's troops fired into the crowd and about a thousand people were hurt. The day became known as Bloody Sunday.

Revolution

The massacre sparked off a revolution. Strikes and peasant risings broke out all over Russia. For a while it looked as though Nicholas would be toppled from his throne. But then at the last moment he agreed to establish an elected *Duma* (parliament) which would make laws and help govern Russia. The promise of a Duma took the steam out of the revolutionaries and order was gradually restored.

The Dumas

The Duma turned out to be a great disappointment. The first two Dumas called in 1906 and 1907 lasted only a few months until the Tsar dissolved them. Nicholas was not prepared to give up enough of his power. For the third Duma, Nicholas changed the electoral law. The peasants and workers were given fewer members while the land-owners were given many more. Not surprisingly, the third and fourth Dumas (1907–12) and (1912–17) got on much better with Nicholas. In the meantime, the Tsar used the police and the army to stamp out all opposition.

(A) *The marchers' petition to the Tsar asked for*:
- An eight-hour day
- A minimum wage of one rouble (10p) a day
- Better working conditions and housing
- A parliament for Russia

(B) *A police report of 1905*:

'Very often the peasants do not have enough allotment land, and cannot during the year feed themselves, clothe themselves, heat their homes, keep their tools and livestock, secure seed for sowing and, lastly [pay] all their taxes and [other debts].'

(Quoted in L. KOCHAN, *Russia in Revolution*, 1966)

(C) *'Bloody Sunday' – Tsarist soldiers shoot down the crowd of demonstrators led by Father Gapon outside the Winter Palace*

(D) *The effects of Bloody Sunday*

'All classes condemn the authorities and more particularly the emperor . . . . The present ruler has lost absolutely the [love] of the Russian people . . . whatever the future may have in store for the dynasty, the present Tsar will never again be safe in the midst of his people.'

(US consul in Odessa, 1905, quoted in L. KOCHAN, *Russia in Revolution*)

Questions

1 List seven problems the peasants faced in 1905. (**B**)
2 Which of the petitioners' demands, if accepted, would have forced the Tsar to give up some of his power? (**A**)
3 What evidence is there in the painting to suggest Bloody Sunday was a massacre and that the troops had no reason to fear the crowd? (**C**) and (**T**)
4 What additional evidence would you need, to discover whether the painting gives an accurate picture of what actually happened? (**C**)
5 What does the US consul claim was the result of Bloody Sunday? (**D**)

The First World War and the March Revolution of 1917

World war

When the First World War broke out in 1914, opposition to the Tsar seemed to dissolve. The Russian people enthusiastically rallied behind their emperor. But the early victories were soon followed by massive defeats. Inept leaders sent troops into battle without weapons, or enough equipment. Discipline was poor and soldiers often deserted.

Back home, conditions became unbearable. Food was scarce and the cost of living rocketed. Refugees fleeing from the front added to the general chaos.

As a mood of despair spread across Russia, Nicholas made a stupid mistake. He decided to become commander-in-chief of his armies. He therefore dismissed his popular commander and went to the battlefront to take control. This removed him from the seat of power in Petrograd.

Rasputin

With the Tsar away from the capital, power passed to the empress. She in turn was under the influence of a drunken monk called Rasputin who advised her on everything, including the appointment of ministers and the conduct of the war. This 'mad monk', as he was called, owed his position to the fact that the empress believed Rasputin had been sent by God to save her son Alexei, the heir to the throne, from the incurable blood disease of haemophilia. Soon Nicholas's best advisers were replaced.

March Revolution

In December 1916, Rasputin was assassinated. But it was too late. In March 1917, revolution broke out (according to the old Russian calendar, the month was February).

In Petrograd there were riots and strikes because of food shortages. Soldiers were ordered to crush the disturbances but joined the rioters instead.

The Duma now met and set up a provisional (temporary) government. On 15 March, Nicholas was forced to abdicate (give up) his throne. As the army would no longer follow his orders, there was little else he could do. Five hundred years of Tsarist rule had suddenly come to an end.

(A) *Letter of the empress to the emperor 28 November 1915*
'. . . I must give you over a message from Our Friend, prompted by what he saw in the night. He begs you to order an advance near Riga . . . otherwise the Germans will settle down through all the winter . . . . He says we can and we must, and I was to write it to you at once.'
(Quoted in F.A. GOLDER, *Documents of Russian History 1914—17*)

(B) *Moscow 1917 – the sign reads 'No Bread Today'*

(C) *Rasputin – the Tsarina's powerful adviser*

(D) *The Petrograd police made a report on troop morale in October 1916*:

'. . . The behaviour of the soldiers, especially in the units located in the rear, is most provocative. They openly accuse military authorities of graft, cowardice, drunkenness, and even treason. One everywhere meets thousands of deserters perpetrating crimes and offering violence to the civilian population. These express their regret that "the Germans did not arrive," that "the Germans would restore order," and so on . . . .'

(Quoted in M.T. FLORINSKY, *The End of the Russian Empire*, 1971)

(E) *Movement of prices*

1913	100
1915	130 (1913=100)
Jan 1916	155
Jan 1917	300
Oct 1917	755

(M. McCAULEY, *The Russian Revolution and the Soviet State 1917–21*, 1975)

Questions

1   Why did Rasputin exercise so much influence at court? (**C**) and (**T**)
2   How did Rasputin try to influence the running of the war? (**A**) What problems did he create for the Russian government?
3   Describe the problems the Russian army faced by late 1916. (**D**) and (**T**)
4   Draw a line graph to show rises in prices between 1913 and 1917. (**E**)
5   How many times did prices increase in this period? (**E**)
6   At what time did prices really begin to rocket? (**E**)
7   What other problem did housewives have to face? (**B**) and (**T**)
8   Review question: Draw up two lists. On one, list the long-term causes of the 1917 revolution; on the other, list the short-term causes. Is there one cause that is far more important than others? How far can Nicholas be blamed for his overthrow?

Dual power

The Provisional Government

From the very start the provisional government led by Prince Luov did not enjoy much support. All across Russia, thousands of groups of soldiers, workers and peasants had joined together to form their own mini-governments called Soviets. In fact, the Petrograd Soviet was even more powerful than the provisional government. It controlled the army, factories and the railways. For the time being however, it was willing to give the provisional government a chance to prove itself. This time of shared power between the Petrograd Soviet and the provisional government is called the period of *Dual Power*.

Unpopularity

In July 1917 Alexander Kerensky took over from Prince Luov as Prime Minister of the Provisional Government. He was a Socialist and also a member of the powerful Petrograd Soviet. Under Kerensky the Provisional Government did little to solve the problems Russia faced.

- It continued the war even though the soldiers were war-weary and deserting in their thousands.
- It did not give the peasants the land which they so badly wanted.
- It could not solve the terrible food shortages which left thousands starving.
- It continued to delay the first meeting of the Constituent Assembly or new Russian Parliament, intended to draw up a new constitution for Russia.

Inexperience

The poor record of achievement of the Provisional Government is in many ways not surprising. Most members of the Government had little experience of power. Moreover they were reluctant to make important decisions because they felt these should be made by the Constituent Assembly when it was elected. Yet the weak and indecisive impression the Provisional Government gave people encouraged even more instability, strikes and mutinies.

(A) *Discontent among the troops*
'Until the revolution in March, the number of registered deserters from the army was about 3500 every two weeks. But with the outbreak of the revolution this figure jumped abruptly to about 17 000 – almost five times as many. The number of unregistered deserters was of course even larger.

"The army is sick," ran one report on military morale. "The spirit of the officers is low, the troops are restless." Their sole preoccupation and "chief desire" was to receive additional grants of land. When reinforcements arrived at the front, they refused to take up their rifles. "What for?" they asked. "We are not going to fight."'
(L. KOCHAN, *The Russian Revolution*, 1970)

(B) *Between 1914 and 1917 Lenin, the Bolshevik leader, lived in exile in Switzerland. In January 1917 Lenin told a group of Swiss students*:
'Revolution in Europe is inevitable [unavoidable]. We of the older generation will not live to see it, but you youngsters will see it.'
(Quoted in A.J.P. TAYLOR, *Revolutions and Revolutionaries*, 1980)

(C) *From April 1917 onwards, peasants began to loot their landlords' manor houses and then set them on fire*

(D) *Peasant uprisings*

1917 March	34
April	174
May	236
June	280

(E) *The peasants' reaction to the March Revolution*
'It is interesting to see the situation through the eyes of a large landowner, Prince Volkonsky, whose estate was in Borisoglebsk. He recalled that there was not a single arrest in the first three weeks of the revolution. But in the second month, trouble began – "and gradually all restraints were broken." Timber was cut illegally, the peasants grazed their cattle on the landowner's pastures, and Bolshevik deserters from the armed forces busily encouraged the peasants. And there was nothing that Volkonsky could do. Whenever he complained to the local authorities, the reply came that they had lost all power and control.'
(LIONEL KOCHAN, *The Russian Revolution*, 1970)

Questions

1 What evidence is there to show that the March Revolution in Russia caught Lenin by surprise? (**B**)
2 What evidence is there to suggest that the peasants took a while to take advantage of the March Revolution and seize their landlords' property? (**E**)
3 Draw a line graph to show the rise in peasant risings following the March Revolution. (**D**)
4 Why do you think it took a couple of months after the revolution before the peasants began to rise up against the landlords in large numbers? (**D**) and (**E**)
5 What do these uprisings tell us about how many peasants felt about the landowners? (**C**), (**D**) and (**E**)
6 What effect did the March Revolution have on the army? (**A**)
7 Talking point: To overthrow the government is the easy part of a revolution. The hard part is to find an able government to replace it. What would you have done if you had been in charge of the Provisional Government in the first few months after the revolution?

The November Revolution

Lenin returns

In April Lenin returned from exile overseas and called on the Soviets to overthrow the provisional government. The war, he said, must be ended. The peasants must be given their land. Food must be given to the hungry. These ideas were soon adopted and turned into popular slogans such as 'All Power to the Soviets' and 'Peace, Bread and Land'.

July days

In July 1917 armed mobs took to the streets shouting Bolshevik slogans. Kerensky, the prime minister, suspected a Bolshevik plot and arrested a number of Bolsheviks. Luckily, Lenin managed to escape to Finland. Even so, it looked as if the Bolsheviks were finished.

But then came a lucky break. In September, the Russian army commander-in-chief, General Kornilov, tried to overthrow Kerensky and set up a military dictatorship. In desperation Kerensky turned to anyone who would resist Kornilov. He even gave arms to the Bolsheviks, who came out of hiding.

The November Revolution

Kornilov was easily defeated but Kerensky's hold on the country continued to weaken. By the end of September the Bolsheviks had won control of the key Petrograd and Moscow Soviets. In October, Lenin secretly returned to Petrograd and persuaded the other party members to stage an armed rising.

Leon Trotsky, the Bolshevik chairman of the Petrograd Soviet, drew up the plans. On the night of 6 November Bolshevik Red Guards started seizing key points in Petrograd. By the next evening the headquarters of the provisional government had been captured. Most of the government ministers were arrested but Kerensky managed to escape overseas. Lenin and the Bolsheviks were now the new rulers of Russia.

(A) *In the days prior to the revolt, the Bolsheviks tried to build up their support among the Petrograd workers. In one speech Trotsky said:*

'The Soviet Government will give everything that is in the country to the poor and to the people in the trenches. You well-to-do folk have two coats – hand one over to the soldiers who are cold in the trenches. You have warm boots? Sit at home; the worker needs your boots.'

(Quoted in D. MACK, *Lenin and the Russian Revolution*, 1970)

(B) *Petrograd: the main objectives of the November Revolution, 6/7 November*

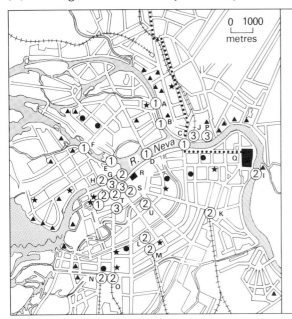

0 1000
metres

● Garrisons loyal to Provisional Government

★ Garrisons which supported the Bolsheviks

▲ Factories which were pro-Bolshevik and anti-war

····· Lenin's route on 6 November; HQ at Smolny Institute

① Night of 6 November: first objectives, including main bridges and telegraph station, seized

② Day of 7 November: second objectives, including railway stations, seized

③ Evening of 7 November: third objectives, including Winter Palace (HQ of Provisional Government) seized

A Grenaderskii Bridge
B Sampsonievskii Bridge
C Puteinyi Bridge
D Troitskii Bridge
E Birzhevoi Bridge
F Tuchkov Bridge
G Dvortsovyi Bridge
H Nicholas Bridge
I Okhtenskii Bridge
J Finland Station
K Nicholas Station
L Electrical Station
M Tsarskoye Selo Station
N Baltic Station
O Warsaw Station
P Prison
Q Smolny Institute
R Winter Palace
S Telegraph Station
T Head Post Office
U State Bank

Questions

1 What is Trotsky promising that the Bolsheviks will do if they gain power? (**A**)

2 Which groups of people would such promises appeal to? Why? (**A**)

3 Study the map of the November Revolution. (**B**)
   (i)   Where did Lenin set up his headquarters?
   (ii) What parts of the city did the Bolsheviks seize on the evening of 6 November, during the day of 7 November and on the evening of 7 November?
   (iii) The plan to overthrow the provisional government was a three-part plan. (**B**) Suggest why Trotsky decided to seize (a) those parts of the city labelled (1) first, (b) those parts of the city labelled (2) next, and left the headquarters of the provisional government till last?

4 What evidence is there in (**C**) to suggest that the provisional government was weak and too poorly organised to stop a revolution?

5 Talking point: No one ever photographed the actual capture of the Winter Palace, but films and paintings have recreated the event. Many of the Soviet pictures show a large group of soldiers storming the palace against fierce resistance.
   Can you suggest why the Soviet government should want the capture of the palace portrayed in this way?

(C) *A description of the capture of the Winter Palace (the headquarters of the provisional government) on November 7, 1917*

'By 7 November 1917 the provisional government had dwindled to a meeting of ministers in the Winter Palace ... the provisional government was not overthrown by a mass attack on the Winter Palace. A few Red Guards climbed in through the servants' entrance, found the provisional government in session and arrested the ministers in the name of the people. Six people, five of them Red Guards, were casualties of bad shooting by their own comrades.'

(A.J.P. TAYLOR, *Revolutions and Revolutionaries*, 1980)

Civil war 1918–21

The Bolsheviks had seized power. Now they had to hold on to it. It was going to be tough. Out of a population of 170 millions, the Bolsheviks numbered less than 300 000.

When the elections for the first Constituent Assembly were held in December 1917, the Bolsheviks won only 175 of the 707 seats. Lenin had no intention of sharing power, and after one meeting, the Assembly was closed down.

Land and peace

To win over the people Lenin made two announcements. First, he said that the peasants could take over the lands of their landlords. Secondly, he made peace with the Germans and the Treaty of Brest-Litovsk was signed in March 1918.

Land and peace increased the Bolsheviks' popularity but they still had more enemies than friends. In December 1917 Lenin set up a secret police force called the Cheka. That summer, thousands of opponents were rounded up and shot. The Bolsheviks also changed their name to the Communist Party of the Soviet Union.

Civil war

In 1918 civil war broke out between the communists (called Reds) and the anti-communists (called Whites). The Whites included everyone from nobles and landlords to Socialist Revolutionaries. The only thing they had in common was a hatred of the communists.

Early victims of the civil war were the ex-Tsar and his family. In July 1918, while being held captive by the Bolsheviks, they were executed.

For three years the war raged. It looked for a time as though the White armies, helped by Britain, France and other countries opposed to communism, would win.

But the Red Army fought back. Trotsky, the Red commander, was a brilliant leader. His troops were better organised, better armed and better fed. The Reds also had the support of most of the peasants.

By the end of 1920, the Reds had won and the foreign troops had withdrawn. Lenin was now firmly in control.

Questions

1 What foreign countries gave aid to the White armies in the civil war? (**A**)

2 If you were a Bolshevik commander, how could you use the fact that foreigners were fighting with the Whites to your benefit?

3 Why did the Bolshevik position look so grim at the end of 1918? (**A**)

4 How far were the various White armies from each other? (**A**) What problems would this have created?

5 Why do you think Trotsky used a train from which to lead the Red Army? (**B**)

6 Why was it important for Trotsky to travel personally to the various battle fronts? (**B**)

7 What was the problem the Red Army faced on the southern front, as shown by Trotsky's orders? (**C**)

8 Talking point: Are commanders justified in shooting deserters in wartime? What would you do, as a commander, to solve the problem?

(A) *The civil war 1918–21*

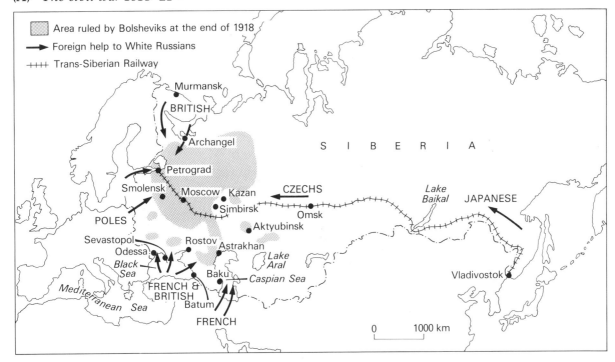

(B) *Trotsky, on how he led the Red Army*:

'For two and a half years I lived in a railway coach.... There I received those who brought reports, held conferences ... dictated orders.... The train included a Secretariat, a printing press ... a radio station ... a library, a garage, and a bath.... It was armoured ... and the crew could handle guns....

The work of the train was to build up the army, to educate, administer and supply it.... Out of bands of irregulars, of refugees escaping from the Whites, of peasants mobilized in neighbouring districts, of detachments of workers sent by industrial centres – out of these we formed at the front companies, battalions.... The train took care of all this; we always had a few zealous communists to provide leadership, a small stock of boots, medicine and bandages, machine guns....

When they were aware of the train just a few miles behind the firing line, even the most nervous units would summon up all their strength.... Often a commander would ask me to stay for an extra half-hour so that news of the train's arrival might spread far and wide.'

(C) *Trotsky's orders to the Red troops on the southern front*

'1. Every scoundrel who incites anyone to retreat, to desert, or not to fulfil a military order, will be shot.
2. Every soldier of the Red Army who voluntarily deserts his military post, will be shot.
3. Every soldier, who throws away his rifle or sells part of his equipment, will be shot.
4. Military police detachments to arrest deserters will be stationed in the whole front line strip.
5. All local soldiers and committees of the poor are obligated on their part to take all measures to capture deserters.
6. Those guilty of harbouring deserters are liable to be shot.
7. Houses in which deserters are found will be burnt down.'

(Quoted in M. McCAULEY [ed.], *The Russian Revolution and the Soviet State 1917–21*)

War communism and NEP

When the communists seized power in 1917 industrial output was falling rapidly while the cost of living was spiralling upwards. For the first six months the communists lived from day to day. Some factories were taken over by the government; others were taken over by the workers themselves. Output, however, continued to fall.

War communism

The outbreak of civil war brought a new set of problems. The Red Army had to be equipped and fed and so had the workers. Yet the White forces controlled most of the best grain-producing areas. In desperation the government placed the whole economy under its control. This policy was later called *war communism*.

Under war communism most factories were nationalised and made to produce goods for the war. To solve the food shortages in the towns, armed squads were sent into the villages to seize food from the peasants. The result was economic chaos. Factory output slumped. By 1921 it was only 15 percent of its 1913 total. On the farms, peasants hid food from collection squads or simply stopped growing it. Food output fell to half the 1913 level. Famine followed and 4 million people died.

By 1921 Russia was exhausted and bankrupt. Discontent erupted with peasant risings and workers' strikes. Even sailors at the Kronstadt naval base revolted.

NEP

Clearly, the communists had to change their policy if they were to stay in power. In 1921 Lenin introduced the New Economic Policy (NEP). Under this policy private trade was allowed once more. Smaller industries were given back to private owners. The peasants were allowed to sell their produce for the best price they could get, so long as they paid 10 percent of what they produced in tax.

The state still kept control of heavy industry (iron, coal, steel, etc.), large factories, transport, banking and foreign trade. By 1928 production was back to its 1914 level.

(A) *The effect of the civil war and starvation is described by Boris Pasternak in his novel, Dr Zhivago:*
'Trudging on foot, loaded with sacks, bundles and babies, exhausted young mothers who had lost their mills, driven out of their minds by the horrors ... abandoned their children.... A quick death, they said, was better than a slow death by starvation.'

(B) *An anti-communist poster put out by the Whites in 1919*

(C) *Peasants were often unwilling to hand over food*:
'... a small company was sent to the village to requisition the bread reserves.... The men were disarmed ... by the peasants.... Another company with two machine guns was sent, and they returned without the machine guns. A third expedition was ordered out ... the peasants opened fire [and] killed six.... A fourth and much better armed force was sent.... It arrested the local soviet, [and] recaptured the machine guns and rifles ....'

(J. BUNYAN AND H.H. FISHER, *The Bolshevik Revolution*, 1934)

(D) *Output of selected goods*

Products	1913	1921	1928
Oil (million tons)	9.2	3.8	11.6
Coal (million tons)	29.1	9.5	35.5
Steel (million tons)	4.2	0.2	4.2
Machine tools (1000 units)	1.8	0.8	2.0
Leather shoes (million pairs)	60.0	28.0	58.0
Grain (million tons)	86.0	36.2	73.3
Cows (million)	28.8	24.8	29.2

(OXENFELDT and HOLUBNYCHY, *Economic Systems in Action*, 1965)

(E) *A communist placard ridiculing the Russian church*

Questions

1 What message about life under the communists is the White poster putting across? (**B**)

2 How did the communists get food from peasants who refused to hand over their crops? (**C**)

3 Why did mothers abandon their children during the famine following the civil war? (**A**)

4 Do you think you would have abandoned your child if you had been in the same situation? Give reasons.

5 What happened to the output of the goods shown in (**D**) between a) 1913 and 1921 b) 1921 and 1928? For each period explain why there was such a great change in output.

6 How are the priests portrayed in the communists' placard against the church in Russia? (**E**)

7 Why do you think communists attacked religion so fiercely? What threat might the churches have posed to the communist party? (**E**)

The rise of Stalin

Lenin died in 1924 after a long illness. A fierce struggle for power now developed among the communist leaders. The two main rivals were Leon Trotsky and Josef Stalin.

Stalin versus Trotsky

Trotsky had successfully planned the November Revolution of 1917 with Lenin. In the civil war he had brilliantly led the Red Army to victory. He was also a gifted thinker and a superb speaker.

Stalin had a much less impressive personality. He was a cold dull character and a poor speaker. But he did know how to gain power. In 1922 he became General Secretary of the communist party. He then appointed his own supporters to key positions within the party.

Trotsky claimed that communism could not succeed in Russia until there had been a world-wide revolution. He therefore wanted Russia to use its resources to organise revolutions throughout the world. Stalin argued that communism could be made to work in Russia alone. Once proven there, it would soon spread throughout the world.

Stalin's plan of 'socialism in one country', as it was called, was much more appealing to the party members. After so many years of hardship they wanted to get on with the job of rebuilding Russia.

In 1927 Stalin had Trotsky expelled from the communist party. Two years later he was sent to live in exile overseas. There he continued to attack Stalin and his policies until 1940, when he was murdered in his own home in Mexico, by one of Stalin's agents.

A picture is worth a thousand words

Once Stalin was established as dictator he was made out to be one of the key leaders of the Russian revolution. He was said to be Lenin's choice as his successor. All mention of the leadership struggle with Trotsky, Kamenev and Zinoviev was forbidden.

In the pictures opposite, you can see how Stalin misled the Russian people about his past.

(A) *Lenin's 'Testament' – before he died, Lenin made notes on who should succeed him*:

25 December 1922
'... Comrade Stalin, having become Secretary General, has concentrated [great power] in his hands and I am not certain *whether he will always be capable of using that [power] with sufficient caution.* On the other hand, Comrade Trotsky ... is distinguished not only by *outstanding abilities.* As a person, he is probably *the most capable man on the CC at present,* but he ... [is often too self-confident and spends too much time on administrative work].'

4 January 1923
'Stalin is too rude and this defect ... [is unacceptable] in the post of Secretary General. That is why I suggest that comrades think of a way of removing Stalin from that post and appointing another man to replace him who in all other respects differs from Comrade Stalin in having only one advantage, namely, that of being tolerant, more loyal, more polite and more considerate to his comrades ....'

(Quoted in M. McCAULEY (ed.) *The Russian Revolution and the Soviet State 1917–21*, 1975)

(B) *In April 1917 Lenin returned from exile in Switzerland, by train, to Russia. In this painting a crowd has gathered to welcome Lenin home at the Finland station. Stalin has been painted in behind him. In fact, Stalin was never there.*

(C) *A painting of Lenin and Stalin speaking to Red Guards at the Smolny, the Bolshevik headquarters during the November Revolution. It is doubtful whether Stalin was there at all.*

(D) *Lenin recovering from a stroke, 1922. Stalin's picture was added to the photograph some years later.*

Questions

1 Give two reasons why Lenin distrusted Stalin. (**A**)
2 What evidence is there that Lenin did not want Stalin to succeed him? (**A**)
3 In Lenin's view what were Trotsky's
  a) strengths
  b) weaknesses? (**A**)
4 Why do you think Stalin's picture was painted in behind Lenin? What impression about Stalin is the artist trying to give? (**B**)
5 Who does (**C**) suggest were the key leaders in the November Revolution?
6 Why do you think this photograph of Lenin recovering from a stroke was selected as one to which Stalin's picture should be added? (**D**)
7 Talking point: The camera cannot lie. A picture is worth a thousand words. How did Stalin use these ideas to mislead the Russian people? How can we protect ourselves from being misled in this way?

The five-year plans: industry

For 'socialism in one country' to work, Russia had to change from a backward agricultural country into an advanced industrial power.

The end of NEP

The NEP was not producing enough industry so it was scrapped. Instead Stalin replaced it with a series of five-year plans. A state planning commission called Gosplan was appointed to set five-yearly targets for industry and agriculture.

The five-year-plans

In the first five-year plan (1928-32) all the stress was on the heavy industries such as steel, coal and machinery. These basic industries were essential to the growth of other industries. In 1932, the first five-year plan was completed a year ahead of time – industrial output had doubled and some 1500 new industrial plants had been built.

Under the second (1933-7) and third five-year plans (1938-43 until interrupted by war preparations), the emphasis remained on heavy industry. In these later plans there was a switch from the production of goods such as tractors to military equipment, to counter the growing threat from Hitler.

Again the results were impressive. By 1939, Russia had passed Britain as an industrial nation and was bettered only by the USA and Germany.

Everyday life

Wages were kept very low and all surplus profits were ploughed back into building more industry. Because so much money was spent on heavy industry there was little money for the manufacture of consumer goods such as clothes and furniture. Sometimes even food was rationed.

Workers who failed to meet their targets or slackened off on the job were treated as criminals and sent to work in labour camps. On the shop floor, bonuses were paid to the best workers.

(A) *In his speech to managers of industry, February 1931, Stalin explained the need for more five-year plans*

'No, Comrades, the pace must not be slackened. On the contrary, we must increase it. This is dictated to us by our obligations to the working class of the whole world. If we slacken we shall fall behind and be beaten.... You are backward, you are weak – therefore you are wrong and can be beaten and enslaved. Or else you are mighty and therefore you are right, hence we must be wary of you. We are fifty years behind the advanced countries. We must make good this distance in ten years or we shall be crushed.'

(B) *The start of the Stakhanovite movement. Stakhanov was made a national hero and other workers were urged to become Stakhanov workers.*

'In August 1935, a miner, Alexei Stakhanov ... had the idea that he could cut more coal during his six-hour day, if he could concentrate all his effort and attention continuously on cutting, enabling others ... to concentrate similarly on their own particular process.... Instead of the six or seven tons per shift in the Donets mines, or the 10 tons of the highly organised German mines in the Ruhr, Stakhanov began at once to cut 102 tons per shift, an amount that was later increased.... The idea spread to other industries.'

(S. AND B. WEBB, *Soviet Communism*, 1959)

(C) *Percentage increase under first five-year plan, 1928–32*

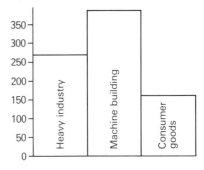

(D) *Industrial production 1927–39 (million tonnes)*

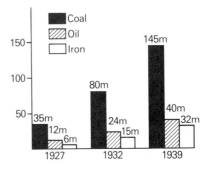

(E) *A Russian 'before and after' cartoon. In the top half of the cartoon, the foreign capitalist calls the 1928 five-year plan a ridiculous dream.*

Questions

1. Why was Stalin so keen to speed up the growth of Russia's industry? (**A**)
2. By what percentage did a) heavy industry b) machine building c) consumer goods increase under the first five-year plan? (**C**)
3. Why were low targets set for consumer goods compared to heavy industry and machine building? (**C**) and (**T**)
4. By what percentage did Russian production of a) coal b) oil and c) iron increase between 1927 and 1939? (**D**)
5. Who was Stakhanov? Why do you think the Russian government turned him into a national hero? (**B**)
6. If you had been a Russian worker and had found out that Stakhanov's effort had been staged as a publicity stunt and that the best workers in the mine were in his team, what would your reaction have been?
7. Write a brief description describing the 'after' part of the cartoon. (**E**)
8. Talking point: Is it a good idea for a government to control and plan a nation's economy?

The five-year plans: agriculture

The key to the success of the five-year plans lay in the countryside.

(1) The peasants were the only group who could be taxed to provide the money to build industry.

(2) The peasants would have to supply cheap food to feed workers in the growing industries.

(3) The peasants would have to supply food for export overseas in order to pay for imported machinery.

(4) Large numbers of peasants would have to leave their farms to go and work in the new factories.

Collectivisation

To solve these problems Stalin decided to end private farming. Instead of farming their own tiny plots, the peasants would be encouraged to hand over their land to a large village farm called a *collective*. Since the collective would be state-controlled, the peasants would then produce whatever the government wanted. Large collectives would also be able to afford to buy modern equipment, such as tractors, to further increase production. This would free peasants to work in the factories.

At first Stalin tried to persuade the peasants to volunteer for the collectives. But many, especially the richer peasants or Kulaks, refused. They had no wish to share their wealth with their poorer neighbours.

So Stalin made collectivisation compulsory. War was declared on the Kulaks and troops were sent to the countryside. Those who resisted – some 5 million in all – were rounded up, shot or deported to distant parts of Russia. In protest the Kulaks burned their crops and slaughtered their stock.

The result of all this was a terrible famine. During 1932–4, some 10 to 15 million Russians died of starvation.

As a concession, Stalin allowed collective farmers to own small private plots of land. They could keep and sell whatever they grew on these plots. The produce from the collective farms had, however, to be sold to the government.

(A) *Protesting against collectivisation – a description from a Russian novel*
'Men began slaughtering their cattle every night . . . as soon as it grew dusk, one could hear the muffled bleating of sheep, the death squeal of a pig piercing the stillness, the whimper of a calf. Both the peasants who had joined the collective farms and the individual farmers killed off their stock. . . . "Kill, it's not ours now. Kill, the state butchers will do it if we don't. Kill, they won't give you meat to eat in the collective farms."'
(M. SHOLOKHOV, *Virgin Soil Upturned*)

(B) *One of many letters sent to village newspapers complaining about collectivisation*
'Comrade editor . . . if, as you write, the peasants join the kolkhoz [collective farm] voluntarily, why do you send brigades who send you to prison for the slightest resistance against the kolkhoz? Did the people think that they would live this way after they received freedom? Now it happens that freedom is not a word, but prison is a word. Say something against collectivisation and you are put in prison, . . . If you took a vote, you would only find half of a percent who joined the kolkhoz voluntarily. Each one thinks that it is a terrible thing, each one wants to be a master and not a slave . . . it is better to hang yourself than to join a kolkhoz; it's better not to be born than to join the kolkhoz.'
(M. FAINSOD, *Smolensk Under Soviet Rule*, 1958)

(D) *Percentage of farm households collectivised 1928–40*

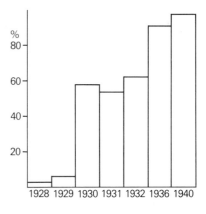

(C) *Livestock numbers* (million head)

	1928	1933
Cattle	70.5	38.4
Pigs	26.0	12.1
Sheep and Goats	146.7	50.2

(A. NOVE, *Stalinism and After*, 1975)

Questions
1. How long did it take to get a) 50 percent and   b) 90 percent of farm households into collectives? (**D**)
2. How was the government able to collectivise agriculture so quickly? (**T**)
3. What did the richer peasants (Kulaks) do rather than join the collectives? What effect did their action have on agricultural output? (**A**), (**C**) and (**T**)
4. Draw three bar graphs to show the effects of collectivisation on the cattle, pig, sheep and goat population between 1928 and 1933 (**C**)
5. How unpopular does the letter claim collectivisation was? (**B**)
6. Why did the peasants hate collectivisation so much? (**A**) and (**B**)
7. Talking point: The famine of 1932–34 which followed the burning of the crops and the killing of animals is never reported in the official Russian history books. Can you suggest why?

The purges

Opposition

By the mid 1930s opposition to Stalin had begun to mount. Within the party an increasing number of the old Bolsheviks, who had been associated with Lenin, had become bitter over Stalin's harsh and brutal methods.

In December 1934 Kirov, a leading communist and possible successor to Stalin, was assassinated. An opposition plot was uncovered and Stalin snatched at the chance to start a purge (a thorough clean-out) to remove anyone from the party who might threaten his power. Over the next few years, practically every important Bolshevik who had been in the 1917 revolution was arrested and shot.

Great show trials were staged, where old Bolsheviks like Kamenev and Zinoviev confessed to incredible crimes such as plotting to kill Stalin or spying for the Nazis.

The Great Terror

In 1937 the purge was extended to the army and thousands of officers were arrested, shot or sent to prison camps.

An estimated one million party-members died in these purges. But the Great Terror, as it became known, also claimed millions of ordinary Russians as victims.

Stalin finally called a halt to the Great Terror in 1938. All of his enemies – and many more besides – had been removed and replaced by his own supporters. His power was now total and unchallenged.

The constitution

Just as the purges were getting under way, Stalin introduced a new constitution. He called it 'the only truly democratic constitution' in the world. This was a lie. Russians were only allowed to vote for candidates selected by the communist party, and the Supreme Soviet, or parliament, was given little say in the running of the country. All real power remained in Stalin's hands.

(A) *Stalin's victims (in millions)*

Victims of Collectivisation 1930–6

Perished during collectivisation	3.5
Died in prison and labour camps	3.5
Victims of the Great Terror 1936–50	
Executions	1.0
Died in prisons and labour camps	12.0
Total (estimate)	20.0 million

(Figures taken from R. CONQUEST, *The Great Terror*, 1968)

(B) *Large scale massacres became common as the Great Terror gained pace. V. Petrov, who was a NKVD officer (a member of the secret police) in Moscow during the purges, handled hundreds of telegrams like the one printed here. The Petrovs later sought political asylum in Australia, after working at the Russian embassy in Canberra.*

Telegram from Yezhov (Chief of Russian NKVD) to NKVD Head at Frunze, capital of Kirghizia:
'YOU ARE CHARGED WITH THE TASK OF EXTERMINATING 10,000 ENEMIES OF THE PEOPLE ... REPORT RESULTS BY SIGNAL.
Reply:
IN REPLY TO YOURS OF ... THE FOLLOWING ENEMIES OF THE PEOPLE HAVE BEEN SHOT...'
(V. AND E. PETROV, *Empire of Fear*, 1956)

(C) *A Russian joke on the purges:*
'According to the story, Stalin lost his pipe. He thereupon telephoned the NKVD [secret police] and demanded it be found immediately. Two hours later, he found the pipe himself – it had merely fallen into one of his boots behind the sofa in his apartment. He telephoned the NKVD again and asked what progress had been made.

"We have arrested ten men already," the Minister reported, "and the investigation is continuing."

"As it happens," said Stalin, "I have found my pipe. So free them instantly."

"But, Comrade Stalin, seven of them have already confessed!"'
(H. MONTGOMERY HYDE, *Stalin*, 1971)

(D) *One of those executed in 1936 was Stalin's old rival Kamenev. The top photo taken in 1915 shows Stalin (back row centre) beside Kamenev (back row right). The bottom photo was published after Kamenev's fall.*

Questions

1. What does (**B**) tell us about the way the purges were carried out? Why do you think local officials obeyed orders such as these?
2. What point about the purges is the Russian joke making? (**C**)
3. Compare the two pictures in (**D**). How has the one on the left been altered? Explain why it was changed in this way. (**D**)
4. Why should we be very careful when using figures like those shown in (**A**)?
5. If you had been an important Russian during the purges what action would you have taken?
6. Talking point: If a dictator gained control in this country, the same things that happened during the purges could happen here. Do you agree?
7. Research: Alexander Solzhenitsyn, a Russian author, spent 10 years in a prison camp. He wrote about his experiences there in a book called *One Day in the Life of Ivan Denisovich*, which was published after Stalin died. Borrow a copy of the book from the library and use it to find out what life in a prison camp was like. Do you think the book is reliable evidence of what really happened?

The Great Patriotic War

During the 1930s Stalin became worried about Hitler's aim to add parts of Russia to the German empire. Approaches were therefore made to the Western European countries to sign agreements to hold Germany in check. In 1935 Russia signed treaties with Czechoslovakia and France.

But Stalin still did not trust Britain and France. He felt they were encouraging Hitler to expand eastwards, towards Russia. If true, Russia would face the Nazis alone. These fears increased when Britain and France turned down a Russian bid for an alliance to resist Hitler.

The Nazi-Soviet Pact

Stalin had no intention of sacrificing Russia to save the Western countries so he quickly made a deal with Hitler. In 1939 the Nazi-Soviet Non-Aggression Pact was signed. Germany and Russia agreed not to make war on each other.

The Western democracies were shocked by the agreement but it suited both the dictators. For Hitler, peace with Russia left him free to attack Western Europe. For Stalin, the deal gave Russia valuable time to build up her defences.

The Second World War

A week after the pact had been signed, German troops invaded Poland and the Second World War began. Soon after Russian troops moved into East Poland and took over the Baltic States – Estonia, Latvia and Lithuania. (See p. 87.)

For two years, events went as Stalin planned. The Western countries and the Nazis fought each other while the Russians furiously rearmed.

Then on 22 June 1941 the Germans invaded Russia. For a while it looked as though the Soviet Union would be defeated. However, with great courage and determination the Russians fought back until in 1945 the last German troops were expelled from Russia.

The war turned Stalin into a national hero. His leadership had rescued Russia from defeat. Even many of those who had suffered in the purges, came to accept him.

(A) *A Russian general tells of the homecoming of one of his sergeants*:

'When Remenyuk got home . . . the cottage had gone – only ruins left. The orchard was burned. Only one old apple tree still standing, and on it his father hung and under it his mother lay dead. Yarinka [his wife] and Oksana [his daughter] the Germans had taken away.'

(Quoted by M. ARNOLD-FORSTER in the *Guardian* 28 June 1981)

(B) *The caption to this poster read*:

'Napoleon suffered defeat. The same will happen to the conceited Hitler.'

(C) *USSR's losses in the Second World War (Soviet statistics)*

Human casualties . . .	20 million killed
Property destroyed:	
cities and towns	1710
villages	70 000
farms	100 000
industrial plants	32 000

(D) *Stalin and his generals*

'Sometimes, in the early days of the war, [Stalin] was savage [with his generals]. He would ring up perhaps half-a-dozen generals whose armies had retreated during the day, and tell them to come to Moscow at once. Immediately on arrival in Moscow, they were brought before a court martial and then, in the evening, shot. Stalin was the only war lord of the Second World War who shot his generals for failure in the field. Hitler, of course, shot some generals who conspired against him, but that was something very different.'

(A.J.P. TAYLOR, *The War Lords*, 1977)

(E) *Russia, 1942: 'Excel yourselves to produce better help for the front.'*

Questions

1. How do Russia's war dead losses compare with America's and Britain's? (**C**)
2. Describe how you would have felt if you had been Remenyuk and had just returned home. (**A**)
3. Memories of the war seem to live on in Russia much more strongly than in Britain and the USA. Can you suggest why? (**A**) and (**C**)
4. What does (**D**) tell us about Stalin as a war leader? Would Stalin's treatment of his generals have encouraged or discouraged good leadership on the battlefield? Explain.
5. Who is the pitchfork aimed at in the poster? (**B**) How is Hitler drawn? What is the torn document in Hitler's hand? What message is the poster trying to get across?
6. Who are the two figures in the flag in (**E**)? What is the poster calling on the Russian people to do?
7. Talking Point: The Russians lost more dead in the Second World War than all the military and civilian deaths in the First World War. Because of these losses the Russians are determined that they will never be invaded again. This is why they have large armed forces today and why they keep countries such as Poland, Czechoslovakia, Hungary and Rumania under tight control. Does this argument seem convincing to you?

Stalin's last years

The war had left Russia in ruins. Twenty million Russians had died. Over half her cities, railways, mines and factories had been destroyed and much of her farming land had been ruined.

Recovery

Now the country had to be rebuilt. In 1946, a fourth five-year plan was started. Like the other plans the stress was on heavy industry. This meant there were few goods for the workers to buy, so living standards remained low. Agriculture was also neglected. The peasants were paid low prices for their produce and food output was well below target. Nevertheless there was a rapid recovery. Sheer hard work plus reparations (machines, equipment, etc.) taken from the defeated countries soon restored production to its old levels. By 1953 Russia's output was higher than it had been before the war.

More purges

During the last seven years of his life, Stalin became more and more suspicious of the people around him. Arrests began to mount and the prison camps to fill up again though not to the levels of the Great Terror.

The cult of personality

At the same time Stalin was turned into a god-like figure. The cult of personality – the worship of Stalin – reached ridiculous heights. Every victory in the war was credited to Stalin. Every socialist success was said to have been planned by Stalin. Everywhere there were statues, paintings and photographs of Stalin.

Then in March 1953, Stalin died suddenly. For many Russians it was hard to think of the Soviet Union without Stalin. For nearly 30 years he had ruled as a dictator. In that time, he had helped turn Russia from a backward agricultural state into the world's second greatest military and industrial power.

Stalin: great leader or evil tyrant?

Below are set out two arguments. One argues that Stalin was a great leader; the other argues that Stalin was an evil tyrant. Read them both, then write an essay of 200–300 words on the topic: 'How should Stalin be remembered?' Start with the words: In my opinion, Stalin deserves to be remembered for ....

Stalin was a great leader

(1) When Stalin took control, Russia had been through revolution, war and was just recovering from near economic ruin. When he died, Russia was one of the world's two superpowers with an industrial output second only to the USA.

(2) By concentrating on heavy industry and armaments, Stalin helped save Russia from the Nazis. During the war, his strong leadership held the Russians together.

(3) Under Stalin, nearly all of the territories lost by the Treaty of Brest-Litovsk in 1918 were recovered. After 1945, communist governments were set up in central Europe, giving Russia extra protection from attack.

(4) For the first time all Russians were given a free basic education. By 1950 only the elderly could not read and write. Workers and peasants were also encouraged to go on to higher education.

(5) In health and welfare there was tremendous progress. Huge numbers of hospitals were built while doctors were trained in their thousands. By 1940 there were more doctors in Russia for every thousand people than in Britain. Russian workers were also given paid holidays and a pension on retirement.

(6) In short, Stalin modernised Russia.

Stalin was an evil tyrant

(1) Stalin was not even a good communist. He destroyed the communist party of Lenin and filled it with his own supporters. There was no thought or discussion within the party.

(2) Those who rose in Stalin's party were often second-rate. Anyone with talent who dared point out mistakes was quickly replaced. Mistakes, instead of being corrected, were simply covered up. Stalin's economic success has been greatly exaggerated. In industry, lots of the goods produced were of poor quality.

(3) In agriculture Stalin's policies proved disastrous. The war on the Kulaks robbed Russia of her best farmers. Collectivisation was a mistake and led to low harvests and food shortages.

(4) Life for the workers and peasants under Stalin was grim. Living standards remained low during the whole of his rule. Shortages of basic goods like bread and vegetables were common. And while workers were putting up with terrible housing, money was being wasted on prestige projects e.g. underground railway stations were built to look like palaces.

(5) Stalin was not the great war leader that he made out. The Russian army would have been much better prepared if most of the best officers had not been purged in the Great Terror. Stalin misjudged the date when Germany would attack, and ignored warnings that Germany was preparing for an attack in early 1941. He needlessly wasted his soldiers in futile attacks. Generals who retreated or failed in battle were recalled to Moscow and shot.

(6) In short, Stalin was one of the most evil dictators who ever lived. He was obsessed by power, and millions of innocent Russians died as a result of his rule.

The rise of Khrushchev

Collective leadership

On Stalin's death a leadership struggle broke out. At first, Malenkov took over as prime minister and party secretary. But within two weeks he had to hand over the important post of party secretary to Nikita Khrushchev. All important decisions were now made by a *collective*, or shared leadership, made up of several men.

This lasted until 1955 when Malenkov was forced to resign and was replaced by Bulganin, a Khrushchev supporter. In 1958 Khrushchev had Bulganin sacked and then he became prime minister as well as party secretary. Khrushchev never became as powerful as Stalin. Nevertheless he did dominate Soviet politics until he was forced to retire in 1964.

Destalinisation

Soon after Stalin's death the newspapers stopped worshipping Stalin. This was a sign that some of Stalin's policies were about to be reversed. In one early move, Stalin's secret police chief Beria was arrested and shot. Later most of the prison camps were closed and the prisoners freed.

Then in February 1956, at the 20th Congress of the Communist Party, Khrushchev made a fierce attack on Stalin. He accused Stalin of murdering thousands of innocent communists and of making serious mistakes during the war. Khrushchev also attacked the personality cult, which had made Stalin out to be a superman.

Khrushchev's speech was followed by a *destalinisation* programme. Stalin's economic policies were criticised and his statues were demolished. At the same time, Russia became a freer place in which to live. This period during which the government slightly loosened its grip on the people, is often called the *thaw*.

Watching the newspapers — the rise of Khrushchev

Russian newspapers rarely report what is going on behind the scenes in Government. Sometimes however it is possible to pick up clues about this by examining what they publish. The two photographs opposite provide an example of this.

(A) *The leadership on 6 March 1953 gathers to pay its respects to Stalin. Malenkov is closest to Stalin, Khrushchev is furthest left.*

Two days later, on 8 March, Khrushchev is closer to Stalin's body.

(B) *Extracts from Khrushchev's secret speech*:
The war
'Stalin [sold himself] as a great leader. In various ways he tried to [convince] the people that all victories gained by the Soviet Nation during the Great Patriotic War were due to the courage, daring and genius of Stalin and to no one else . . . .

Not Stalin, but the Party as a whole, the Soviet Government, our heroic army, its talented leaders and soldiers, the whole Soviet Nation – these are the ones who [won] the victory in the Great Patriotic War.'

Stalin's suspicions
'Stalin was a very distrustful man, sickly suspicious, we knew this from the work with him. He could look at a man and say: "Why are your eyes so shifty today?" or "Why are you turning so much today and avoiding to look me directly in the eyes?" The sickly suspicion created in him a general distrust even toward [important] party workers whom he had known for years. Everywhere and in everything he saw "enemies", "two facers" and spies.'

Purges
'Of 139 members of the Party's Central Committee 70 percent were arrested and shot. Of 1966 delegates to the Party Congress 1108 were arrested on charges of anti-revolutionary crimes. Now when the cases of some of these "spies" and "saboteurs" were examined it was found that the cases were fabricated. Confessions of guilt were gained with the help of cruel and inhuman tortures.'

(Adapted from N. KHRUSHCHEV, reported in *Manchester Guardian Supplement*, 1956)

Questions

1 What do the two photographs suggest was happening among the Russian leaders following Stalin's death? Who appears to be on the rise? (**A**)

2 What did Khrushchev accuse Stalin of doing during the war? (**B**)

3 What mental problem does Khrushchev claim Stalin suffered from? (**B**)

4 What does Khrushchev suggest was the main cause of the great purges? (**B**)

5 Khrushchev's speech (**B**), when it was printed in other parts of the world, amazed many people. Can you suggest why?

6 Talking point: Khrushchev was bound to have attacked Stalin at some time. No one wants to be compared to a person who has been turned into a virtual God. Do you agree?

Khrushchev's domestic policies 1953–64

When Khrushchev came to power, the USSR was one of the world's super-powers. Yet the Soviet people enjoyed a standard of living well below that of the USA. Khrushchev hoped 'to catch up and take over the USA' and prove that communism was the better way of life. More consumer goods, better housing and more food were promised.

Industry

Production of items such as clothing, appliances, and housing materials was increased. Meanwhile Russia continued to make advances in other areas. In 1957 she launched the world's first space satellite.

To make industry more efficient, some decision-making was *decentralised*. Regional economic councils were given some power to make decisions for local industries. Even so, all important decisions still came from Moscow.

Agriculture

Khrushchev promised to increase food output. More money was injected into agriculture and better prices were paid for crops. A number of new schemes were begun. The grandest was a plan to plough up and cultivate some 90 million acres of previously uncultivated land called the 'Virgin Lands'. At first Khrushchev's experiments were successful. Food production jumped 50 per cent between 1953 and 1958. But after that it stagnated.

Much of the improvement has been because agriculture was still recovering from previous neglect and wartime damage. The climate of the virgin lands was unfavourable for good grain crops. And in many areas, bad planning led to crops being planted in the wrong kind of soil.

The fall of Khrushchev

By 1963 it was clear that many of Khrushchev's policies were failing. That year Russia had to import grain. Industry was not reaching its targets. These facts plus Khrushchev's foreign policy failures led to his dismissal in 1964.

(A) *From Khrushchev's report of livestock production figures 1916–53 (in millions)*:

	1916	*1928*	*1941*	*1953*
Large horned cattle:				
Total	58.4	66.8	54.5	56.6
Cows	28.8	33.2	27.8	24.3
Pigs	23.0	27.7	27.5	28.5
Sheep and goats	96.3	114.6	91.6	109.9
Horses	38.8	36.1	21.0	15.3

(J.P. NETTL, *The Soviet Achievement*, 1967)

(B) *The Soviet Seven-Year Plan 1958–65*

	1958	1965 (planned target)	1965 (actually achieved)
Industrial output	100	180	184
Farm output	100	170	114
Sales of consumer goods	100	162	159

(J.P. NETTL, *The Soviet Achievement*, 1967)

(C) *Distribution of consumer goods in the USSR and the USA*

	Number of each item per thousand of the population		
	USSR, 1955	USSR, 1966	USA, 1966
Radios	66	171	1300
Cars	2	5	398
TV sets	4	82	376
Refrigerators	4	40	293
Washing machines	1	77	259
Sewing machines	31	151	136

(J.N. WESTWOOD, in *Purnell's History of the Twentieth Century*, 1968)

(D) *Khrushchev's views on Communism and living standards*:

'We must help people to eat well, dress well and live well. You cannot put theory into your soup or Marxism into your clothes. If after forty years of Communism, a person cannot have a glass of milk or a pair of shoes, he will not believe that Communism is a good thing, no matter what you tell him.'

Questions

1. Which items in (**A**) reveal increases? Which show decreases?
2. What evidence is there to show Soviet livestock production had made little progress since before the Russian Revolution? Quote figures. (**A**)
3. In what areas could Khrushchev's policies be judged a) successful b) a failure? Give reasons. (**B**)
4. Why does Khrushchev think it is vital for the communist government to provide its people with a high standard of living? (**D**)
5. Roughly how many times did the output of the various consumer goods shown in (**C**) increase between 1955 and 1966? What evidence is there in (**C**) to show that there was a big improvement in the standard of living under Khrushchev?
6. Judging by the figures (**C**) do you think the Russians were a) close to b) equal c) ahead or d) far behind the USA in the output of consumer goods?
7. Talking point: Even today Russians have a lower standard of living than most people in the Western world. Does this prove that communism is a failure?

After Khrushchev

After his fall, Khrushchev's powers were shared between two men – Leonid Brezhnev, who became head of the communist party, and Alexi Kosygin, who became premier (head of the Council of Ministers). By the early 1970s Brezhnev was by far the most powerful man in Russia.

Economic policies

Since Khrushchev the economy has grown rapidly. Today Russia has the largest economy after the USA and leads the world in industries such as coal mining and steel.

Trade with western countries has increased. Living standards have risen rapidly but shortages of consumer goods remain. Agriculture is still the weak point of the economy. In times of bad harvest, large amounts of food have to be imported.

Social welfare

Huge amounts of money are spent on social welfare. The wide range of benefits includes loss of breadwinner allowances, student grants and maternity benefits. Retirement pensions are paid to men at 60 and women at 55. All medical services and treatment are free. So is education which is compulsory for 10 years from the age of seven. Large numbers of houses have been built too.

Changing attitudes

The public attacks on Stalin which had been common under Khrushchev have ended.

Censorship has become much stricter. Writers who have not been prepared to follow the exact party line have found it difficult to get their work published. Some who have dared openly to express their beliefs, have been sent to labour camps and mental homes.

Freedom of worship is only barely tolerated. But even this is a big improvement on the days of Khrushchev and Stalin, when the churches were openly attacked.

The communist party is still the only legal party and controls the government at every level.

(A) *Some prices in state stores, 1979 (in rubles):*

Cafeteria meal	0.75–1.25
Cigarettes (20)	0.30
Beer (mug)	0.22
Coffee (cup)	0.08
Bread (lb.)	0.06–0.12
Potatoes (lb.)	0.05
Sugar (lb.)	0.44
Haircut (man's)	0.50
Travel fares:	
bus	0.05
metro	0.05
trolley	0.04
street car	0.03
Beef (lb.)	1.00
Ready-made man's suit	100.00

(V. MEDISH, *The Soviet Union*, 1981)

(B) *The disastrous grain harvest of 1972*
As historians we must be careful to weigh up all the facts and figures before making a general statement. Take for example the so-called disastrous grain harvest of 1972. Western newspapers pointed out that the Russians had to buy record amounts of grain from the USA. The Minister of Agriculture had been dismissed for poor results and foreign observers noted the weather had been unfavourable.

But was this evidence strong enough to label the harvest disastrous? Look at the grain harvest statistics, then answer the questions that follow.

1 The 1973 grain harvest was the highest in history. Where does the 1972 harvest rank?
2 Do you think the 1972 harvest should be labelled as disastrous? Give reasons for your answer.
3 'The 1972 weather was at least as bad as that of 1963' (Alex Nove). Taking this fact into account, how does the 1972 grain harvest compare with the 1963 harvest?

Grain harvest variations (in million tons)

1960	1961	1962	1963
125.5	130.8	140.2	107.5

1964	1965	1966	1967
152.1	121.1	171.2	147.9

1968	1969	1970	1971
169.5	162.4	186.8	181.2

1972	1973		
168.2	222.5		

(A. BROWN and M. KASER, *The Soviet Union since the fall of Khrushchev*, 1975)

(C) *Living standards for a Moscow family*
'Their monthly income consists of two, better-than-average salaries and a pension and totals 450 rubles. Out of this sum they pay a low income tax of 30 rubles (about 7 percent) and a small charge of 20 rubles (4 percent to 5 percent) for their modest apartment and utilities. They pay 4 rubles for labor union membership. About 12 rubles is spent on inexpensive public transportation (their children walk to school) and approximately 60 rubles on lunches and pocket money. Basic foods for a family of five cost about 250 rubles per month. By now our hypothetic family has spent more than three-fourths of the budget: 30+20+4+12+60+250 = 376. They are left with less than 75 rubles to cover all other expenses: the purchase and repair of clothing, shoes, household appliances, furniture, and other manufactured goods.'
(V. MEDISH, *The Soviet Union*, 1981)

(D) *Average monthly salary compensation (includes such invisible income as free education, medical care and various subsidies):*
(Taken from *Soviet Statistics*)

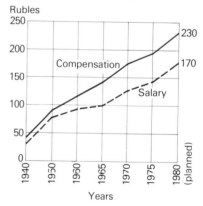

Questions
1 Why is the compensation higher than the average level of wages? (**D**)
2 How many times has the average wage roughly increased since 1940? (**D**) What does this tell us about the changes in the Soviet standard of living?
3 Work out the average weekly income. How many   a) 1 lbs of beef   b) ready-made suits would it purchase? (**A**)
4 What is the average weekly wage in this country? How many   a) 1 lbs of beef   b) ready-made suits would you be able to purchase? Are these items less or more expensive than in Russia? (**A**)
5 Draw a pie graph to give a breakdown of how a Russian family might spend its income using the figures in (**C**).

123

The American system of government

The United States is a *democratic republic* with a *federal* system of government.

Democracy

In a democracy every adult has the right to vote; to choose between the candidates of different political parties. Regular elections are held to make sure that the voters are ruled by the government of their choice. To help them to choose wisely, Americans enjoy a large number of individual rights. These include freedom of speech, freedom of assembly (the right to meet and form groups) and freedom of the press.

Republic

The USA is also a republic, i.e. the head of state is a *President* who is elected by the people every four years. The federal system of government means that power is shared between the central or federal government in Washington and the various (50) state governments.

Constitution

This system of government was laid down by the founders of the USA in 1787 in a written document known as the *Constitution*. The constitution divides the powers of the government among three separate branches – legislature, executive and judiciary (see the diagram opposite). Each branch has the power to check and balance the other two.

Political parties

The Democratic and Republican parties are by far the largest. The Democrats tend to be fairly *liberal* and interested in reforms to help the weak, old and jobless. Republicans on the other hand are more *conservative* and tend to support the interests of businessmen and richer Americans.

(A) *The United States system of government, which is laid down in a written document called 'The Constitution'*

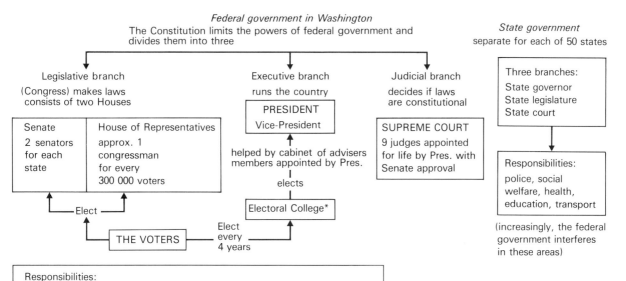

Federal government in Washington
The Constitution limits the powers of federal government and divides them into three

State government
separate for each of 50 states

Legislative branch
(Congress) makes laws consists of two Houses

Senate	House of Representatives
2 senators for each state	approx. 1 congressman for every 300 000 voters

Executive branch
runs the country

PRESIDENT
Vice-President

helped by cabinet of advisers
members appointed by Pres.

elects

Electoral College*

Judicial branch
decides if laws are constitutional

SUPREME COURT
9 judges appointed for life by Pres. with Senate approval

Three branches:
State governor
State legislature
State court

Responsibilities:
police, social welfare, health, education, transport

(increasingly, the federal government interferes in these areas)

Elect

THE VOTERS — Elect every 4 years

Responsibilities:
National defence, foreign policy, collecting taxes, trade, some social welfare

* a body of electors chosen by the voters who formally elect the Pres. and Vice-Pres.

Questions

1 Match the terms on the left with their correct meanings:

1	President	A	A document which states how the USA must be governed
2	Congress	B	Government elected by the people
3	Supreme Court	C	Carries out the laws passed by Congress
4	Federal Government	D	A country where the head of state is a president
5	State Government	E	Draws up and passes laws
6	Voter	F	A council of advisers to the President
7	Constitution	G	Explains and interprets the federal laws
8	Republic	H	Mainly responsible for looking after education and health
9	Democracy	I	Responsible for looking after the armed services
10	Cabinet	J	Selects his or her choice for President every four years

2 Talking point: 'You can fool all the people some of the time, and some of the people all the time, but you cannot fool all the people all the time' (Abraham Lincoln). What point about democracy is Abraham Lincoln making?

The Roaring Twenties

For many Americans the 1920s was an age of gaiety when they tried to forget the horrors of the First World War. Indeed, the 1920s are often called the 'roaring twenties' or the 'jazz age'.

During this time, the economy boomed. In the ten years between 1919 and 1929 industrial output doubled. Business profits also rocketed upwards, and wage earners had a little more money to spend.

Much of this new wealth came as old-established industries expanded. But there were also important new industries. Refrigerators, radios and vacuum cleaners began to appear in many homes. The first talkie arrived in 1927 and by 1930 the talkies were attracting 90 million viewers a week. Then there was the motor car – the most important of all the rising industries. In 1919 there were only 7 million cars in America; by 1929 there were nearly 24 million – one for every five people.

Politics

In these good times Americans voted for the conservative Republicans. Warren Harding was President during 1920–3, Calvin Coolidge between 1923 and 1929 and Herbert Hoover from 1929 to 1933. The Republican claim, that anyone could succeed in America as long as he worked hard, appealed to those who had made it. Besides, the Republican belief that prosperity would come to America without any government action, seemed to be true.

Poverty

But not all Americans shared in this prosperity. There were great extremes of income. For example, in 1929 the richest 10 percent of families received nearly 40 percent of all personal income, while the poorest 10 percent got only 2 percent. A survey in 1929 showed that four in every 10 American families were living in poverty. For those on farms, life was especially tough. Farmers were producing more food than they could sell, so prices began to drop. As a result, the 1920s saw farm incomes fall by two-thirds.

(A) *Economic indicators, 1922 and 1929*

Indicator	1922	1929
National income (billions of 1926 dollars)	61.2	75.9
Income per head (1926 dollars)	563.0	625.0
Employment (millions)	40.0	47.9
Average hourly earnings in manufacturing (dollars)	0.52	0.57
Bank deposits (billions of dollars)	41.1	57.9
Business profits (billions of dollars)	3.9	7.2

(G. FITE AND J. REEGEE, *An Economic History of the United States*, 1965)

(B) *Henry Ford and the cheap motor car*

'What was needed was a cheap, sturdy, simple car that could get the traveler *through* the morasses. Ford gave the answer in 1908 with his Model-T, which influenced not merely ways of life but the whole system of industrial production. Ford pioneered the assembly line. He paid men the incredible wages of five dollars a day to put cars together as they went by on moving lines. By 1914, one hour and 33 minutes of a man's time would assemble a chassis – a revolution in mass production.

The car which emerged from this process was probably the best-loved car ever made. In 1908 it cost $850, but by 1917 it was $360, and in 1925 one model sold for $290. This was stripped down, of course; when you bought a Ford it was only a point of departure. Its color was always black. It had no bumpers, no speedometer, no rearview mirror (why would you want to see what was coming from behind?); no accelerator, no temperature indicator (you could always tell when the engine boiled); no spare tire. Shortly after purchase, you began to order from the Sears, Roebuck catalog the accessories which were to adorn simplicity and make it comfortable.'

(J. DODDS, *Everyday Life in Twentieth-Century America*)

(C) *'Another Modern Improvement'* – *a cartoon showing the current feeling of optimism*

(Orr in the Chicago *Tribune*, 1929)

Questions

1 Which of the following statements for the period 1922–9 can be supported by the statistics in (**A**)?
   (a) America's wealth increased
   (b) There were less jobs available
   (c) People were saving more
   (d) Factory workers' wages increased faster than businessmen's profits.

2 Describe how Ford brought about a revolution in mass production. (**B**)

3 Who do the characters in the cartoon represent? (**C**)

4 What has happened to them over the years? (**C**)

5 What is the general message of the cartoon? (**C**)

6 In your opinion, has the cartoonist drawn an accurate picture of life in the 1920s? Comment. (**C**) and (**T**)

7 Talking point: Harding, the American President between 1920 and 1923, once admitted, 'I am not fit for this office and never should have been selected'. Why are such admissions so rare among politicians?

Social problems of the 1920s

The Red Scare

In the 1920s anyone who was not a white native-born American was distrusted. When several violent strikes broke out in 1919, foreign communist immigrants were blamed. Americans were so scared of communism that they hardly protested when 6000 suspected of communism, mainly immigrants, were arrested in 1920. Later most had to be released for lack of evidence.

The Sacco-Vanzetti case

In 1920 two Italian immigrants, Sacco and Vanzetti, were convicted for murder despite insufficient evidence and executed. To this day, many Americans believe they died because they were foreigners and held radical beliefs.

Anti-foreign feeling and the fear of communism resulted in the Quota Immigration Law of 1921. This reduced the flood of immigrants to a mere trickle.

The 1920s also saw the revival of a secret racist group called the Ku Klux Klan. Originally the Klan had been formed to oppose black rights and maintain white supremacy in the South. Now the Klan also attacked Catholics, foreigners, Jews and communists. By 1925 membership had swelled to nearly 5 million.

Prohibition

In 1920 the USA went 'dry'. It became illegal to make or sell intoxicating liquor. The ban was the result of a long campaign against drink by a number of *prohibition* groups. But the law proved impossible to enforce and many drank illegally in secret bars called 'speak-easies'. Gangsters like Al Capone took over the liquor trade and crime increased. Prohibition was finally ended in 1933.

(A) *A comment by Al Capone*:
'When I sell liquor, it's called bootlegging; when my patrons serve it on silver trays on Lake Shore Drive, it's called hospitality.'

(B) *Overcoming the prohibition law*

'Many people made their own home brew; in large cities, hardware stores openly displayed copper stills along with yeast, hops, and other ingredients. Other people bought their whiskey from bootleggers who claimed they were selling the best imported brands from Canada or Scotland, and sometimes did. More often, they passed off inferior products – at worst substances like Jamaica ginger, better known as "jake", which paralyzed thousands of people, Jackass Brandy, which caused internal bleeding, ... or Yack Yack Bourbon from Chicago, which blended iodine and burnt sugar.'

(W.E. LEUCHTENBURG, *The Perils of Prosperity*, 1958)

(C) *Prohibition and the gangsters*

'Bootlegging (selling illegal alcohol) produced the chief income for gangs which infested the large cities and frequently bought or forced their way into city governments. In 1920 "Scarface" Al Capone, a New York hoodlum from the Five Points Gang, moved to Chicago and set up an empire in alcohol, gambling, prostitution, and drugs. By 1927 he was operating a $60 million business and had a private army of close to one thousand hoodlums who "rubbed out" rival bootleggers attempting to cut into Capone's "territory". In 1926 and 1927 there were 130 gang murders in Cook Country, and not a single murderer was apprehended. Capone drove the streets of Chicago in a $30 000 armor-plated automobile, convoyed by scout cars, and went to the theater with a score of bodyguards.'

(W.E. LEUCHTENBURG, *The Perils of Prosperity*, 1958)

(D) *Ben Shahn's 'Prohibition Alley': Under a diagram of the workings of a still, bootleggers stack whisky smuggled in by ship, an operation eyed by Chicago gangster Al Capone. At left is a victim of gang warfare, at right, patrons outside a speak-easy.*

(*Museum of the City of New York*)

Questions

1 How did people get around the prohibition law? (**B**)

2 What effects did prohibition have on law and order? (**C**)

3 What evidence is there to suggest that high profits were being made out of bootlegging? (**C**)

4 What problems brought about by prohibition does Ben Shahn's painting show? (**D**)

5 Is the painting (a) enthusiastic (b) neutral or (c) against prohibition? Say why.

6 What point about prohibition is Al Capone making? (**A**)

7 Talking point: Prohibition was bad law. It turned normally law-abiding citizens into criminals. Do you agree?

The Great Depression

The Wall Street Crash

When Herbert Hoover became President in 1929 America's future looked bright. There was plenty of money around. In fact thousands of Americans were using their savings to buy shares in businesses on the American stock exchange (the headquarters of the stock exchange is in Wall Street, New York).

Share prices were spiralling upwards, so it was a simple matter to buy some shares, wait for the price to rise and then sell them off at a profit. It was a surefire way to make a fortune – so long as there were people who wanted to buy the shares and the price kept rising. But it couldn't last.

Suddenly in October 1929, panic set in. Nobody wanted to buy and everyone wanted to sell. Share prices crashed and millions of people were ruined. The Great Depression had come to America.

Causes of the depression

Even before the 1929 collapse, business had begun to decline because of four basic weaknesses in the economy:

- Much of the new wealth was in the hands of a few. Not enough Americans had sufficient money to buy all the cars, houses and other goods being produced.
- Factories were turning out more goods than they could sell. Unable to sell their stock, businessmen closed down their plants and laid off workers. This led to further cuts in the demand for goods as the unemployed had little money to spend.
- America's foreign trade was in a bad way. Since the First World War the USA had lent large sums of money to other countries to allow them to buy American goods. Suddenly, in 1928, foreign loans dried up and instead, the money was invested on the booming stock exchange. The result was a sharp fall in American exports.
- The American banking system was weak so when large numbers of people tried to withdraw their savings at the same time, a lot of banks were forced to close.

(A) *Unemployment 1920–41* *Business failures 1920–41* *Bank failures 1920–41*

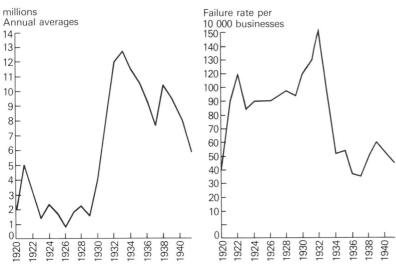
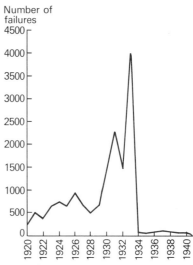

(B) *Henry Ford said in March 1931*:
'The average man won't really do a day's work unless he is caught and cannot get out of it. There is plenty of work to do, if people would do it.'

(C) *A tenement dweller on 113th Street in East Harlem wrote to his Congressman in Washington*:
'You know my condition is bad. I used to get pension from the government and they stopped. It is now nearly seven months I am out of work. I hope you will try to do something for me.... I have four children who are in need of clothes and food.... My daughter who is eight is very ill and not recovering. My rent is due two months and I am afraid of being put out.'

(Quoted in H. ZINN, *A People's History of the United States*, 1980)

(D) *An unemployed car worker*

Questions
1 Which of the following statements is true according to the graphs? (**A**)
   (a) There was no unemployment before the crash of 1929
   (b) All businesses were prospering in the 1920s
   (c) The worst year of the depression was 1930.
2 In what year did (a) unemployment (b) business failures (c) bank failures reach their peak? (**A**)
3 Imagine you are a newspaper editor in 1931. You have just received a copy of the photograph (**D**) and the latest unemployment figures (**A**). Write an editorial attacking Henry Ford's statement (**B**).
4 Why was the tenement dweller in such a desperate position? (**C**)
5 If you had been President what would you have done to provide work or help for the millions of hungry and unemployed? Design an election manifesto setting out your programme.

Hoover and the depression

By the winter of 1932 there were 10 million out of work. Over 5000 banks had closed their doors and 32 000 businesses had gone bankrupt. Farmers were hit by drought and a further drop in prices.

All across America millions were crying out for government help. But Hoover was a strong believer in the theory of *laissez-faire*, that is that governments should not become involved in business affairs.

Hoover's programme

Nevertheless as the depression deepened, Hoover realised that the federal government had to do something. In 1930 federal money was set aside for public works to employ idle workers. In 1932 the Reconstruction Finance Corporation (RFC) was set up to loan money to save some near-bankrupt banks and businesses. But Hoover refused to set up federal relief programmes to aid the unemployed. He insisted it was the job of private charities and local state-governments to look after the needy.

Protest

As the depression dragged on, the protest movement grew. The jobless marched in the streets demanding work or unemployment insurance. The hungry marched for more food and angry farmers demonstrated about low prices. Perhaps the most dramatic protest of all was the Bonus Army march on Washington, to try and get the government to make an advance payment of the veterans' bonus that was due to them in 1945. But Hoover refused to pay the bonus and he ordered the army in to destroy the camps and to drive the veterans out of the city.

For the 1932 presidential election, the Republicans re-nominated Hoover. To oppose him, the Democrats put up Franklin D. Roosevelt who promised a 'new deal for the forgotten man on the bottom of the economic pyramid'. On election day, Roosevelt swept to an easy victory.

(A) *During the depression, Hoover's name took on a number of new meanings*:

- *Hoovervilles* were shanty towns built on the outskirts of towns where the homeless sheltered.
- *Hoover Stew* was the thin soup distributed at emergency kitchens.
- *Hoover Blankets* were old newspapers used for warmth.
- *Hoover Apples* was the fruit sold by the unemployed on the streets.
- *Hoover Leather* was the cardboard with which people patched their shoe soles.

(Adapted from J. RUBLOWSKY, *After the Crash*, 1970)

(B) *Roosevelt shaking hands with a coal-miner during the 1932 election campaign*

(C) *What Roosevelt planned to do if he got into power. An extract from a campaign speech*:

'The country needs and, unless I mistake its temper, the country demands bold, persistent experimentation. It is common sense to take a method and try it. If it fails, admit it frankly and try another. But above all, try something.'

(Quoted in J. RAY, *Roosevelt and Kennedy*, 1970)

(D) *A Hooverville in Central Park, New York. In the background are blocks of luxury flats.*

Questions

1 Why do you think Hoover's name came to be used in these ways? (**A**)
2 What kind of person does Roosevelt seem to be, judging by this photograph? (**B**)
3 What evidence is there in this extract to show that Roosevelt had no detailed plan for solving the depression if he became President? (**C**)
4 If you had been living in a shanty town like the one in New York, who would you have voted for in the 1932 election? (**D**) Explain why.
5 Talking point: Was Herbert Hoover responsible for bringing misery and hardship to millions of Americans?

The New Deal Laws I

Once in power Roosevelt acted fast. Relief and recovery measures were the most urgent. They therefore dominated what is called the First New Deal – the years 1933–5. After 1935 the New Deal was mainly concerned with reform measures, the Second New Deal (1935–9).

The banking crisis

Roosevelt spent much of his first year trying to restore the shattered economic system. The Emergency Banking Act (1933) enabled the government to lend money to banks so they could carry on trading. Another act insured bank deposits up to $5000 to reassure small savers.

The unemployed

To provide immediate relief the Federal Emergency Relief Administration was set up. FERA spent $3 billion dollars feeding the hungry and on wages for men on public works.

During the winter of 1933–4, four million people were given jobs working for the Civilian Works Administration (CWA) building roads, schools, playgrounds and airports. Unemployed young men were given jobs working for the Civilian Conservation Corps (1933), in forestry, flood control and soil conservation.

The largest New Deal agency was the Works Progress Administration (1935). In its seven-year history, the WPA spent $10 billion and employed eight million workers.

Industry and labour

To revive industry the National Recovery Administration of 1933 was set up. This agency hoped to increase production by reducing hours of work and raising wages. It also guaranteed workers the right to join trade unions and negotiate with their employers. But in 1935, the Supreme Court ruled that the NRA was unconstitutional.

In reply, Congress passed the Wagner Act of 1935. Workers could bargain with their employers through the union of their own choice. As a result the number of trade unionists doubled between 1935 and 1941.

(A) *'Looks as if the new leadership was really going to lead.' A cartoon about the early years of the New Deal.*

(B) *Cartoon showing the increased federal powers during the first New Deal.*

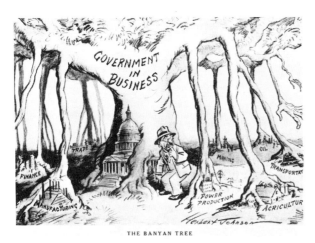

THE BANYAN TREE

(C) *Roosevelt speaks*:
'... This nation asks for action, and action now. Our greatest primary task is to put people to work.'

His wife, Eleanor, wrote about him:
'His voice lent itself remarkably to the radio. It was a natural gift, for in his whole life he never had a lesson in diction or public speaking. His voice unquestionably helped him to make the people of the country feel that they were an intelligent and understanding part of every government undertaking during his administration.'

(J. RAY, *Roosevelt and Kennedy*, 1970)

(D) *This Christmas card was put into pay envelopes, and was headed 'Merry Christmas from Santa Claus'.*

'I am sending this card to
    tell you
That the New Deal has
    taken away
The things that I really
    needed
My workshop – my rein-
    deer – my sleigh
Now I'm making my
    rounds on a donkey
He's old and crippled and
    slow
So you'll know if I don't
    see you Christmas
That I'll be out on my ass
    in the snow.'

(Quoted in G. WOLFSKILL AND J A. HUDSON, *Franklin D. Roosevelt and his Critics, 1933–39*, 1969)

Questions

1 What did Roosevelt consider to be his most urgent task on taking office? (**C**)
2 Why would it be unwise to rely solely on the opinion expressed in (**C**) about Roosevelt's impact on the radio?
3 Who is the character pulling the mule and cart? Who do the people in the cart represent? Who are following on behind? What is the message of the cartoon? (**A**)
4 From where is the tree growing in cartoon (**B**)? What point about the New Deal is the cartoonist making?
5 Describe the attitude of the writer of the Christmas card towards the New Deal. (**D**)
6 Talking point: The idea behind the New Deal was that the government was going to reshuffle the cards and give the people with 'bad hands' a chance to do better. Why were the supporters of laissez-faire so opposed to this idea?

The New Deal Laws II

Farmers

When Roosevelt took office, incomes were so low that many farmers were being forced to leave the land. To make matters worse, drought in the mid-West meant that 300 000 farmers had to abandon their 'dustbowl' farms.

To increase farm incomes, the government passed the Agricultural Adjustment Act (AAA) of 1933. Farmers were paid to produce less. At a time when millions were going hungry, it seemed a terrible waste but by 1936 farmers' incomes were 50 percent higher than they had been in 1933. In 1936 the AAA was declared unconstitutional and the government replaced it with the Soil Conservation Act.

The TVA

Perhaps Roosevelt's boldest plan was to set up the Tennessee Valley Authority. The Tennessee Valley was a poor, badly eroded region which was often flooded. The TVA built a network of dams to control the floods and give the area a supply of cheap electricity. More industry was attracted and gradually the whole region began to prosper.

Housing and security

To stop people from losing their homes because they were unable to pay their mortgages, the government set up the Home Owners Loan Corporation (HOLC) in 1933. Money was lent to home owners at very low rates of interest.

In 1934 the Federal Housing Administration (FHA) was established. Low interest loans made it possible for millions of people to obtain better housing. In 1937 the National Housing Act was passed. Money was lent to local public housing agencies for slum clearances and low-cost housing.

The Social Security Law of 1935 provided pensions for most people over 65 years old and benefits for the unemployed. It also provided funds for the crippled, the blind, dependent mothers and children.

How do we remember the depression?

Over the years, two pictures have come to represent what the depression meant to Americans. Perhaps the most famous of all is Dorothea Lange's *Migrant Mother and Children*. (C) This one photograph has appeared in over 10 000 different books.

The second most popular picture is probably Arthur Rothstein's *Dust Bowl*. (B)

(A) *Two of the 5000 to 8000 letters that Roosevelt received every day at the White House*:

'Dear Mr. President:

This is just to tell you that everything is all right now. The man you sent found our house all right, and we went down to the bank with him and the mortgage can go on for a while longer. You remember I wrote you about losing the furniture too. Well, your man got it back for us. I never heard of a President like you.'

'Dear Honored Mr. Roosevelt:

I never saw a President I would write to until you've got in your place, but I have always felt like you and your wife and your children were as common as we were.'

(Quoted in *The Fabulous Century, vol IV, 1930—40*)

(B) 'Dust Bowl'
A farmer and his sons run for cover in a dust storm, Oklahoma, 1936

(C) 'Migrant Mother and Children'
A mother and children who have moved to California in search of a better life, 1936

(D) *The New Jersey Color Cases Company circulated this handout*:

Confidential Report of Conditions of the Nation Under the New Deal	
Population of the United States	124 000 000
Eligible for Old Age Pensions	30 000 000
That leaves to do the work	94 000 000
Persons working for the government	20 000 000
That leaves to do the work	74 000 000
Ineligible to work under the Child Labor Law	60 000 000
That leaves to do the work	14 000 000
Number unemployed in the nation	13 999 998
That leaves to do the work	2

ME AND THE PRESIDENT
HE HAS GONE FISHING
AND I AM GETTING DAMN TIRED

(Quoted in G. WOLFSKILL AND J.A. HUDSON, *Franklin D. Roosevelt and his Critics, 1933—39*, 1969)

Questions

1 Compare (**A**) and (**D**). Which (a) supports the New Deal (b) opposes the New Deal (c) uses humour to make its point?
2 What message is (**D**) trying to get across?
3 Describe how have (a) Dorothea Lange and (b) Arthur Rothstein managed to capture the hopelessness and despair of the depression in their photographs. (**B**) and (**C**)
4 Which of the two pictures (**B**) or (**C**) best sums up the depression for you? Say why.
5 Talking point: If you were a photographer for your local paper and were asked to take pictures to illustrate an article on the effects of poverty, where would you go? What sort of pictures would you take?

Opposition to the New Deal

Most Americans supported the New Deal. In the 1936 presidential election, Roosevelt won 46 of the 48 states. Even so, there were millions of Americans who hated Roosevelt.

Conservative opposition

The business and upper classes complained that the New Deal:
- was costing far too much and was driving the country into bankruptcy
- interfered too much in business affairs
- encouraged trade unions
- put too much power into the hands of the central government
- was making people lazy
- was bleeding the rich dry with high taxes.

Radical opposition

Then there were those who thought Roosevelt had not done enough to help the poor. Governor Huey Long of Louisiana attracted a large following with his plan to take from the rich and give to the poor. In California Dr Francis Townsend won over many with his promises of a pension of $200 a month for everyone over 60.

The Supreme Court

Opposition from the Supreme Court nearly wrecked the New Deal. Between 1935 and 1937, the Court judged seven important New Deal laws to be *unconstitutional*. It said that the federal government was going beyond the powers given to it in the constitution. What was Roosevelt to do? The laws had the support of the people but were being blocked by a few old conservative judges. In fact, most of them had been appointed by Republican presidents.

To overcome this problem, Roosevelt asked Congress to increase the number of Supreme Court judges from nine to fifteen. Fortunately, while the debate over this raged, the Court suddenly changed its mind and brought about a number of pro-New Deal decisions.

The New Deal: success or failure?

The New Deal is still hotly debated. On one side there is a group of historians who praise the New Deal. In their writings they concentrate *on what the New Deal did*. On the other side there is a group who often the criticise the New Deal. They concentrate *on what the New Deal left undone*.

Below is a collection of jumbled pieces of evidence on the New Deal. Some provide support for the argument that the New Deal was a great success. Other pieces of evidence support the opposite point of view. Some irrelevant information has been added also, to distract you. Be careful to ignore it.

A The New Deal helped workers organise themselves into trade unions. Between 1935 and 1941 union membership doubled.

B Roosevelt was one of America's most popular presidents.

C The New Deal set up the Welfare State. For the first time the federal government accepted that it was responsible for guaranteeing every American a minimum standard of living. To do this the government provided old-age pensions, unemployment insurance, minimum wages, maximum hours, cheap home and farm loans and public works for the unemployed.

D The New Deal did not abolish poverty. In 1939 one in three Americans was still ill-fed, ill-clad and ill-housed.

E The New Deal never solved the unemployment problem. As late as 1939 there were still 9 million jobless.

F Little was done to share out the country's wealth more fairly. In 1941 the richest 20% were earning 49% of the national income. The poorest 20% were earning only 4%.

G Little was done to change the way negroes were treated. Negroes were segregated (separated) on federal projects. Roosevelt would not even fight for a law to make it a federal crime to lynch a negro.

H The Social Security Act excluded 20% of the work force, including 5 million desperate farm-workers and domestics. Also, there was no provision for state-paid medical care.

I During the hard times of the 1930s many turned to crime.

J There was an enormous change in the role of the federal government. The government decided it was its job to manage the economy and end the depression. It regulated banking and businesses, set up the TVA, and provided public works for the jobless in hard times. The economy did recover, wages rose and unemployment fell.

Activities

1 Write down the letters of the paragraphs which provide support for the proposition that the New Deal was a great success.

2 Do the same for the opposite point of view. Remember to leave out the irrelevant paragraphs.

3 Reorder the letters so that they form two easy to follow, logical arguments. Now write a full essay either in support or against the proposition. Don't forget to provide your own introductory statement, paragraph-linking sentences and a conclusion.

US foreign policy 1920–41

Despite President Wilson's hopes, the American Senate refused to agree to the Peace Treaty of Versailles. America also refused to join the League of Nations. Instead she *isolated* herself from world affairs throughout the 1920s and 1930s.

Isolationism

Under this policy, the USA avoided commitments to other powers wherever possible. When dictators took control in Italy, Germany and Japan and began conquering weaker neighbours, Americans chose to ignore the danger. Between 1935 and 1937 a series of *neutrality* laws were passed to keep America free of foreign wars. No Americans were allowed to trade or give financial aid to any country at war.

Isolation ends

In the late 1930s American public opinion began to change. When the Second World War broke out in September 1939, many Americans realised that if Western Europe fell to Hitler, then the USA might be next. In November 1939, Roosevelt changed the Neutrality Acts to allow the sale of arms and equipment to friends. After the fall of France Congress passed the Lend–Lease Act (1941) which allowed America to lease or give any goods to any country whose survival was vital to America. Under this Britain and the other allies were given billions of dollars-worth of arms and vital supplies.

Pearl Harbour

Meanwhile the Japanese empire was spreading into South-East Asia at an alarming rate. To bring the Japanese to heel, Roosevelt in July 1940 froze all Japanese assets in the United States, and later banned exports of oil and steel to Japan. This caused the Japanese mood to harden and on 7 December 1941, Japanese bombers attacked Pearl Harbour. The next day Congress declared war on Japan; three days later Germany and Italy declared war on America.

(A) *In a radio chat to the American people, on 29 December 1940, Roosevelt explained why it was necessary to help Britain with the Lend–Lease scheme*:

'If Great Britain goes down, the Axis powers will control the continents of Europe, Asia, Africa, Australia and the high seas – and they will be in a position to bring enormous military and naval resources against this hemisphere.... There is far less chance of the United States getting into the war if we do all we can now to support the nations defending themselves against the Axis.... We must be the arsenal of democracy.'

(Quoted in J. RAY, *Roosevelt and Kennedy*, 1970)

(B) *Graphs showing the results of polls carried out in 1940 and 1941 to see how Americans felt about going to war:*

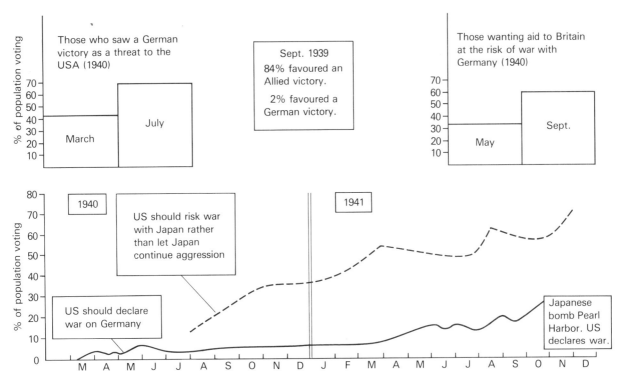

Those who saw a German victory as a threat to the USA (1940)

% of population voting

70
60
50
40
30
20
10

March

July

Sept. 1939
84% favoured an Allied victory.

2% favoured a German victory.

Those wanting aid to Britain at the risk of war with Germany (1940)

70
60
50
40
30
20
10

May

Sept.

80
70
60
50
40
30
20
10
0

% of population voting

1940

1941

US should risk war with Japan rather than let Japan continue aggression

US should declare war on Germany

Japanese bomb Pearl Harbor. US declares war.

M A M J J A S O N D J F M A M J J A S O N D

Questions

1   Here are seven statements about the American attitude to war:
   (i)   The American people saw Japan as a greater danger than Germany.
   (ii)   The fall of France had an important effect on American opinion.
   (iii) The USA would not have entered the war but for Pearl Harbour.
   (iv)   Support for US involvement in the war increased steadily throughout 1941.
   (v)   From the start of the war, US feeling favoured the Allies.
   (vi)   Only a minority of Americans wanted to declare war on Germany.
   (vii) Between March and September 1940, there was a major change in US opinion.
   Which of these statements are:
   (a)   supported by the charts
   (b)   proved incorrect by the charts
   (c)   neither supported nor proved incorrect by the charts? **(B)**
2   Suggest why American ships were so prominently marked with huge flags printed on their sides. **(C)**
3   Why did Congress agree to pass the Lend-Lease Act? **(A)**
4   How did Lend-Lease help the Allies? **(A)** and **(T)**

(C) *An American ship leaving England late 1939*

War and the Fair Deal

America's involvement in the Second World War (1941–5) caused government spending to rise rapidly from 9 billion dollars in 1940 to 100 billion dollars in 1945. Record spending led to:
- higher taxes to pay for the war effort
- a sharp fall in unemployment because the new war industries and armed forces took on millions of men and women
- an increase in the standard of living for most Americans.

In April 1945 Roosevelt died and his vice-President Harry S. Truman took over.

Post-war boom

After the war America enjoyed an economic boom. People spent their money on houses, cars, washing machines and all the other goods which had been unavailable in wartime. The GI Bill of Rights, passed in 1944, prevented unemployment from becoming a major problem. War veterans were given readjustment allowances, loans to start businesses and education grants to retrain.

The Fair Deal

In the field of social welfare Truman called for a package of new reforms known as 'The Fair Deal'. His programme included a national health scheme, federal aid to education, higher minimum wages and a big expansion of social security.

Yet Truman had little success. A Republican-controlled Congress blocked much of his legislation. Congress also passed the Taft-Hartley Act of 1947 which outlawed the *closed shop*. No longer were employers forced to employ only union men. Truman vetoed the bill but Congress overrode his objections.

In 1948 most opinion polls predicted that Truman would be defeated and that the next president would be Thomas E. Dewey, the Republican candidate. But after a hard fought campaign Truman eventually won.

(A) *Government spending, 1929–45*

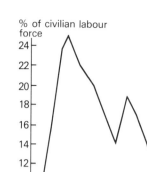

billions $

(B) *Unemployment 1929–45*

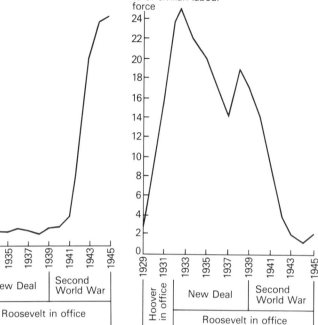

% of civilian labour force

(D) *In early 1949 Truman declared*:

'In a nation as rich as ours it is a shocking fact that tens of millions lack adequate medical care. It is equally shocking that millions of our children are not receiving a good education – millions of them are in over-crowded, obsolete buildings . . .'

(C) *Historian, Eric Goldman, on the 1948 election campaign*:

'Dewey campaigned six weeks; Truman eight. Dewey covered 16 000 miles; Truman 22 000. Dewey made 170 speeches; Truman 271. Up and down the country the President went, clambering out of the confusion of his campaign train to talk to any crowd that gathered at 7 a.m. or 11 p.m. "Give 'em Hell, Harry", somebody would yell. And Harry Truman, the Missouri twang shrill, both hands pumping up and down, would pour it on in the roughest English spoken by a Presidential campaigner since frontier days.'

(Quoted in M. BASSETT, *The American Deal*, 1975)

Questions

1 How many times did government spending increase between 1939 and 1945? (**A**) What caused this increase?
2 What effect did the Second World War have on the level of unemployment? Why? (**B**)
3 Was it (a) the New Deal or (b) the Second World War which most reduced unemployment? Quote figures. (**B**)
4 In your own words describe Truman's 1948 election campaign. (**C**)
5 The *Chicago Daily Tribune* declared Dewey to be the winner before all the results were in. Why do you think they did this? (**T**)
6 What social problems remained unsolved in the USA according to Truman? (**D**)
7 Why did he consider this to be so shocking? (**D**)

McCarthyism

The Cold War

After the war Americans were worried at the spread of communism. Russia was now the number two world power and was rapidly expanding. By 1948 Russia controlled Eastern Europe. In 1949 the Russians exploded their first atomic bomb. That same year the Chinese communists took control of China. Then in 1950 the USA became involved in a war against communism in Korea (see p. 202).

For Americans, who were used to success in foreign affairs, these setbacks seemed unbelievable. For some, the reason had to be that there were traitors working inside America.

In 1947 Truman ordered an investigation into the loyalty of America's 3 000 000 civil servants. Three hundred were sacked and nearly 3000 resigned. Those looking for further proof of treason found it when Alger Hiss, a top government official, was jailed in 1950 after being accused of being a Soviet spy. Two weeks later the British arrested one of their top atomic scientists for leaking secrets to the Russians.

McCarthy

A wave of 'red fear' now swept America. A young Senator named Joseph McCarthy claimed that the State Department was full of communists. It was a giant lie but it turned McCarthy into a national politician. He became the head of a government committee and used his power to smear civil servants. Officials were branded communists without the slightest proof.

Public feeling was so strong that few dared oppose McCarthy. In many parts of America teachers, trade union officials, reformers and other 'suspicious' characters were made to take oaths of loyalty.

McCarthy's campaign lasted until 1954 when he unwisely attacked the army. The hearings were televised. Americans saw that McCarthy was an unfair, rude bully. Public opinion turned against him and McCarthy was finished.

(A) *A cartoon from the early fifties showing a communist taking an oath of loyalty*

YEAH — SO HELP ME GOD!

LOYALTY OATH

(B) *Trends in support of free speech for communists. Results taken from selected public opinion polls:*

'[In peacetime,] do you think members of the communist party in this country should be allowed to speak on the radio?'

	Yes	Yes, qualified	No	Undecided
		(In percent)		
November 1945	48		39	13
March 1946	45		44	11
April 1948	36		57	7
November 1953	19	9	68	4
January 1954	14	8	73	5
January 1956	16	6	76	3
December 1956	20	4	72	4
April 1957	17	5	75	3
November 1963	18	10	67	5

(Quoted in J.E. MUELLER, *War Presidents and Public Opinion*, 1973)

Question

The early 1950s were 'bitter years of fear and distrust'. Which of the sources (**A**)-(**E**) would provide support for the statements:

(a) politicians used the fear of communism to smear their opponents

(b) many Americans had their careers ruined because of the fear of communism

(c) communists could not be trusted to be loyal Americans

(d) many Americans believed American communists should not be allowed the same rights as their fellow citizens

(e) there was a belief that American communists were helping the spread of communism overseas.

(C) *Joseph McCarthy claimed:*

'The communists within our borders have been more responsible for the success of communism abroad than Soviet Russia.'

(D) *Statistics from the McCarthy period:*

- 9500 federal civil servants were dismissed
- 15 000 federal civil servants resigned while under investigation
- 2000 industrial workers were fired
- 3800 seamen were fired
- 600 teachers were dismissed
- 300 were *blacklisted* in films, television and radio
- 500 state and city employees were sacked
- 500 were arrested for *deportation* because of their political beliefs
- Hundreds of scientists and university teachers also lost their jobs

(D. CAUTE, *The Great Fear*, 1978)

(E) *Victimisation:*

One victim of the Red Scare was Senator Tydings of Maryland. His opponent, John Butler, joined a picture of Earl Browder, the communist leader, with a picture of Tydings. The new picture was then printed in an election brochure attacking Tydings. On election day Tydings lost.

Eisenhower and prosperity

In 1952 twenty years of Democratic rule came to an end. Americans felt it was 'time for a change' and elected Republican Dwight D. Eisenhower as President by a huge majority over his Democratic rival, Adlai E. Stevenson. 'Ike' was a war hero and was well liked. In 1956 he again beat Stevenson for a second term.

Some Republicans expected Eisenhower to reverse the New Deal and Fair Deal policies. But Eisenhower made few changes. Like most Americans he believed that social welfare and government management of the economy were essential.

In social welfare, Eisenhower made moderate progress. Social security was given to several new groups of workers; federal spending on public health was doubled.

In 1957 Americans were stunned when the Russians beat them in the race to put a satellite (*sputnik*) in space. American scientific and technical education was blamed so Congress passed the National Defence Education Act in 1958. Over $600 million was provided for low cost loans to university students.

Civil rights

Perhaps the most important reforms were to help the negroes win their civil rights (see pp. 148, 150).

Prosperity

For most Americans, the Truman and Eisenhower years were prosperous times. Between 1945 and 1960 the *Gross National Product* (which is the total of all the nation's goods and services) more than doubled. The average family income also climbed steadily to give the typical American the highest standard of living in the world.

Houses, cars and electrical appliances were built in their millions to keep up with the demand. Televisions began to appear in most American homes. New technology such as computers, electronics and automated assembly lines helped produce the large number of goods needed to satisfy all the demand.

(A) *Eisenhower was the first President to make extensive use of television*

(B) *Luxury goods owned by American households, 1960:*

| | CARS | | TELEVISION | | | | | | |
	One or more	Two or more	Black and white	Color	Washing machine	Clothes dryer	Refrig- erator or freezer	Dish- washer	Air condi- tioner
1960 All house- holds	75.0	16.4	86.7		74.5	17.4	86.1	4.9	12.8

(US Dept. of Commerce, *Statistical Abstract of the United States*, 1971, table 511)

(C) Time *magazine's coverage of the 1952 Presidential campaign*

'Time magazine selected twenty-one photographs of Dwight D. Eisenhower during thirteen weeks of the 1952 presidential campaign; all showed the candidate in a favourable light. During the same period, thirteen photographs of his opponent, Adlai Stevenson were selected for publication. About half of these showed him in an unfavourable manner – eating, drinking or grimacing.'

(R. CIRINO, *Power to Persuade. Mass Media and the News*, 1974)

(D) *Who was the best President?*

In 1956 an opinion poll asked Americans to rank their Presidents from best to worst. In 1962 a similar poll was conducted among historians. Here are some of the results.

Presidents	Public 1956	Historians 1962
Lincoln	2	1
Washington	3	2
F.D. Roosevelt	1	3
Truman	5	9
Hoover	9	19
Eisenhower	4	22

(Figured from J.E. MUELLER, *War Presidents and Public Opinion*, 1973)

Questions

1 Which presidential candidate do you think *Time* magazine supported in the 1952 election? Why? (**C**)
2 List all the ways in which you think a newspaper could influence a reader's choice of whom to vote for.
3 What sort of person does Eisenhower appear to come across as? (**A**)
4 How important is television to a modern politician?
5 How did Hoover rank as a President with the American public in 1956? How did he rank with the historians? (**D**) What reasons can you suggest for the large difference between their views?
6 What percentage of American households owned (a) a car (b) a television (c) a washing machine in 1960? (**B**)
7 What do the figures in (**B**) tell us about the standard of living for most Americans?
8 Local study: Make up your own class survey on who was the best ever prime minister. You may like to compare your parents' views with your teacher's.
9 Talking point: Should newspapers and news magazines be required by law to give each candidate or party equal space in their election coverage? Is it right for newspapers and magazines to come out in support of one particular candidate or party?

The negro problem I

From the 1600s onwards negroes were brought to America to work as slaves on the southern plantations. Slavery lasted in the South until 1863 when they were freed.

In practice however negroes remained second-class citizens. In the 1890s the all-white southern state governments passed a series of Jim Crow laws *segregating* (i.e. separating) negroes from whites in schools, hotels, parks and on public transport. In 1896 the Supreme Court made racial segregation legal with its decision in *Plessy* v. *Ferguson*. It said separate facilities were legal as long as they were equal.

Economically the blacks always got the worse jobs and were the first to be laid off in bad times.

The Second World War

The turning point for negroes was the Second World War. Labour was in short supply and many found skilled jobs in the war industries. Over a million blacks also served in the forces in segregated black units. Large numbers returned home determined to improve their lot.

After the war President Truman tried to tackle the negro problem at a national level. In 1948 he ended segregation in the armed services and government. But his other reforms to end racial discrimination were rejected by Congress.

Brown v. Topeka

A giant step forward was taken by the Supreme Court in 1954 with its decision in *Brown* v. *Topeka Board of Education*. The court held that public school segregation of negroes from whites was unconstitutional. Congress also passed Civil Rights Acts in 1957 and 1960 in an effort to try to protect the negroes' right to vote.

But enforcing the law proved difficult. Often there was strong resistance from the southerners. In 1957 for example the governor of Arkansas used state troops to stop negroes from entering high school at Little Rock. In response President Eisenhower sent in federal troops to escort the negro children past a howling mob into school.

(A) *Voting in the Southern States*

'There are numerous instances of Negroes who attempted to register or vote being driven away, beaten up, or killed. More generally the opposition took the form of intimidation. For example, a Negro went to the registration booth in his county and asked if he could register. The white official replied: "Oh, yes, you can register, but I want to tell you something. Some God-damn niggers are going to get killed about this voting business yet." In Dennison, Texas, in the fall of 1932, handbills were scattered throughout the town reading as follows:

NIGGER!

The white people do not want you to vote Saturday.
Do not make the Ku Klux Klan take a hand.
Do you remember what happened two years ago, May 9?
George Hughes was burned to death, the county courthouse destroyed
. . . . For good reason.

Riots on election day in which both whites and Negroes were killed occurred in various sections of the South.'

(M.R. DAVIE, *Negroes in American Society*)

(B) *Negro students being escorted into Little Rock Central High School by federal troops*

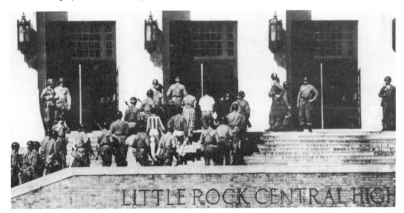

(C) *Merry-Go-Round*

Colored child at carnival:
Where is the Jim Crow section
On this merry-go-round,
Mister, 'Cause I want to ride?
Down South where I come from
White and colored
Can't sit side by side.
Down South on the train
There's a Jim Crow car.
On the bus we're put in the
   back –
But there ain't no back
To a merry-go-round!
Where's the horse
For a kid that's black?

(*Selected Poems of Langston Hughes*, 1959)

(D) *Little Rock*

'Few incidents in recent American history can match the courage shown by the nine teen-age Negroes of Little Rock. They risked their lives for the sake of establishing a principle: the right to attend an integrated high school. They did it in the face of ugly and determined opposition . . . .

This was the most severe test of the law. The Federal courts paved the way; Federal troops held the angry mob at bay. But the nine Negro pupils . . . went ahead, despite jeers and bitter invectives.'

(*Chicago Daily Defender*, 28 May 1958)

Questions
1 List the various ways negroes were prevented from voting in the South. (**A**)
2 Why do you think it was so important for the southern whites to stop the negroes from voting? (**A**)
3 What were the Jim Crow laws? (**T**)
4 How does the poet use a young child at a carnival to show the Jim Crow laws as ridiculous? (**C**)
5 Is the extract (**D**) sympathetic, neutral or hostile towards negroes? Give reasons.
6 How would you have felt if you had been one of the negro students being escorted into Little Rock High School? (**D**) and (**B**)
7 Talking point: There is no negro problem in the USA; there is only a white problem. Do you agree?

The negro problem II

After the war negroes began to grow impatient and started
to take more action themselves. By the 1960s their protest
action had become more militant. Groups of blacks organised 'sit-ins' in segregated lunch counters, 'wade-ins' at
beaches and 'kneel-ins' at churches. Other negroes went on
'freedom-rides' to put an end to segregation on interstate
transportation. In 1963 'freedom marchers' were organised
all over the country and the Rev. Martin Luther King organised a 200 000-strong march on Washington.

New Civil Rights Acts

In 1964 Congress passed a Civil Rights Act which outlawed segregation in public places. The next year it passed
the Voting Rights Act. This law gave the federal government enormous powers to overcome all the restrictions
southerners were using to stop negroes from voting.

But for some, change was coming far too slowly. In 1965
negroes rioted in the Watts district of Los Angeles. During
the summers of 1966 and 1967 there were similar riots in
cities all across America. It was clear that many negroes
were fed up with ghetto life. Then in 1968 King was
assassinated by a white man, James Earl Ray. Racial
rioting erupted in 125 cities. Congress was moved to pass
the Civil Rights Act of 1968. Most discrimination in
housing was made illegal.

Black Power

Despite the slow improvements, young negro leaders in the
mid-sixties began to preach the doctrine of *Black Power*.
They urged blacks to be proud of their colour and called on
them to run their own businesses and communities. Some,
like Stokely Carmichael, believed blacks would have to use
violence to gain their rights. The most feared group – the
Black Panthers – clashed with the police in several shoot-
outs.

But violence proved futile and, by the mid 1970s, even
the most militant blacks had returned to political action.

(A) *Negroes in public schools with whites in 11 southern states – estimated number, 1956–62*

(B) *Percentage of the same, December 1961*

State	(A) Estimated number Academic Year 1956–57	1961–2	(B) Percentage Dec. 1961
Mississippi	0	0	0
Alabama	0	0	0
South Carolina	0	0	0
Georgia	0	9	0.003
Louisiana	0	12	0.004
Florida	0	552	0.258
Virginia	0	533	0.246
North Carolina	0	203	0.061
Tennessee	6	1142	0.734
Arkansas	34	152	0.142
Texas	3400	4300	1.420
	3440	6903	

(D) *In 1964 Martin Luther King won the Nobel Peace Prize for his non-violent campaigns for negro civil rights. This is how one black power leader, Malcolm X, reacted to it:*

'He got the peace prize, we got the problem. I don't want the white man giving me medals. If I'm following a general, and he's leading me into battle, and the enemy tends to give him rewards, or awards, I get suspicious of him. Especially if he gets a peace award before the war is over.'

(Quoted in PETER GOLDMAN, *The Death and Life of Malcolm X*)

(C) *How White Views of the Negro Have Changed 1963–70:*

WHITES WOULD MIND	ALL WHITES 1963	1966	1970	SOUTHERN WHITES 1963	1966
Sitting next to Negro in restaurant	20%	16%	11%	50%	42%
Sitting next to Negro in movie	24	20	—	54	46
Using same rest room as Negro	24	21	—	56	56
Trying on same clothing Negro had tried on	36	28	—	57	54
Sitting next to Negro on bus	20	16	—	47	44
If teen-age child dated a Negro	90	88	83	97	94
If Negro family moved next door	51	46	41	74	69
If a close friend or relative married a Negro	84	79	72	91	92

(Quoted in L. CUBAN AND P. RODEN, *Promise of America, An Unfinished Story*, 1971)

Questions
1 Explain what is shown in resources (**A**) and (**B**), and use figures to support your answer.
2 Why was Malcolm X opposed to King taking the Nobel Peace Prize? (**D**)
3 Do you agree with Malcolm X's reasoning? Give your reasons.
4 Talking point: Many blacks are still poor, badly educated and housed in ghettos. If you were President, what would you do to solve these problems?

The Kennedy years

Poverty in the midst of plenty

Americans entered the 1960s richer than ever before. But although most Americans were wealthier, many lived in poverty. In his book called *The Other America* (1962), Michael Harrington shocked Americans by claiming that there were 50 million poor in America.

Kennedy and the New Frontier

In the election of 1960, John F. Kennedy defeated the Republican candidate, Richard Nixon, in a very close contest. Kennedy was keen to build on the New and Fair Deals. His programme known as the *New Frontier* aimed to help the poor, old and the various racial minorities.

Kennedy's ambitious plans included:
- a national health scheme for those over 65
- a big boost in federal spending on education
- a civil rights bill to end segregation in public places such as restaurants
- a big tax cut to boost spending and so cut unemployment.

But all these measures were rejected by Congress. As a result the New Frontier achieved even less than the Fair Deal.

Then on 22 November 1963, after only 1000 days in office, Kennedy was shot. The youngest man ever to become President – and the first Catholic – was dead.

The assassination of President Kennedy: A continuing mystery

On 22 November 1963, President Kennedy visited Dallas, Texas. Mrs Kennedy, the governor of Texas and his wife joined the President in an open-car tour of the city. As the car was passing the Texas School Book Depository Building in Elm Street, shots rung out. Both the President and the governor were hit. Thirty minutes later, President Kennedy was dead.

A special investigation, called the Warren Commission, was set up to look into the assassination.

(A) *A summary of the key findings of the Warren Commission*:
'The shots which killed President Kennedy and wounded Governor Connally were fired from the sixth floor window . . . of the Texas School Book Depository.
. . . There is no [believable] evidence that the shots were fired from the Triple Underpass, ahead of the motorcade, or from any other location.
The weight of the evidence indicates there were three shots fired.
. . . all the shots which hit the President and Governor Connally were fired by Lee Harvey Oswald.
The Commission found no evidence that anyone assisted Oswald in planning or carrying out the assassination.'
(The Warren Commission, 1964)

Not everyone was satisfied with the Warren Commission's findings. In 1976 a House Select Committee on Assassinations was set up by the US Congress to conduct another official investigation into the death of President Kennedy.

(B) *A summary of some of the key findings of the Select Committee*:
'Lee Harvey Oswald fired three shots at President . . . Kennedy. The second and third shots he fired struck the President. The third shot he fired killed the President. The shots that struck President Kennedy from behind were fired from the sixth floor window . . . of the Texas School Book Depository Building.'
Scientific acoustical [sound recording] evidence establishes a high probability that two gunmen fired at President Kennedy. A newly-found tape recording of a motor-cycle policeman's radio transmission has shown that four, not three, shots were fired. Very sophisticated electronic analysis of the tape also suggests one of the shots was fired from a small grassy hill in front of the motorcade.
'The Committee believes . . . that President Kennedy was probably assassinated as a result of a conspiracy [a secret plan involving others]. The Committee is unable to identify the other gunmen or the extent of the conspiracy.'
(Report of the Select Committee on Assassinations, 1979)

(C) *Dallas, Texas, 22 November 1963*

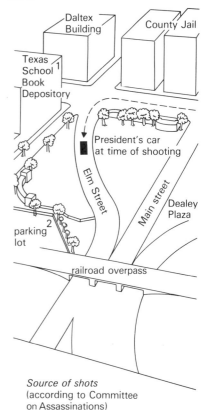

Source of shots
(according to Committee on Assassinations)

1 three shots from sixth floor to rear of President, possibly some from another source to rear

2 one shot from fence to front right of President

Questions

1 Compare the Warren Commission's findings with those of the Committee on Assassinations on the following points:
  (a) Who assassinated Kennedy?
  (b) Where were the fatal shots fired from?
  (c) How many shots, in all, were fired?
  (d) How many gunmen were there?
  (e) What evidence of a conspiracy was there? **(A) (B)** and **(C)**

2 What important questions did the second investigation leave unanswered?

3 Who do you think might have had a motive to kill President Kennedy?

Johnson and the great society 1963–8

When Kennedy died, vice-President Johnson was sworn in as the new President.

The Great Society

In the presidential elections in 1964, Johnson easily beat the Republican, Barry Goldwater. During his campaign Johnson promised to end poverty and racial prejudice and create what he called the Great Society. To achieve this, Johnson introduced a flood of social reforms.

First, there was a big increase in federal aid to education. Much of this went to schools in poor neighbourhoods.

Secondly, Congress passed a Medicare bill which provided medical and hospital care for the elderly through Social Security. It was the first time ever that the federal government had entered the field of national health insurance.

Lastly, Johnson persuaded the Congress to pass the Civil Rights Act of 1964. This act protected the negroes' right to vote.

For a time it looked as though Johnson might rival Roosevelt as a reform leader. But after 1965 Johnson became more and more occupied with the Vietnam War. And as defence spending rose, spending on the poor fell.

Protest movements

Johnson's rule was marred by a wave of social unrest and conflict. All over the country, blacks protested against social injustice. Students also began to demand a greater say – they staged sit-ins, boycotts and demonstrations to back up their claims. At the same time, more and more Americans began to argue that America had no business to be fighting in Vietnam (see p. 216). This led to more marches and demonstrations, some of which ended in violence. Among the victims was Martin Luther King, who was assassinated in April 1968.

The social unrest was so widespread that Johnson's popularity dropped sharply. In 1968 he declared he would not stand again.

(A) *Family personal income received by each fifth of families in 1962. Each bar of the graph shows the income of one-fifth of the population of the USA, from the richest at the top to the poorest at the bottom.*

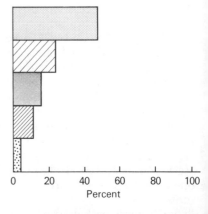

Percent

(B) *A child in a Harlem ghetto*

(C) *MARTIN LUTHER KING RE-JECTED VIOLENCE*

NEW YORK, April 5.

'Dr Martin Luther King, who was shot and killed in Memphis yesterday, won the 1964 Nobel Peace Prize for his non-violent campaigns for Negro civil rights in the United States.

A Baptist minister and son of a Negro pastor, he was the youngest man to win the prize.

Dr King, who graduated doctor of philosophy at Boston University after earlier studies in Atlanta and Pennsylvania, turned his back on a secure career to return to the Southern States and campaign for Negro rights.

The founder of the Southern Christian Leadership Conference, he was the leading advocate of non-violent action and passive resistance.

Dr King won his first major battle in the war on segregation in Montgomery, Alabama, the cradle of the confederacy He organised and led the Montgomery bus boycott, a campaign which led to integrated seating on city buses in the Alabama capital.

It was a victory that many Southerners found difficult to believe and it launched Dr King on a campaign that made him the best-known civil rights leader in the world. . . .

Dr King himself was in gaol more than a dozen times.

When he was in a Georgia gaol in 1960, his wife, pregnant with their fourth child, received a call from the late John Kennedy, then the Democratic nominee for President.

Mrs King told reporters that Mr Kennedy had told her he was "very much concerned for both of us. He wanted me to know he was thinking about us and he would do all he could to help."

Dr King was released from gaol the next day and Mr Kennedy won thousands of Negro votes that helped make him the forty-third President of the United States. . . .

Although his Montgomery home was bombed in January, 1956, Dr King implored the 50 000 Negroes who had united in the bus boycott to use passive resistance. "We believe in law and order," he told them . . . .

Opponent of War

His strong beliefs in civil rights and in non-violence made him one of the leading opponents of American participation in the war in Vietnam, the "New York Times" News Service said. . . .

Dr King's belief in non-violence was subjected to intense pressure in 1966, when some Negro groups adopted the slogan "black power" in the aftermath of civil rights marches into Mississippi and race riots in Northern cities.

At the root of his civil rights convictions was profound faith in the basic goodness of man and the great potential of American democracy.

Scores of millions of Americans – white as well as Negro – who sat before television sets in the summer of 1963 to watch the march of some 200 000 Negroes on Washington were deeply stirred when Dr King, in the shadow of the Lincoln Memorial, said: "Even though we face the difficulties of today and tomorrow, I still have a dream. I have a dream that one day this nation will rise up and live out the true meaning of its creed: "We hold these truths to be self-evident, that all men are created equal".'

(*Christchurch Press*, April 1968)

Questions

1 What percentage of family income did a) the richest fifth and b) the poorest fifth of American families receive? What does this tell us about the distribution of wealth in America? (**A**)

2 How did President Johnson's Great Society programme try to overcome some of the inequalities? (**T**)

3 Many of the poor, especially blacks, live in ghettos (city slums) like (**B**). What social problems would you expect to find in the ghettos? Why?

4 Martin Luther King was one of many Americans who died violently in the 1960s. Write a brief outline of Dr King's life using the headings a) early life   b) ideas and beliefs   c) achievements   d) death. (**C**)

5 King's hopes were summed up in a speech he gave to 200 000 negroes on the Washington march in 1963. What was his dream? (**C**)

6 Do you think this dream will ever come true?

7 Talking point: Does King deserve to be remembered as a great man?

155

Nixon and Watergate

In the 1968 elections, Republican Richard Nixon won a narrow victory over the Democrat Hubert Humphrey.

Nixon inherited Johnson's problems of student and anti-war unrest. The violence peaked in 1969 and 1970 when 4330 bombs were planted, resulting in 40 deaths. But after that the whole protest movement began to quieten down. Vietnam also became less of an issue as Nixon began to make progress towards a ceasefire.

In 1972 Nixon was re-elected after a massive victory over his Democratic opponent George McGovern. His second term was clouded by the bribery, corruption and other illegal activities that were uncovered in the government. In 1973 vice-President Spiro Agnew resigned following charges of bribery and corruption. But this was small fare compared to the Watergate scandal.

The Watergate scandal

This began when seven men were caught breaking into the Democratic Party headquarters in the Watergate Apartment complex during the 1972 presidential campaign. Among those arrested were members of Nixon's re-election committee. In the investigation that followed, it was revealed that Nixon's election committee and other White House staff were involved in illegal activities to discredit the President's enemies and to secure his election.

Nixon denied all knowledge of this but a number of Congressmen refused to believe him. They also believed Nixon was trying to sabotage the Watergate investigations.

The resignation of Nixon

In July 1974 the House of Representatives Judiciary Committee recommended that Nixon be charged with:
  (i) obstructing justice in the Watergate case
 (ii) misusing his office to stage a cover-up
(iii) refusing to produce documents for the Committee.

At first Nixon denied the charges but more evidence was then produced against him. So on 9 August, 1974, he resigned – the first American President to do so.

Nixon: Peacemaker or Crook?

President Nixon will always be remembered as the first American President to be forced to resign as a result of a scandal. But does he deserve to be remembered in this way? Below are a variety of facts and opinions on Nixon's presidency. Consider them carefully. Then answer the questions that follow.

(A) *Foreign Affairs*
- Nixon's chief aim when he came to office was to settle the Vietnam war (see p. 216). American troops were gradually withdrawn from Vietnam and a cease-fire was finally achieved in 1973.
- Critics have claimed Nixon could have ended the war much earlier and saved thousands of lives and billions of dollars. At the same time as he was talking about 'peace with honour', he was secretly ordering the invasion of Cambodia and stepping up the bombing of North Vietnam.
- Under Nixon, America's relations with Communist China improved dramatically. For the first time since 1950, the two nations began to trade with each other. In 1972 Nixon became the first President to visit China while in office. This paved the way for even closer ties between two old enemies.
- Nixon signed an agreement with the Russians, in 1972, to limit the output of nuclear weapons.
- In the Middle East, Nixon's efforts helped bring about a ceasefire to the 1973 Arab–Israeli war.

Domestic Affairs
- Nixon established a revenue–sharing plan in which the federal government gave billions of dollars to state and local governments.
- Inflation spiralled upwards as prices rose at the fastest rate since 1947.
- On 20 July, 1969, Neil Armstrong and Edwin Aldrin became the first men to land on the moon.
- Nixon held back social welfare payments to help the poor. Meanwhile spending on new weapons was increased.
- Above all Nixon gave the office of president a bad name by:
  (1) trying to use the FBI and CIA to spy on his opponents and investigate reporters
  (2) organising smear campaigns to blacken the names of his political opponents
  (3) trying to persuade the tax department to go easy on his friends and to be tough on his enemies
  (4) trying to cover up and delay the investigation of the Watergate burglary
  (5) lying to the American people about Watergate.

(B) *How does Nixon want to be remembered?*

In his first inaugural address Nixon said, 'The greatest honour history can [give] is the title of peacemaker'. In a television interview following his resignation Nixon said, 'I have done some stupid things, particularly in the handling of what was the pip-squeak Watergate thing; but I did the big things rather well'.

Activity

After considering the evidence, how do you think Richard Nixon should best be remembered:
(a) As a crooked politician
(b) As a peacemaker
(c) Neither. In my opinion he was . . . (complete in your own words).
In all cases give reasons to support your choice.

(C) *Historian Henry Steele Commager's judgement*
'Other things being equal, we haven't had a bad President before now. Nixon was the first dangerous and wicked President'.

Ford, Carter and Reagan

Ford

On 9 August 1974, vice-President Ford became President. A month later he pardoned Nixon for all his wrongs. Critics complained that Nixon had got off free, whereas those who had worked for him were jailed for their crimes.

In the remaining two years before the election Ford managed to restore some respect to the presidential office. His simple, honest, commonsense approach won him many friends. But as a President he was ineffective. Unemployment and inflation remained high, and in the 1976 elections Ford was easily defeated by Democrat Jimmy Carter.

Carter

Like Ford, Carter found difficulty in turning his ideas into workable laws. His price, tax and energy reforms were heavily altered by Congress. Rising prices, high unemployment and a temporary shortage of petrol saw Carter's popularity slump even further.

Carter's only success was in foreign affairs. He managed, for example, to get Israel and Egypt to sign a peace treaty. But even this was clouded by the fact that the Iranians were still holding 52 Americans as hostages in Teheran.

Reagan

The Republicans put up an ex-actor and former Californian governor as their candidate. Reagan called for less government and cuts in taxes, and promised to make America great again.

Opponents claimed Reagan's spending cuts would hit the poor and the weak. But it was time for a change and Reagan was elected by a massive majority. On the very day Reagan took his oath of office, the American hostages in Iran were released. No American President could have hoped for a better start.

(A) *Cost of living–consumer price index for all urban consumers (base: 1967 = 100)*

1967	100
1975	161
1976	171
1977	182
1978	195
1979	230

(US Bureau of the Census, *Annual Statistical Abstract of the United States*)

(B) *A sign in Washington, in 1977, reminding people how petrol gauges will look if a start is not made in conserving energy*

(C) *The 1980 presidential election: a look at the voting figures*

	% Popular Vote
Mr Reagan	51
President Carter	41
Other candidates	8

Who voted?
160 491 000 Americans were able to vote – of these:

52.3%	voted
47.7%	did not bother to vote

(D) *Part of a letter to the editor, complaining at President Reagan's 1981 cuts in Social Security:*
'Dear Sir,

My wife and myself are getting by on a combined income of little more than $130 per week. Some people are even on a less income than that. One big worry of ours is medical payments. Out of our Social Security we all pay toward Medicare. To help support that we have to pay many more dollars for other insurance, out of the allowance we receive, which cuts our income down considerably. To date we have to pay the first $60 for doctor's office calls, which I understand is being raised to $75 in January.

On top of this we have to buy the medicine prescribed by the doctor. Just recently my wife had to have a prescription which cost $35, which is a medication which has to be renewed every few weeks. A week or two ago I had to have a prescription which cost $29 to be refilled in three weeks' time. Several people we know are ill enough to go to the doctor, but say "what is the use? We cannot afford to buy the medicine anyway"....

It grieves me to hear Mr Stockman and the president say that they will have to make further cuts into various social programs....

Recently, as was very much in the news, Mrs Reagan was not happy because the china in the White House did not all match.

I wonder, does she realize that many people do not possess even odd dishes and if they did they do not have sufficient food to put on them?...

The president has said many times that his family were poor when he was being raised. I wonder just how poor, as he does not seem to have too much feeling now for the poor people....

My wife and myself both voted for Mr Reagan as we thought he would be good for the country generally. Not realizing that now, he and Mr Stockman are making the rich richer and the poor poorer....'

(Quoted in GUARDIAN WEEKLY, 3.1.82)

Questions
1. Ask your teacher to explain what a price index is and how one is compiled. (**A**)
2. Draw a line graph to show the price increases between 1975 and 1979. (**A**)
3. What problems do rapidly rising prices create for politicians?
4. What problem is the sign telling Americans to think about before it is too late? (**B**)
5. What will happen if people choose to ignore the warning? (**B**)
6. If you were a supporter of Mr Reagan, what figures could you quote to prove that he had won a massive election victory and clearly had the support of most Americans? (**C**)
7. What figures could you cite to show Mr Reagan's support might not be as great as the election results would at first seem to indicate? (**C**)
8. Why is the writer in (**D**) angry at President Reagan's cuts in social welfare?
9. Why does the writer think that President Reagan does not understand what it is to be poor? (**D**)

China to 1900

Government

Because of its vast size and huge population China had always been a difficult country to rule. For two thousand years she was ruled by a series of *dynasties* or ruling families. The head of the dynasty was called an emperor. Like the Tsar of Russia, the Emperor of China was an *autocrat*. That is, he could make what laws he liked and there was no parliament to represent the people.

Society

At the top of Chinese society was a small select group of highly educated officials, large landowners and rich merchants. At the bottom were the poor – the peasants who made up 80 percent of the population. Most of them lived in villages, owned a little land and kept a pig and a few chickens. For the peasants, life was a constant struggle.

By the nineteenth century, it was becoming clear that the power of the ruling Manchu dynasty was breaking down. It became more difficult to keep order and peasant revolts became more frequent. The local officials, who were responsible for collecting taxes and keeping law and order, began to neglect their duties. They took bribes and often pocketed part of the tax collection.

Foreign influence

From the 1840s onward the European powers took advantage of the government's weakness and started carving China up among themselves. China was forced to open special *Treaty Ports*, within which foreigners controlled the customs and the trade. Soon the Europeans also controlled most of China's key industries.

Defeat by Japan

China's humiliation at the hands of foreigners reached a climax in 1895 when she was defeated in war by Japan. China could no longer even claim to be the strongest power in Asia. Furthermore, China's defeat was the signal for a scramble among the Western powers to take further valuable privileges from China.

(A) *Population distribution in China*

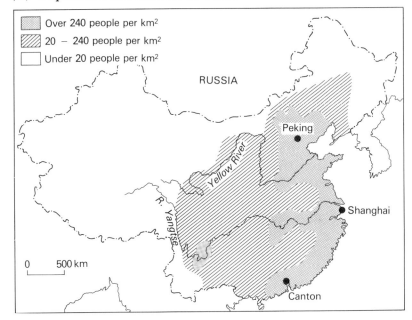

- Over 240 people per km²
- 20 – 240 people per km²
- Under 20 people per km²

RUSSIA

Peking

Yellow River

R. Yangtse

Shanghai

Canton

0   500 km

(C) *'China in Distress'*

(From *La Silhouette*, Paris)

(B) *Cheng Kuan-ying, a Chinese businessman, writing around 1892, described how the Westerners do as they please in China:*

'When a foreign ship collides with and destroys a Chinese boat, the latter . . . is blamed for being slow in avoiding the collision. . . . When a foreign stage-coach hurts a Chinese, the latter . . . is charged with not knowing how to [give] way. . . . Chinese employed by foreign companies or as sailors . . . frequently have their wages cut on some [excuse] or are beaten to death. . . . When a Chinese merchant owes money to a foreign merchant, as soon as he is accused, his property is confiscated. . . .

[Foreign] stage-coaches rush along our thoroughfares, they carry weapons in time of peace, they reduce the wages of their employees, . . . [They] control the customs . . . kidnap and sell our people . . . all the various kinds of wrongdoing that should be forbidden by Western law. . . .'

(Quoted in N. CAMERON, *From Bondage to Liberation, East Asia 1860–1952*)

(D) *A favourite song of revolutionary students in the late 1890s*

'We are only afraid of being like India, unable to defend our land;
We Chinese have no part in this China of ours.
This dynasty exists only in name!
Being slaves of the foreigners,
They force us common people to call them masters!'

(Quoted in L. BIANCO, *Origins of the Chinese Revolution*)

Questions

1 In what parts of China do most Chinese live? (**A**) Why? You may need to consult an atlas.
2 Who are the people sitting down in the cartoon? (**C**)
3 What are they doing?
4 What does the Chinese person think of it?
5 Why did the Chinese seem to hate foreigners? (**B**), (**D**) and (**T**)
6 Talking point: To the ancient Chinese, China was the centre of the world – the Middle Kingdom. The Chinese saw themselves as superior to everyone else. Foreigners were uncivilised barbarians. What encouraged the Chinese to think like this?

The end of the Manchus

The Boxer Rebellion

In 1900 one of China's many secret societies, the Boxers, organised a rising to get rid of the foreigners. The Boxers killed two hundred foreign missionaries and thirty thousand Chinese Christians, and attacked the foreign embassies in Peking. The Western powers reacted swiftly and sent in an international police force to crush the Boxers.

Reforms

This setback led to further criticism of the Manchus. For years, educated Chinese had argued that the cause of China's weakness was her outdated government.

Now under pressure, the Empress decided to introduce various reforms. The education system, the civil service and the army were all improved. There were even plans to set up a parliament. But the days for reform had passed. An entirely new system of government seemed the only answer to China's problems.

Sun Yat-sen

In 1894 a Western-educated doctor named Sun Yat-sen founded the Revive China Society. His aim was to overthrow the Manchus and set up a *republic* with a democratic form of government. During the next few years Sun went abroad and organised a series of unsuccessful attempts to overthrow the Manchus.

In 1908 the powerful Empress Dowager died. Then came three years of poor harvests, floods, droughts and rising taxes. Suddenly on 10 October 1911 (the Double Tenth) revolutionaries seized control of the military headquarters at Wuchang. Within a month, fifteen of China's eighteen provinces had rebelled in support of the revolutionaries. On 29 December 1911, representatives from these provinces proclaimed a republic. Sun Yat-sen returned home from abroad and was elected President.

(A) *A Boxer print. Christians are shown as pigs; the goats represent Westerners*

(B) *The Empress Dowager speaks about herself. Remarks she made one day to Princess Der Ling;*

'Do you know, I have often thought that I am the most clever woman that ever lived, and others cannot compare with me....

'Now look at me. I have 400 000 000 people, all dependent on my judgment. Although I have the Grand Council to consult with, they only look after the different appointments, but anything of an important nature I must decide myself. What does the Emperor know? I have been very successful so far, but I never dreamt that the Boxer movement would end with such serious results for China. That is the only mistake I have made in my life. I should have issued an Edict [order] at once to stop the Boxers practising their belief, but both Prince Tuan and Duke Lan told me that they firmly believed the Boxers were sent by Heaven to enable China to get rid of all the undesirable and hated foreigners'.

(Quoted in K. PELISSIER, *The Awakening of China, 1793–1949*)

(C) *This woodcut, 'The Starving People Seize the Grain', shows hungry peasants attacking a landlord – one of a wave of peasant riots between 1909 and 1911*

Questions

1. Suggest why the Boxer print should attack Chinese Christians as well as Westerners. **(A)**
2. What did the Empress think of her brains, power and success? How do you think this would have affected her ability to rule wisely? **(B)**
3. Sun Yat-sen wanted to overthrow the Manchu government. What is shown in this woodcut that would have helped him? Explain. **(C)**
4. What do you think were the three most important causes of the 1911 revolution? Give reasons for your choices.

Yuan Shi-kai and the warlords

When Sun returned to China, he found that the northern provinces near Peking had stayed loyal to the Manchus. In a final effort to save the dynasty, the Manchus had handed power over to a powerful local general named Yuan Shi-kai.

In order to avoid war, Sun offered to give up the presidency to Yuan if Yuan would force the Emperor to give up the throne. Yuan accepted. On 12 February 1912 the Emperor *abdicated*. Three days later Yuan became President of the Republic of China.

The Kuomintang

China's new government was supposed to be a democracy with an elected parliament.

It was expected that Sun's old revolutionary group, now named the Kuomintang or Nationalist party, would have most of the say. But Yuan ignored parliament and terrorised the Kuomintang. In desperation Sun's supporters staged a 'second revolution' to overthrow Yuan. It failed and Yuan now ruled as a dictator.

The Twenty-One Demands

In 1915 Japan presented China with a list of Twenty-One Demands. These proposed to give Japan control of much of China's industry. China also had to accept Japanese advisers to help run her affairs. The Chinese were shocked. These terms would turn China into a Japanese *satellite*, unable to act as a free country. Yuan was able to get some of the demands dropped but had to accept others. Once more China had been humiliated by the foreigners. Yuan was blamed for giving way. Public reaction was so violent that Yuan was forced to give up his plan to become emperor. In mid-1916 he died, 'a broken-hearted man'.

Yuan's death was followed by chaos. Real power fell into the hands of the various generals or warlords who ran the provinces and were always fighting each other. Robberies, killings and lootings became everyday events. The years from about 1917 to about 1928 are known as the warlord era.

(A) *After a town had been captured, soldiers went on a rampage of looting. One reporter saw them:*
'staggering along under their loads of watches, dollars, and other small but valuable loot they had taken. In every case they had their guns in position ready for use.... They would step up to a man on the street, point their guns at him and demand his money. If he refused they threatened to fire.... A number of soldiers went into the city temple, drew their guns on the shopkeepers, peddlers, customers, tea-drinkers, etc., and ordered that their dollars and banknotes be put into handkerchiefs and towels spread on a table.'

(Quoted in O. SCHELL AND J. ESHERICK, *Modern China*)

(B) *Refugees fleeing from a battle between two warlords*

(C) *Yuan Shi-kai, first President of the Chinese Republic*

(D) *A peasant recalls the visit of the northern warlord, Hu Tsung-nan to his village in the 1920s:*
'When Hu Tsung-nan came, almost everyone left Liu Ling. We went up into the hills. I was in the people's militia [citizens' army] then. We had buried all our possessions and all our corn. Hu Tsung-nan destroyed everything, and his troops ate and ate. They discovered our grain stores, and they stole our cattle.'

(J. MYRDAL, *Report from a Chinese Village*, 1965)

Questions

1 Describe Yuan's uniform. What does this suggest about his character? Would such a judgement be fair and accurate? (**C**)

2 How does the evidence (**A**), (**B**) and (**D**) help to explain why the warlords were so hated throughout China?

3 (**D**) is taken from an interview with an old peasant conducted in 1962. Why should historians be extra careful when using this sort of evidence?

4 Imagine you were one of the parents in the photograph (**B**). Write a short conversation between you and your partner. Begin with the sentence: 'What are we going to do now?'

5 Talking point: Foreign nations such as Japan and Britain gave money and arms to a number of warlords. Why was it in their interests to do so?

The rise of the Kuomintang

The First World War

In 1917 China entered the First World War on the Allied side in the hope that, once peace came, the foreign powers would give up some of their Chinese acquisitions. In particular the Chinese wanted to expel Japan from Shantung. (Japan had captured Shantung from the Germans in 1914.)

In 1919, news arrived from Paris that the peace-makers had allowed Japan to keep Shantung. To make matters worse, the warlord government in Peking had agreed to Japan's claim as part of a deal for a secret loan.

The May 4th Movement

A storm of protest known as the May 4th Movement or 'Student Revolution' swept China. Demonstrations, strikes and *boycotts* of Japanese goods were held in all the major cities. The government was forced to dismiss three 'traitor ministers' and the Chinese delegation in Paris refused to sign the peace treaty. 'China's first mass movement had won its first victory.'

The May 4th Movement was a turning point in China's history. For the first time students, workers, teachers and merchants had combined in a national movement.

Sun Yat-sen and the Kuomintang

In the meantime Sun had been working in southern China trying to gain a base from which the Kuomintang could operate. But it was slow going. Twice Sun had set up a government in Canton (1917–18, 1920–22) and twice he had been driven out by local warlords. Sun needed a strong army. Only then could he hope to defeat the warlords and unite China under his control.

Russian help

In 1923 Sun turned to Russia for help. Russia agreed to supply money and arms and advisers. With this help the Kuomintang was reorganised and strengthened. Then in 1925 Sun died. His successor was a young general named Chiang Kai-shek.

(A) *Student Slogans of the May 4th Movement*

1	DON'T FORGET OUR NATIONAL HUMILIATION
2	THROW OUT THE WARLORD TRAITORS
3	BOYCOTT FOREIGN GOODS

(B) *Sun's hopes for China were set out in a plan called 'The Three Principles of the People'*

People's Rule (Nationalism)	People's Authority (Democracy)	People's Livelihood (Socialism)
China should be a strong, proud, united nation. China must free itself of foreign controls.	China must be ruled by all its people. Democracy will come after a period of Kuomintang rule [dictatorship] to prepare the people for self-government.	Give land to those who work it. The state will have to run some of China's industries to ensure a fair standard of living for all.

(C) *Leaders of the Kuomintang, 1923 – Chiang Kai-shek (left) and Sun Yat-sen*

(D) *Part of an interview given by Sun Yat-sen to the* New York Times *in 1923:*

'The real trouble is that China is not an independent country. She is the victim of foreign countries. . . .

If the foreign countries leave us alone, China will have her affairs in shape within six months. . . . The Peking Government could not stand twenty-four hours without the backing it receives from the outside, from foreign governments. . . . We have lost hope of help from America, England, France or any other of the Great Powers. The only country that shows any signs of helping us is the Soviet Government of Russia.'

Questions

1. Explain the purpose behind each of the three slogans. (**A**)
2. Which of Sun's ideas (**B**) would have a) appealed to the peasants b) appealed to Chinese patriots c) upset the foreign powers? Explain why in each case.
3. Where did Sun initially hope to get help for his revolution to overthrow the warlords? Suggest why he failed. (**D**)
4. Look at the picture (**C**). What are your first impressions of Sun and Chiang?
5. Draw up a recruiting poster to attract members to join the Kuomintang.

Mao Tse Tung and the birth of Chinese communism

Mao's early life

Mao was born in 1893 into a moderately well-off peasant family in Hunan province. His father was a hot-tempered man. He frequently beat Mao and his brother and refused to give them any money. Mao's mother was more kind. She was a generous and sympathetic woman who was always ready to share whatever she had with her sons.

When the revolution of 1911 overthrew the Manchus, Mao enlisted in the revolutionary army but saw little action. In 1913 he enrolled in a five-year course to train as a teacher in Changsha. From Changsha, Mao went to Peking to work in the university library. Here he made contact with professors and students who were looking for new ways to solve China's problems.

The founding of the Chinese Communist Party

At this time Mao began studying the writings of Karl Marx, the chief founder of communism. In an ideal communist society, all property and goods would be shared and no one would be allowed to own property of his own. Such a society appealed to Mao. It seemed much fairer than the China in which he lived, where a few lived in luxury while the great majority lived in poverty.

Eventually Mao became a communist. Like most communists he looked towards Russia, then the only communist state, for help. In 1920, a Russian agent arrived in Peking to help found a Chinese Communist Party. The following year, Mao and 12 others formed the Chinese Communist Party in Shanghai.

The tiny party worked hard to help workers form unions to improve their miserable wages. In time, it was hoped, the workers would rise up, overthrow their employers and establish a communist state.

The Communist-Kuomintang alliance

In the meantime it seemed a good idea to work with the Kuomintang to drive out the warlords and unite the country. Russia was especially keen on this move. Mao and his comrades therefore joined the Kuomintang.

(A) *Mao's family background*

'As middle peasants then, [Mao later recollected] my family owned 2½ acres of land. On this they could raise 3½ tons of rice a year. The five members of the family consumed 2 tons – about 2½ pounds per day per head, on average – which left an annual surplus of 1½ tons. Using this surplus, my father accumulated a little capital and in time purchased another acre, which gave the family the status of "rich" peasants. We could then raise 5 tons of rice a year . . . .'

(Quoted in D. WILSON, *Mao the People's Emperor*)

(B) *Mao recalls a famine in Changsha*

'There had been a severe famine . . . and in Changsha thousands were without food. The starving sent a delegation to the civil governor to beg for relief, but he replied to them haughtily, "Why haven't you food? There is plenty in the city. I always have enough." When the people were told the governor's reply, they became very angry. They held mass meetings and organized a demonstration. They attacked the Manchu yamen, [the office of a public official] cut down the flagpole, the symbol of office, and drove out the governor. . . . A new governor arrived, and at once ordered the arrest of the leaders of the uprising. Many of them were beheaded and their heads displayed on poles as a warning to future "rebels."

This incident was discussed in my school for many days. It made a deep impression on me. . . . I never forgot it. I felt that there with the rebels were ordinary people like my own family and I deeply resented the injustice of the treatment given to them.'

(Quoted in R.H. SOLOMON, *A Revolution is not a Dinner Party*)

(C) *The room where Mao spent his childhood*

(D) *A folk song from Mao's village*

' Layer on layer of silt in the Shaoshanchung
Nine families out of ten are poor,
Three dangling knives hang above the heads of peasants:
Heavy debt, heavy rent and heavy interest.
Three roads are there for the peasants:
Flight from famine, beggary or prison.'

(Quoted in D. WILSON, *Mao the People's Emperor*)

Questions

1 What sort of life does the folk song suggest most of Mao's neighbours lived? (**D**)

2 How would you check whether this song gives a true picture of peasant life? (**D**)

3 Mao's parents were rich peasants by Chinese standards. What made Mao's family 'rich' peasants? (**A**)

4 How was Mao treated by his parents during his childhood? How might this have affected his attitude to injustices later on in life? (**T**)

5 What sort of impression do we get of Mao's home life in this picture of his bedroom? (**C**)

6 Why did the Changsha famine make such a deep impression on Mao? What does this incident tell us about Mao? (**B**)

7 What experiences in Mao's life made him sympathetic to communist ideals? (**B**), (**D**) and (**T**)

8 Talking point: As a youngster, Mao loved to read Robin Hood type stories where bands of rebels robbed the rich to give to the poor. At 10, he ran away from school to escape a harsh schoolmaster. How much weight should historians give to facts such as these when they try to explain why Mao became a revolutionary?

The Kuomintang defeats the communists and the warlords

After Sun Yat-sen's death in 1925, the leadership of the Kuomintang passed to Chiang Kai-shek. Chiang was born in 1887 into a rich land-owning family. As a young man he trained as an army officer in Japan. While there he fell under the influence of Sun Yat-sen and joined the revolutionary movement. In 1923 Sun appointed him head of the Kuomintang army.

The Northern Expedition

In the summer of 1926, Chiang led his forces north from Canton on an expedition to defeat the warlords. Everywhere people rallied to the Kuomintang. In the areas captured from the warlords, the communists quickly organised peasant groups and labour unions. As a result peasants began to demand a cut in their rent and in some cases seized their land. In the towns, strikes increased as workers demanded higher wages and shorter hours.

The purge of the communists

As a wealthy man, Chiang had never trusted the communists. He was afraid that the communists would soon rise to overthrow him. So he struck first. In April 1927 a blood bath began. Thousands of communists were butchered in Shanghai. Similar massacres followed in other Kuomintang-held cities.

The defeat of the warlords

In late 1927 Chiang's armies marched on Peking as the second stage of the Northern Expedition. By the end of 1928 Peking had been captured and the warlords had been defeated. It seemed that Chiang had succeeded in uniting China under Kuomintang control.

(A) *Northern Expedition 1926–8*

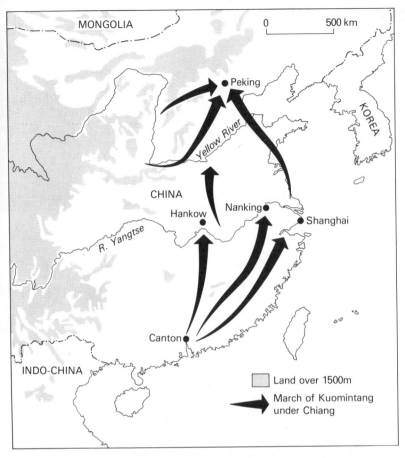

(C) *Massacre in Canton, December 1927. An account by an official at the American consulate:*

'Many private scores were paid off. Two lots of 500 and 1000 men each were taken out and machine-gunned. Realising that this was a waste of ammunition, the soldiers loaded the victims on boats, took them down the river below the city, and pushed them overboard in lots of ten or twelve men tied together. The slaughter continued for four or five days, during which some 6000 people [said to be] Communists, lost their lives in the city of Canton.'

(B) *The 'Execution Patrol' in Shanghai. Groups of soldiers like these patrolled the streets of Shanghai during the disturbances in 1927. The man in the centre is carrying a bare blade, ready to decapitate (behead) any communists he sees.*

Questions

1 Where did the Northern Expedition (a) begin (b) finish? (**A**)

2 Roughly how far did Chiang's armies travel? (**A**)

3 Why did Chiang decide to turn against the communists? (**T**)

4 Imagine you are Chiang's press officer. The picture and the comment, (**B**) and (**C**), have appeared in a foreign newspaper. Write a letter to the editor defending the attacks on the communists.

The communists regroup 1927—34

Many communists escaped the massacres of 1927. The Central Committee of the Party went underground in Shanghai. The largest group fled to a mountain stronghold on the borders of the Kiangsi and Hunan provinces. This group was headed by Mao Tse-tung and the Red Army leader, Chu Teh.

The appeal to the peasants
In Kiangsi, Mao worked hard to govern the countryside. Land was seized from the landlords and *redistributed* to the poor peasants. All debts were wiped out. *Soviets* (councils of peasants, workers and soldiers) were organised to govern the countryside.

The Red Army
At the same time the Red Army was trained in hit and run or *guerilla* warfare. This involved ambushing the enemy at its weakest point and then retreating quickly into the countryside. The idea was to avoid taking on the Kuomintang (who had more men and were better armed) in open battle. The Red soldiers were instructed to pay for all their food, help the peasants wherever they could, and act as model soldiers. This way they won over the local peasants, who were used to soldiers stealing their food and raping their women. Soon the communist republic in Kiangsi had grown into a large territory with a population of 2 000 000.

Differences in policy
Mao believed the countryside was the key to the communist takeover of China. Once aroused, the peasants, led by the Red Army, would surround the cities and conquer all of China. But the Central Committee in Shanghai disagreed. They followed Marx's teaching that the city workers (proletariat) would lead the revolution. To prove its point, the Central Committee ordered Chu Teh's Red Army to attack several large cities. These attacks, which took place in 1930, were disasters. The Kuomintang were too strong and few city workers rose to support the communists.

(A) *Chiang Kai-shek's army on the march to attack Kiangsi and the communists, who were led by Mao*

(From the Viollet Collection)

(B) *General Chu Teh recalls life in Kiangsi when the communists arrived*:

'Most of Kiangsi is mountainous, and the crops are poor. The landlords took as much as 70% of the crop as rent, and most peasants had to borrow from them at high rates of interest each year, so that they and their sons and their sons' sons were bound by debt in . . . [slavery] to the landlords. The peasants were so poor that they sopped up every drop of fat in cooking pans and could afford to buy only a handful of salt at a time. They would dissolve a pinch of salt in a bowl of water and dip their bits of vegetable in it when they ate. They were [boney], half-naked, and illiterate, and lived in dark, insanitary hovels in villages surrounded by high mud walls which had only one gate.'

(Quoted in A. SMEDLEY, *The Great Road*)

(C) *A peasant recalls first hearing about the communists*:

'In February 1934, people began whispering about the Red Army, and how it was saying: "The poor will not have to pay taxes. The poor will not have to pay rent. Poor people's children shall go to school, and landlords will disappear." Then the landlords said: "Don't listen to rumours. The Communists are bandits. They want to kill you and take your wives."'

(J. MYRDAL, *Report from a Chinese Village*, 1965)

(D) *Red army discipline was condensed into 'three rules' and 'eight points' that were tirelessly taught and explained.*
'The three rules were:
Obey orders.
Take nothing from the people, not even a needle and thread.
Return "confiscated goods" to the authorities.
And the eight points were:
Speak with courtesy.
Be fair in your purchases.
Return everything that you borrow.
Compensate for the damages that you have caused.
Do not strike or insult the people.
Do not damage the harvests.
Do not bother the women.
Do not mistreat prisoners.'

(Quoted in J. CHESNEAUX *et al.*, *China from the 1911 Revolution to Liberation*)

(E) *Then there were the four rules of tactics*:
'When the enemy advances we retreat.
When he escapes we harass.
When he retreats we pursue.
When he is tired we attack.'

(Quoted in H. PURCELL, *Mao Tse-Tung*)

(F) *A Red Army marching song*
'You are poor, I am poor
Of ten men, nine are poor
If the nine poor men unite
Where then are the tiger landlords?'

(Quoted in A. SMEDLEY, *The Great Road*)

Questions

1. What do you think was the purpose of the three rules and the eight points? (**D**)
2. Explain why the communists adopted guerilla tactics. (**E**)
3. What is the message of the marching song? (**F**)
4. What problems did Chiang Kai-shek face in moving his troops quickly into battle against Mao? (**A**)
5. Give three reasons why Kiangsi peasants were so poor. (**B**)
6. If you had been a peasant, would you have supported the communists in Kiangsi? (**C**)

China under the Kuomintang

From 1928 until 1934 Chiang Kai-shek had the chance to carry out Sun Yat-sen's 'Three Principles' (see p. 167) and so turn China into a modern powerful state.

Problems

Although the nationalists dominated China they only effectively controlled one part of China – the Lower Yangtse Valley:

- The north-east was occupied from 1931 by the Japanese
- Warlords remained in control of many provinces
- Large areas of Kiangsi were under communist rule from 1931–4. By 1936 they had a new base in Shensi.

Achievements

Chiang was *recognised* by the foreign powers. He shifted his capital from Peking to the more centrally located Nanking.

A modernisation programme was begun. New Chinese-owned factories were built. Railways and road communications were improved. More Chinese were educated than ever before. Foreign trade was increased. China also regained control of her customs service and some foreign concessions were returned to her.

Failures

Yet all these reforms meant little to the great majority of China's peasants. They remained poor, deeply in debt and over-burdened with taxes. For most tenant farmers, rent alone took 40–60 percent of the crop.

No attempt was made to train the people for democracy. Chiang ruled as a dictator and positions in the government were given to his rich friends. Moreover Chiang made little effort to oust the Japanese from the north-east.

(A) *People on the land*

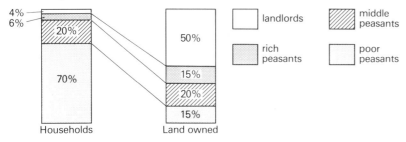

4%
6%
20%
70%
Households

landlords
rich peasants
middle peasants
poor peasants

50%
15%
20%
15%
Land owned

(B) *Reforms*

'Among the new laws passed in Nanking were a number of excellent-sounding reforms. Hours, conditions and pay in factories were to be regulated. Peasants were to be helped to own their land. But Chiang's government was never powerful enough to enforce these laws against the warlords and landlords who were his own main supporters'.

(LOIS MITCHISON, *Chinese Revolution*, 1971)

(C) *Victims of famine, July 1930*

(D) *Edgar Snow, an American, was in China during the 1930s:*

'The shocking thing was that in the cities ... there were grain and food, and had been for months; ... [but it] could not be shipped to the starving. Why not? Because in the North-West there were ... [generals] ... who wanted to hold all their railway [engines and trucks] and would release none of it towards the east, while in the east there were other Kuomintang generals who would send no [railway engines and trucks] westward – even to starving people – because they feared they would be seized by their rivals.'

(E. SNOW, *Red Star Over China*, 1972)

Questions

1   What percentage of land did the richest 10 percent own? (**A**) What problems would this sort of distribution create?

2   What does extract (**B**) tell you about the power of Chiang's government in this area?

3   Famine victims like these in (**C**) were a common sight in Kuomintang China. What does the surrounding land suggest may have caused this particular famine?

4   What stopped food for the starving people getting through? (**D**)

5   Divide your page into two columns. Label one *Chiang Kai-shek's failures*, and the other *Chiang Kai-shek's successes*. Use the text and resources on these pages to help you fill in each column.

The Long March

The extermination campaigns

Chiang Kai-shek was determined to end the communists' rule in Kiangsi. Between 1930 and 1934 Chiang launched five massive attacks against the Red base. But despite being outnumbered ten to one, the communists repelled the first four attacks. Their guerilla tactics were highly successful.

For the fifth campaign, Chiang changed tactics. The Red base was ringed and blockaded by large forces. The plan was to cut off all supplies to the Red base and so starve the communists to death.

The Long March (October 1934 – October 1935)

Rather than risk being wiped out, the communists broke out of Kiangsi. In October 1934 well over 100 000 men, women and children broke through the Kuomintang blockade. Their destination was a communist base in Northern Shensi at Yenan. In order to give the pursuing Kuomintang troops the slip, a zigzag course was followed through some of the wildest country in China. This incredible journey on foot, covered 6000 miles and lasted one year. Fewer than 30 000 lasted the journey. The cost was huge. But the communist party and the Red Army had survived and now had a base in north China.

Moreover, the March had brought the communists into contact with millions more Chinese. All along the route the Red soldiers had taken time to spread their ideas among the people they met.

Mao established as leader

The Long March also established Mao as the unchallenged leader of the communists. It was Mao who led the marchers. And in future it would be Mao's ideas that would be followed in the battle to take control of China.

(A) *Part of a tapestry commemorating the Long March – across the mountain ranges of northern China*

(B) *Crossing the grasslands*

'... When we entered the marshlands ... most men drank the bitter black water ... and wild grass and vegetables were now plucked and eaten. When no green things were to be found the men would gather dried grass and chew the roots.... One day someone dug out a kind of aqueous plant the size of a green turnip; it tasted sweet and everybody at once searched for it. It proved poisonous. Those who ate it vomited after half an hour and several died on the spot. Death, however, could not be allowed to delay our progress.'

(Quoted in C.P. FITZGERALD AND M. ROPER, *China, a World so Changed*)

(C) *An overview of the Long March*

'This [unbelievable] feat of endurance ... led across eleven provinces, over remote regions inhabited by suspicious peoples ... through murderous marshy lands overgrown by grass, and in the face of danger from local and government forces. It is claimed that the Communists crossed eighteen mountain chains, twenty-four large rivers, broke through armies of ten warlords and defeated dozens of KMT regiments; they took, temporarily, sixty-two cities. The basic aim – to save the revolution – was achieved. But the price was high. Of the 130 000 men who left fewer than 30 000 arrived in North Shensi [to join the guerrillas already in the region].'

(T. MENDE, *The Chinese Revolution*, 1961)

(D) *The route of the Long March*

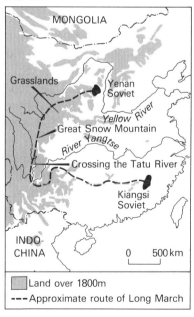

- Land over 1800m
- - - Approximate route of Long March

Questions

1. Describe the route of the march using compass directions. (**D**)
2. What was the countryside like for the latter part of the journey? (**C**)
3. The Long March has been described as one of the greatest feats of human endurance. What evidence is there in resources (**A**) to (**D**) to support such a conclusion?
4. Imagine you are a reporter. Using the text and all the evidence (**A**) to (**D**), write an article on the Long March. In it include:
   a) the reasons for the march
   b) the journey itself.

War with Japan 1937–45

Communist – Kuomintang alliance

In December 1936, Chiang flew to Sian to order renewed attacks against the communists. Here he was kidnapped by soldiers of his own army. To win his freedom, Chiang was forced to agree to a Communist-Kuomintang united front against the Japanese. For the communists, the united front was a major victory. They expected the Kuomintang to exhaust themselves in the coming war with Japan.

The Marco Polo Incident

In July 1937 Japan attacked Chinese troops at the Marco Polo bridge near Peking. This was the start of a full-scale war which lasted until 1945. Within eighteen months the Japanese had occupied many of China's great ports and her industrial and commercial centres. After putting up a fierce struggle, Chiang's forces were forced to retreat to Chungking. There they remained for the rest of the war.

In the north-west the communists conducted a highly successful guerilla war. Small Red Army units struck deep into Japanese-held territory, hit important targets and then retreated back into safety.

By the end of 1939, China was split into three parts:
• Occupied China
• Kuomintang China, centred on Chungking
• Red China in the north-west.

After taking over an area, the Red Army immediately set about winning over the people. To secure peasant support, land rents and interest payments were reduced. Schools were opened and medical care was provided. Where possible the Red Army helped in the fields and around the villages. In these ways the Red troops came to be seen as defenders and friends of the people. By 1945 there were 95 million peasants under communist rule within nineteen *liberated* regions.

The Second World War
After conquering the richest parts of China, Japan turned elsewhere. In December 1941, she attacked the United States base at Pearl Harbour. Soon after, China declared war on Germany and Italy and joined the Allies in the Second World War.

(A) *Japanese invasion of China, showing movements of Chinese forces*

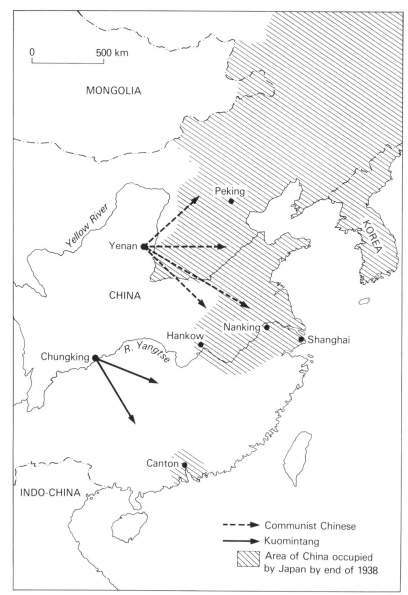

(B) *Communist guerilla troops in training*

(C) *Japanese tactics*

'The Japanese slogan was: "Kill all, Burn all, Loot all". As they moved into an area on their mopping-up campaigns, they killed all young men, destroyed or stole all cattle and broke or made off with all farmers' tools and grain. Their object was to create a no-man's land in which nothing could live. At the same time they reinforced their economic blockade, halted all salt and cloth from entering the guerrilla regions and tried to starve the population out of resistance.'

(Quoted in C.P. FITZGERALD AND M. ROPER, *China, a World so Changed*)

Questions

1 What advantages did Yenan have as a base in the fight against the Japanese compared to Chungking? (**A**)
2 What evidence is there in the photograph that the communists were poorly equipped for the fight against the Japanese? (**B**)
3 Describe how the Japanese tried to wipe out all resistance. (**C**)
4 Talking point: How did the communists use the Second World War to spread their influence and control throughout China?

Communist victory 1945-9

Japan's defeat set off a race between the Kuomintang and communists for Japanese-held territory. Communist guerillas moved into Manchuria. With the aid of American ships and planes, Chiang transported thousands of his troops into key cities in north and east China. Clashes between the two sides broke out. Civil war seemed likely.

In December 1945 the USA sent General Marshall to China to try and get Mao and Chiang to form a *coalition* government. A truce was called.

Civil War 1946-9

In July 1946 the truce collapsed; neither side was willing to trust the other and a civil war began. At first the Kuomintang made spectacular advances into north China and Manchuria. In mid-1947 the communists counterattacked. The Kuomintang were forced onto the defensive.

In 1948 the communists took Manchuria and won decisive battles in north China. By the end of the year, the Kuomintang forces were falling apart. In the Kuomintang areas, there was an acute shortage of food. Prices rocketed and money became almost worthless. Crooked government officials often pocketed money sent from abroad for food and arms. In January 1949 Tientsin and Peking fell. Nanking, Shanghai and Canton soon followed. On 1 October 1949 the People's Republic of China was proclaimed. The Kuomintang government fled to Taiwan.

What made communist victory possible?
At the start of the civil war the communists were outnumbered 4 to 1 by a better-armed Kuomintang army, supported by large doses of American aid. Why did the communists win?
- The nationalist forces were poorly led. The communists had able leaders.
- The nationalists tried to occupy too large an area. Supply lines became stretched. Communist *strategy* was to move around and destroy the enemy not defend territory.
- Kuomintang troops lacked the will to fight whereas it was regarded as an honour to fight for the Red Army.
- Popular support went to the Red Army, largely an army of peasants who tried to win other peasants over.

(A) *Famine riot in Shanghai, Christmas Eve 1948*

(B) *Chinese communist advance, 1946–51*

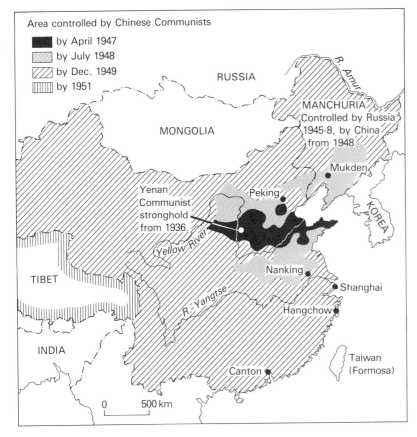

Area controlled by Chinese Communists
- ■ by April 1947
- ▨ by July 1948
- ▧ by Dec. 1949
- ▥ by 1951

RUSSIA

MONGOLIA

MANCHURIA
Controlled by Russia
1945-8, by China
from 1948

R. Amur

Mukden

Yenan
Communist
stronghold
from 1936

Peking

KOREA

Yellow River

Nanking

Shanghai

Hangchow

R. Yangtse

TIBET

INDIA

Canton

Taiwan
(Formosa)

0   500 km

(D) *Rising prices*:
'It was impossible to live on one's wages as [money lost its value] from hour to hour or even from minute to minute. In 1948 a lunch at the Palace Hotel, Shanghai, cost millions of Chinese dollars. Soup was $800 000 and chicken liver with mushrooms $3 500 000.'
(Quoted in C.P. FITZGERALD AND M. ROPER, *China, a World so Changed*)

Questions

1 Where were most of the communist controlled areas located in 1945? What advantages did this give to the communists? What problems did it pose for Chiang? (**B**)

2 Give three reasons why Kuomintang soldiers might have lacked the will to fight the communists. (**C**)

3 Why might the evidence in (**C**) be more reliable than a Chinese account?

4 What is the economic term for describing what is happening in (**D**)?

5 What effect would scenes like those in (**A**) and (**D**) have on morale in Kuomintang areas?

6 Divide your page into two columns. On one side, list the reasons why the Kuomintang lost control of China. On the other, list what the communists did to win the support of the people. Compare your list with the rest of the class.

7 Debate: 'The communists did not win China, the Kuomintang lost it.'

(C) *Chiang's army*
An American, William Lederer, wrote:
'. . . as early as 1941 I personally have seen long lines of con-scripts chained together on their way from their villages to training camps. . . .'

And the wartime correspondent Jack Belden reported:
'. . . Sons of the rich never entered the army; sons of the poor could never escape. An impoverished widow's only son was always drafted; the numerous offspring of the landlord, never.'
(Quoted in F. GREENE, *A Curtain of Ignorance*)

Two other American reporters, Theodore White and Annalee Jacoby, wrote:
'. . . Recruits ate even less than the starving soldiers; sometimes they got no water. Many of them were stripped naked and left to sleep on bare floors. They were whipped. Dead bodies were allowed to lie for days. In some areas less than 20 per cent lived to reach the front. . . . Near Chengtu one camp had received some 40 000 men for [training]. Many had already died on the way; only 8000 were still alive at the camp at the end of the drive. One batch of 1000 [recruits] was reported to have lost 800 recruits through the [carelessness] of its officers.'
(Quoted in F. GREENE, *A Curtain of Ignorance*)

Making China communist

Four major problems faced the new communist government:

- The communists had to prove they were capable of providing a strong, effective government.
- Opposition to the government had to be removed or brought under control.
- The economy had to be restored.
- Most of the world refused to recognise the communists. America continued to recognise the Kuomintang on Taiwan. Only Russia could be expected to provide aid to help rebuild China.

Setting up government

The communists were already experienced in the art of government. For years they had ruled large parts of China.

To win the widest possible support, a number of political parties were invited to work with the communists. In theory this meant that the government was a *coalition* of different parties. In practice it was a single party communist *dictatorship*. The communist party ran the army and the various mass groups of peasants, workers, students and children. Through these bodies party cadres (organisers) persuaded the masses to think and act like true communists. Heading the government, as Chairman of the Communist Party, was Mao Tse Tung.

Many opponents were persuaded to reform their ways and were 're-educated' to communism. Large campaigns of 'thought reform' were launched against enemies: usually landowners or businessmen. As many as a million opponents were executed between 1949–51.

Soviet aid

In February 1950 Mao visited Moscow and signed a Sino-Soviet Treaty of Friendship. Russia agreed to lend China money and provide technical assistance.

(A) *A scene from a Chinese novel,* The Hurricane:

'A landlord called Han is facing a village meeting. The women and children sing: "The wrongs, the hate of a thousand years, can be avenged now the Party's here!

Han number six! Han number six!

The people are out for your blood."

A peasant accuses Han.

"Han number six is my mortal enemy. In 1941, he refused to pay me wages after I'd worked as his farmhand for a year. Instead, he had me sent for forced labour. When I ran away, he put my mother in prison and there she died. Today I want to avenge my mother's death. Can I beat him?"

"Go ahead!"

"Beat him to death."

From all sides the shouts thundered. The peasants raised their sticks and spears in their hands and surged forward. The militiamen held their spears horizontally to stop them, but the crowd burst through.... After more village accusations of rape and murder, Han was shot outside the village gate.'

(Quoted in L. MITCHISON, *China in the Twentieth Century*)

(B) *Chinese workers giving presents to their foreign advisers*

(C) *The economy. A report prepared for the US government in 1967 stated*:

'The economy inherited by the [communists] was a shambles.... Industry and commerce had almost come to a standstill in major urban centers.... Dams, irrigation systems, and canals were in a state of disrepair. Railroad lines had been cut and recut by the contending armies. Inflation had ruined confidence in the money system. And, finally, the population had suffered enormous casualties ... and was disorganized, half starved, and exhausted.'

(*An Economic Profile of Mainland China*)

(D) *Early achievements*

'... In a remarkably short time the new government had:

*   suppressed banditry.
*   restored the battered railroad system to operation.
*   repaired and extended the badly neglected system of dikes.
*   replaced the [crooked local government officials].
*   introduced a stable currency and enforced a nationwide tax system.
*   begun an extensive program of public health and sanitation.
*   provided a tolerably even distribution of available food and clothing.'

(*An Economic Profile of Mainland China*)

Questions

1   Why should historians be careful when using books like *The Hurricane*? (**A**)
2   Who are the foreign advisers shown in this poster? (**B**)
3   In your own words describe the economy inherited by the communists. (**C**)
4   Do you think the communists were successful in getting the economy back on its feet? (**D**) Give reasons.
5   Talking point: Why was it so important for the communists to be successful in these years? Could the communists have kept power without executing or 'brainwashing' their enemies?

Industry and agriculture

Five-year plans

In 1953 Russian style five-year plans were introduced. Under the first plan (1953-7) special importance was placed on *heavy industry* – especially iron and steel production. Russia helped out with machinery, equipment and technical assistance. During this same period much of the remaining private industry was taken over by the state.

Agriculture

Under the Agrarian Reform Law of 1950 land was taken from the landlords and shared out amongst the peasants. Landlords as a class were wiped out. Grain production climbed to a record height in 1952. But even so the average peasant farm was less than 2.5 acres. Larger farms and modern methods would be needed if food production was to be increased greatly.

In 1952 groups of peasant households were encouraged to join together in *mutual-aid* teams. Farmers kept their own land but shared their animals and labour. By the end of 1952, 40 percent of all peasants were members of mutual-aid teams.

In 1953 peasants were called on to take the second step towards full co-operative or collective farming. Mutual-aid teams were joined together and farmed as one unit. Profits were shared out among the members according to the amount of land, tools and hours of work they had put in. Overall, these co-operatives were well received by the peasants, who grew more food and ate better.

The introduction of higher-grade co-operatives or *collectives* began in 1955. All land was handed over to a collective. Private ownership, except for small garden plots, ceased to exist. Instead farmers became wage earners. Although there was opposition, by 1957 over 90 percent of the peasants were in the collectives.

(A) *Production figures for 1952 and 1957*

Production	Best Previous Year	1952	1957
Steel (tons)	900 000	1 350 000	5 400 000
Coal (tons)	62 000 000	66 490 000	130 000 000
Electricity (KwH)	6 000 000 000	7 300 000 000	19 000 000 000
Oil (tons)	320 000	436 000	2 000 000
Raw cotton (bales)	848 000	3 600 000	4 500 000
Cotton cloth (metres)	—	3 300 000 000	5 000 000 000
Grain (tons)	150 000 000	163 000 000	170 000 000

(J. CHESNEAUX, *China the People's Republic 1949–76*, 1979)

(B) *Peasants working a treadmill to irrigate the fields*

(C) *More goods for the consumers, 1952–7*

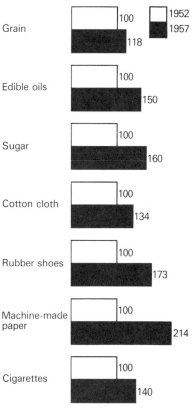

(D) *Population growth*

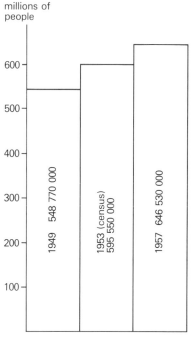

Questions

1 By what percentage did a) steel b) coal and c) electricity increase between 1952 and 1957? (**A**)

2 Suggest why special importance was placed on increasing steel production.

3 What problem facing Chinese agriculture does the picture show? How could this type of problem be overcome? (**B**)

4 What evidence is there that the standard of living increased for most Chinese between 1952 and 1957? Use figures in your answer. (**C**)

5 By how many people did the population increase between 1949 and 1957? What problems might this have created for the communist government? (**D**)

6 Draw a cartoon for a newspaper mainly read by peasants, pointing out the benefits of collectivisation.

7 Using the text and sources (**A**)-(**D**), summarise the successes and failures of the government in industry and agriculture by 1957.

185

The Great Leap Forward

Despite the success of the first five-year plan, serious economic problems remained. First, China's vast pool of manpower was not being fully used. There was unemployment in the cities and in the countryside most peasants had little to do between harvesting and sowing. Secondly, there was the problem of how China could raise enough money to build more industry.

To solve these problems, Mao came up with a new plan called the *Great Leap Forward*. In the countryside peasants would be fully employed if they were set to work on large irrigation and flood control projects. They could also develop small scale industries. One result would be more farm produce, which could be taxed to help build industry. In the cities *labour intensive* industries, which required little money, would be set up to solve the unemployment problem.

Therefore, for the second five-year plan (1958–62) very high targets were set in both agriculture and industry. Record figures in just about everything were reached in 1958.

Communes

At the same time a new way of organising agricultural life came into being. Collective farms were joined into 24 000 communes, with an average population of 30 000 people. Communes seemed the ideal way to organise China's vast peasant labour force. They were large enough to tackle large projects, such as irrigation works and run their own schools, clinics, shops and local *militia* (citizen army). In addition, each one set up its own local industries.

Life on the commune was supposed to be lived communally. Peasants were to eat in mess halls; and nurseries were provided for young children. Family life was cut back. In these ways it was hoped that communes would speed up the change to full communism.

(A) *'Long Live the People's Commune!' – a poster by Ha Chiung-Wen*

(B) *Communes: the three levels of organisation*

Commune
Typical commune might have 20 000 to 50 000 people responsible for big projects like tractor stations, farm machinery repair shops, secondary schools.
Numbers: 1958 around 26 000, early 1960s increased to 74 000; since 1970 cut to 55 000.

Brigade
Ten to twenty brigades in one commune. Responsible for smaller projects, small reservoirs, primary schools and health clinics.

Team
Main level of organisation. Ten to twenty teams in one brigade. About the size of a small village. One or two hundred members. Keeps its own accounts. Shares out income among members.

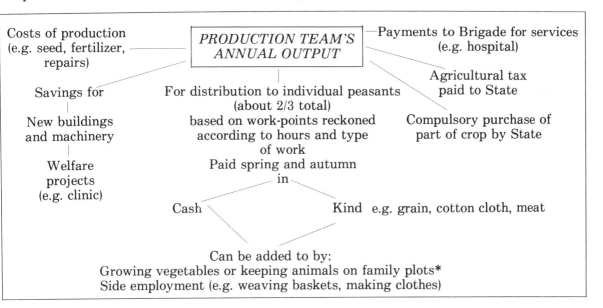

NB private plots were abolished for a time during the Great Leap Forward

Questions

1. What evidence is there to show that communes were established with great speed? (**B**) and (**C**) Quote figures and dates. What problems would such a rapid pace create?
2. What benefits does the poster claim that the People's Commune will bring? (**A**)
3. Which of the following statements are true/false? (**B**)
   - a typical commune would have 30 000 people
   - the brigade pays the peasants
   - peasants are paid wages only
   - all peasants receive the same income
   - part of the crop has to be sold to the government.
4. In your own words explain what a commune is, and how it works. (**B**)
5. Talking point: China had little machinery but vast numbers of people. How did the Great Leap Forward try to overcome this problem and turn China into a rich country?

(C) *The establishment of communes during the Great Leap Forward – Percentage of total peasant population*

August 1958 (end)	30.4
September 1958 (early)	48.1
September 1958 (middle)	65.3
September 1958 (end)	98.0
December 1958 (end)	99.1
1959	

(R.M. BETH, *Mao's China: a Study of Socialist Economic Development*)

Retreat from the Great Leap Forward

The Great Leap tried to do too much too fast, and led to huge mistakes. Thousands of small factories proved to be inefficient and wasteful. Food production also slumped and too many peasants had been moved from agriculture to industry. The communes were not the great success hoped for. Many proved too large to be run efficiently. Peasants resented the loss of their private plots and the attacks on family life.

Mao, it seems, took part of the blame and, in late 1958, resigned as China's head of state. He was replaced by President Liu Shao-chi.

Economic retreat

Under Liu many of the Great Leap policies were abandoned. Thousand of small factories were closed. Millions of peasants were returned from manufacturing to farming. Communes were also reduced in size.

To encourage the peasants to produce more food, private garden plots were returned. Mao was angry at these changes. Liu's policies were creating new farms of social inequality. The government, by bringing back private plots, had created a new class of rich peasants. The payment of prizes and bonuses had resulted in a new privileged class of workers. To make matters worse, party and government officials also were starting to behave like a privileged ruling class.

A problem of evidence: did the Chinese starve?

In 1958 China enjoyed a record harvest. Then followed three disastrous years. The government even had to import large amounts of grain from overseas. In the West, reports began to appear in the press that the Chinese people were starving.

Questions

Read the evidence for starvation and answer these questions.

1 How many calories does Alsop claim the Chinese were living on? (**A**)
2 From where have the newspapers gathered their evidence to prove that the Chinese were starving? (**B**)

Read the evidence against starvation and answer these questions.

1 How does Greene disprove Alsop's claim? (**D**)
2 How does the view given in (**E**) differ from those given in (**B**)?
3 Which evidence, (**B**) or (**E**), is likely to be the more reliable? Why?
4 What picture of Chinese life does the witness in (**F**) give?

The evidence for starvation

(A) *An American journalist's report:*

'On September 13, 1961, the American journalist Joseph Alsop reported that the average Chinese "was being compelled to live on a diet of no more than 600 calories" of food intake a day.... This was "a level of nourishment so low that American doctors require patients needing such severe diets to enter hospitals for the purpose".

Mr Alsop went on to report that a person on 600 calories "can normally expect to lose about 20 pounds a month". Mr Alsop concluded ... that "the population of China is starving".'

(Quoted in E. SNOW, *The Other Side of the River*)

(B) *There were similar reports in other Western newspapers:*

'(May 15) AP reported from Hong Kong: "Refugees rounded up by Hong Kong patrols today claimed that hundreds of Chinese have died of starvation while trying to reach the border. One said it was impossible to get enough to eat to keep alive in his village...."

(May 19) AP reported from Hong Kong: "Some 3000 to 5000 more refugees from hunger-ridden Red China streamed across the border before dawn yesterday."

(May 27) Tillman Durdin, in the New York Times: "The migrants in fact were fleeing grim conditions of hunger.... It is now no longer considered absurd for observers of the China scene to talk of the possibility of a break-up of the Communist regime or revolt against it."

(June 18) *Newsweek* spoke of "the 60 000 hungry workers who swarmed out of China last month...."'

(Quoted in F. GREENE, *A Curtain of Ignorance*)

(C) *Having seen reports of 'famine in China,' Mrs Cookson wrote to a friend who lived in Shanghai. The following are extracts from her friend's reply:*

'That China during 1960 experienced the severest and most widespread natural calamity of the past century is a fact.... To say that China is experiencing a famine is grossly untrue.

... People throughout the country have been and still are co-operating in their efforts to be sparing with food and to avoid waste, so that the supply will go round for all.'

(From *A Curtain of Ignorance*)

Summing up the evidence

After considering all the evidence for and against starvation, which of these conclusions do you support?

Conclusions

(a) There was mass starvation in China in the early 1960s.

(b) The Chinese did not starve in the early 1960s.

(c) There is not enough evidence to prove that the Chinese were starving or were not starving. Compare your evidence with the rest of the class.

The evidence against starvation

(D) *In answer to Mr Alsop's claim that the Chinese were living on 600 calories a day, Felix Greene wrote in 1964:*

'Medically this makes no sense (a baby needs a minimum of 709 calories). The Chinese would now be dead. There are still 700 000 000 of them left.'

(Quoted in F. GREENE, *A Curtain of Ignorance*)

(E) *On 22 May 1962, in the House of Commons, the British Colonial Secretary said:*

'There is little evidence that the Chinese refugees attempting to enter Hongkong were suffering malnutrition.'

(F) *In a letter to the editor of the* New York Herald Tribune, *Sybil Cookson wrote:*

'Having recently undertaken a three weeks' tour of China – visiting six cities and many country districts – my husband and I were astonished to read Joseph Alsop's recent report from Hong Kong suggesting that there is widespread famine in China and even a likelihood of a revolt against the present regime.... [It is] quite contrary to our impression formed in China itself last autumn. We were allowed to travel where we desired – in crowded streets, stores and holiday resorts. We visited communes, schools and technical colleges, hospitals and homes for old folk. Nowhere did we see any signs of [discontent] much less of famine, despite a disappointing harvest.'

(From *A Curtain of Ignorance*)

The Cultural Revolution

In 1962 Mao came out of semi-retirement to launch the 'Socialist Education Movement'. This was a campaign to get the people back on the right path to communism.

But Mao could do little while Liu Shao-chi and his supporters held most of the positions of power. Mao, therefore, turned to the army for help. Soldiers were ordered to study Mao's thoughts contained in the 'Little Red Book' and spread his ideas throughout China. By 1965 Mao had enough support to launch a new super-campaign known as the Cultural Revolution.

The Cultural Revolution

In 1966 attacks against Mao's opponents grew louder. At first the attacks were aimed at unnamed enemies of socialism. Later the attacks were centred on Liu and his followers.

In June 1966 schools and universities were closed down, and the students joined the groups of Red Guards which were springing up. Between August and November 1966, millions of these students were brought to Peking by the army for a series of mass rallies. There they were instructed by Mao to attack the 'four olds': old customs, old habits, old thoughts and old culture. Later they were ordered to rid the communist party of the enemies of Mao's policies. Opponents were humiliated, tortured, or executed and many party officials, including Liu, were removed from office.

By 1967 China was on the verge of civil war. Red Guards were fighting with workers and peasants, and industrial production was dropping. To cope with the chaos the government disbanded the Red Guards. Schools were reopened and millions of youths were sent to the countryside to work among the peasants.

Revolutionary committees, dominated by the army, were set up to run the country. In 1969 the Cultural Revolution was declared over. And Lin Piao was named as Mao's successor.

(A) *Gross National Product 1965–70 [The total wealth of a country is usually called its Gross National Product (GNP)]*

	GNP†	Per cent Annual Change
1965	163	15
1966	177	9
1967	172	−3
1968	173	1
1969	192	11
1970	219	14

† In billions of 1975 U.S. dollars

(F.M. KAPLAN *et al.*, *Encyclopedia of China Today*, 1979)

(B) *A cartoon showing Liu Shao-chi and his wife on a visit to Indonesia*

(D) *Red Guard posters*
'We are the Red Guards of Chairman Mao and we effect the convulsion. We tear up and smash up old calendars, precious vases, US and British records, superstitious lacquers [wood paintings] and ancient paintings, and we put up the picture of Chairman Mao....'
(BBC Radio for Schools, 1974)

(C) *'Chairman Mao Goes to Anyuan'* The caption from Peking reads, 'In autumn 1921, our great teacher Chairman Mao went to Anyuan and personally kindled the flames of revolution there.'
(A collective work by students of Peking universities and colleges)

Questions
1. What effect did the Cultural Revolution have on China's economy? Quote figures. (**A**)
2. Why should the Red Guards wish to smash a) old calendars and vases b) US and British records? (**D**)
3. What sort of people does the cartoon show Liu and his wife to be? (**B**)
4. Do you think the cartoonist would be a supporter or an opponent of Mao? Explain why. (**B**)
5. How is Mao portrayed in the painting? Why do you think he was drawn like this? (**C**)
6. Talking point: Mao tried to get the people thinking like true communists. Is it ever possible that people will think and act like true communists?

After the Cultural Revolution: 1969–76

Many of the abandoned policies of the Great Leap were reintroduced in the countryside and new rural industries were established. Millions of city dwellers were also encouraged to return and work in the country. Medical care was improved as thousands of *barefoot doctors* were trained. An effort was also made to provide every peasant child with primary schooling.

Prizes and bonuses for urban workers were abolished. Instead special importance was placed on teamwork.

Political power

One of the goals of the Cultural Revolution was to give the masses more self-government. Yet in fact 95 percent of party officials were given their jobs back. They, however, were now regularly sent out to work in the fields and factories to keep in touch with the people.

For certain radicals the changes did not go far enough. Lin Piao, it seems, actually believed Mao had betrayed the Cultural Revolution and attempted a *coup* (take-over). In 1971 he along with several military leaders disappeared. Exactly what happened is still unclear.

In January 1976, Mao's lifelong comrade and likely successor, Premier Chou En-lai, died of cancer. After a brief struggle, Hua Kuo-feng, a moderate, was appointed Premier. Then in September 1976 Mao died. His widow, Chiang Ching, with the help of three other *radicals*, tried to seize power. But their attempt failed and the 'gang of four', as they became known, were arrested. In October Hua was appointed successor to Mao as Party Chairman.

(A) *The death of Mao, September 1976*

'Mao Tse-tung, the chieftain of the bandits, who had plagued China and the world for 60 years, died early this morning, thus concluding his evil life.'
(Taiwan radio station)

'. . . a man of great, remarkable ability, skill, vision and foresight.'
(President Ford, the United States)

'One of the greatest leaders ever known.'
(Prime Minister Palme, Sweden)

'Men like Mao Tse-tung come once in a century, perhaps once in a thousand years.'
(President Bhutto, Pakistan)

(B) *Display of Mao flash cards at the China National Games (1975)*

(C) *Mao's Achievements and Failures*

Achievements

- For over 50 years Mao played a key role in China's history. In his lifetime he rose from peasant stock to become ruler of a great nation. He never forgot his peasant origins and always lived simply and plainly.
- Mao's life-long ambition was to change China from a backward corrupt state into a modern just nation.
- In his early days, he helped explain how China had been exploited by foreigners. At the same time he gave Chinese Communism its own special flavour.
- He led the communist forces during the Long March, then helped defeat the Japanese and expelled the Kuomintang in 1949. Without Mao's leadership, success would have come much later.
- For the next quarter of a century he governed a quarter of mankind. When he died, 900 million Chinese were enjoying a much better life. Moreover he had given the Chinese a set of beliefs to guide their daily lives.
- Under Mao, China once again held its head high in the world.

Failures

- Mao believed he was infallible. He could not accept criticism of his ideas and labelled rivals 'class enemies' even when they were loyal and sincere communists.
- Mao could not work with others or adopt a team approach to solving China's problems.
- Mao claimed he was against personality cults. Yet, during the Cultural Revolution he was adored like a God.
- Mao must bear responsibility for the thousands and possibly millions who died during the reforms of the 1950s.
- Mao's two great experiments – the Great Leap Forward and the Cultural Revolution – were failures.
  The Great Leap was an economic disaster and led to food shortages.
  The Cultural Revolution brought chaos and economic hardship.
- In both cases Mao tried to make massive changes in too short a time.

Questions

1 What does (**B**) show about the position of Mao after the Cultural Revolution?

2 Explain why the radio station's opinion of Mao is so critical. (**A**)

3 Look at all the judgements on Mao in (**A**). Then read (**C**) carefully. Which of the opinions is the closest to your view of Mao? Give reasons.

4 Review: You have been asked to write a biography of Mao. What points about his life and achievements would you stress?

China since Mao

Leadership

In 1977 further leadership changes saw the fall of a number of radical 'leftists' while Teng Hsaio-ping, a former top party official, who had earlier been sacked for criticising Mao, emerged as the new party strong man.

China was going through 'demaoisation' just as Russia had gone through 'destalinisation' in the 1950s. The new leaders wanted to end the violent upheavals of Mao's later years and place China on a path of cautious social reform and steady economic growth.

In 1980 Hua Kuo-feng was replaced as Premier by Chao Tzu-hang. In 1981 Hua was replaced as Party Chairman by Hu Yao-Pang.

Economy

The present leadership feels the economy will never be healthy until it solves the basic problems of providing enough food, clothing and consumer goods for China's 1000 million people.

To encourage peasants and workers to produce more, new incentives have been introduced. Prices paid by the state to peasants for grain and other food have been raised. Peasants are allowed to grow more cash crops and sell their surplus produce at market value. In the factories, bonuses are paid for extra output. People are even free to own their own small businesses. To satisfy demand, record numbers of consumer goods such as bicycles, watches and sewing machines, are being produced.

Education

The educational reforms of the Cultural Revolution have been reversed. Examinations are back. Success in academic subjects is once again essential in order to go on to higher education. Special key schools for the best students have been set up to provide China with the skills she needs to make her prosper. On the other hand, the time spent on political education and manual work has been cut.

(A) *Effigies of the 'gang of four' are paraded through the streets of Canton in 1976 during a demonstration to support the new communist party chairman, Hua Kuo-feng*

(B) *Life for the average Chinese citizen, 1979:*
'The life of the average Chinese citizen is spartan at best. Average total earnings last year for its 95 million industrial employees came to about £180 a head, a 6 percent improvement over 1977. Its 800 million peasants had much lower cash earnings. In 1978, the average take-home pay per head for the year (excluding food and payments in kind) was about £24, a 14 per cent rise over 1977.'

(LEO GOODSTADT, *Guardian*, 1979)

(C) *In late 1979 a 'one is fine' birth control programme to encourage single child families was instituted:*
'In keeping with the new outlook of accounts-keeping, profit-making China, the campaign is backed by economic reward,.... Parents who promise to have only one child earn for themselves the private plots, and food and fuel supplies of a two-child family. They are given housing priority over everyone else.

At the same time, having a third child means the loss of 10 per cent of a family's wage packet and an extra 5 per cent levy for every child after that. The message is clear; big families go hungry while the childless and one-child families live in comparative comfort.'

(*The Times*, 1981)

(D) *Food bill estimate (mid-1977):*

	*Yuan per head
Total per head	156.40
Total per family (of 4.5 members)	703.80
plus tea per family	7.20
Total incl. tea per family	711.00
Wage income per person	720.00
Wage income per family (with 1.7 workers)	1 224.00
Total food bill (in % of family wage income)	59.00

* £1 sterling = 3.25 yuan

Questions

1 Since the 'gang of four' were arrested in 1976, blame for virtually everything that has gone wrong recently in China has been heaped on them. Can you suggest why? (**A**)

2 Explain how the 'one is fine' birth control programme is supposed to reduce China's population. (**C**)

3 Already this programme has begun to meet strong resistance from the public. Can you suggest why? (**C**)

4 How much does the average Chinese worker earn in a year? What does this tell us about the standard of living? (**B**)

5 How much would an average Chinese family spend on food per year? (**D**)

6 Draw two pie graphs. On one, show the percentage of its family income that a typical Chinese family spends on food. On the other, do the same for your own family. Compare the two. (**D**)

7 Talking point: 'Over the last thirty years the Chinese have found life tolerable, in spite of the poverty, because of the vast improvement in conditions before Mao Tse Tung came to power in 1949. But now a whole new generation has reached adulthood which has no personal recollection of past miseries' (Leo Goodstadt). What problems is this going to create for governments in the future?

The basis of the Cold War

Superpowers

The United States and Russia emerged from the Second
World War as the world's two *superpowers*. Both were far
more powerful than any other country. France and Britain
on the other hand were exhausted. China was engaged in a
civil war, while Germany and Japan had been utterly
defeated.

Most people hoped that Russia and America would work
together to build a prosperous peaceful world. Both had
fought as allies against Hitler and both joined the United
Nations – a world peacekeeping body – set up in 1945 to
replace the League of Nations. Both however soon quarrelled.

The Cold War

Indeed ever since the Second World War, Russia and the
United States have been deadly rivals locked in a struggle
called the *Cold War*; so called because it has not led to
fighting a 'hot war' on a large scale. The differences
between the two powers are rooted in their very different
beliefs.

Capitalism

Americans believe in private ownership or *capitalism*.
American people are free to own property, to run their own
farms and businesses, and to make as much money as they
can. Americans also live in a democracy. At election time
they can vote for any government they like.

Communism

Russians on the other hand believe in communism. Communists believe that under capitalism a few live in luxury,
while the rest live in poverty. Stalin had destroyed
capitalism in Russia by placing industry and agriculture
under state control. In the process all opposition was
brutally crushed. Russia is not a democracy. There are no
free elections. It is a one party state ruled by the communist party.

(A) *Major foreign invasions of Russia*

The Mongol Occupation ('Yoke') 13th–15th centuries, 250 years;
The German intrusions into Northwest Russia   1280s;
The Polish occupation of Moscow in 'Times of Trouble'   1600s;
The Swedish invasion   1709;
The Napoleon occupation of Moscow   1812;
The German invasion in World War I   1914–18;
The foreign intervention in Russia's civil war   1918–21;
The German (Nazi) occupation during World War II   1941–44.

(V. MEDISH, *The Soviet Union*, 1981)

(B) *Some Cold War jokes. Jokes became one of the weapons with
which the Cold War was fought. Here are two examples*:
(1) *First Russian*: Say what do you think of the regime [govern-
ment], comrade?
Second Russian (playing it very carefully): About the same
as you do, comrade.
First Russian: In that case I've got to arrest you, comrade.
(2) A Frenchman, an Englishman and a Russian were debating
the nationality of Adam and Eve. The Frenchman said that
with all the passion they had, they must have been French.
The Englishman said that with the figleaves, Adam was
obviously an English gentleman. No, said the Russian, they
must have been Russians. Only a Russian could have only a
figleaf and only an apple to eat and yet believe he was in
paradise.

(I. LISTER, *The Cold War*, 1974)

(C) *Military forces in Europe
in 1945 and 1946*

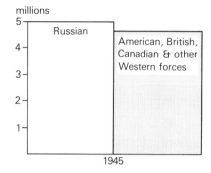

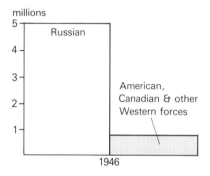

(D) *One early enemy of
communism was Winston
Churchill. In 1924 he warned*:
'From the earliest moment of
its birth the Russian Bol-
shevist Government has declared its intention of using all
the power of the Russian Empire to promote a world revolution. Their agents have pene-
trated into every country.
Everywhere they have endea-
voured to bring into being the
"germ cells" from which the
cancer of Communism should
grow . . .'

(Quoted in H. HIGGINS, *The Cold War*, 1974)

Questions
1   How many major invasions of Russia have there been
   a) since the 13th century   b) in this century? (**A**)
2   How would these invasions help explain Russia's great
   distrust of the West? (**A**)
3   Why were many westerners so afraid of the Russians,
   following the Russian Revolution of 1917? (**D**)
4   'When the war came to an end in 1945, the Red Army,
   instead of being drastically reduced in size to a peacetime
   level, was kept on a war footing.'
   What evidence is there in the graphs to support this idea?
   Quote figures. (**C**)
5   The origins of most Cold War jokes are obscure. Which joke
   in the two examples seems to have originated in the
   Russian purges of the 1930s? (**B**)
6   What aspect of Russian life does the first joke poke fun at?
   (**B**)
7   What comment about the Russian economic way of life
   does the second joke make? (**B**)
8   Talking point: How can jokes help us understand the past
   better? When we laugh at racial jokes, do we reveal our
   prejudices?

The beginnings of the Cold War

By the end of the Second World War, Russia had occupied most of eastern and central Europe. Afterwards Stalin planned to keep this area under Soviet control – to provide a protective *buffer* zone between Russia and its enemies.

Between 1945 and 1947, with help from the Red Army, communist governments were set up in Poland, Bulgaria, Hungary, Rumania and Yugoslavia.

The American response

Worried by this, in March 1947 President Truman announced that the USA would aid 'free peoples' to resist communist aggression. This plan was called the Truman Doctrine. From now on the United States would act as an international policeman working to *contain* the spread of communism.

The Marshall Plan, introduced later in 1947, gave American aid to the shattered European economies to help them recover; American influence would increase and western Europe would be saved from communism. In all, 16 western European countries received $15 billion of aid. In answer to the Marshall Plan, the USSR set up the Cominform in October 1947. This was an organisation of all the various communist parties, set up to plan and promote the spread of communism throughout the world.

Yugoslavia

Until 1948 Yugoslavia under Marshal Tito was considered one of Russia's closest satellites. But then Tito broke away from Soviet control and said Yugoslavia would stay neutral in the Cold War.

Stalin was probably tempted to invade Yugoslavia but held back after the Western powers backed Tito with military and economic aid.

(A) *An extract from Winston Churchill's Iron Curtain speech at Fulton, Missouri, USA, 5 March 1946*:

'From Stettin, in the Baltic, to Trieste in the Adriatic, an *iron curtain* has descended across the continent. Behind that line are all the capitals of the ancient states of central and eastern Europe – Warsaw, Berlin, Prague, Budapest, Belgrade, Bucharest and Sofia. All these famous cities and the populations around them, lie in the Soviet sphere.'

(Quoted in I. LISTER, *The Cold War*)

(B) *The communist take-over in eastern Europe*

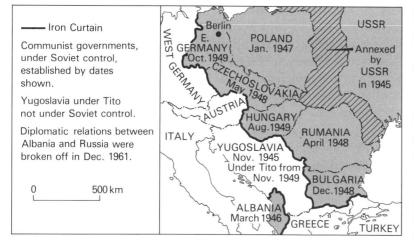

(C) *Countries which received most in Marshall Aid and [inset] progress in countries receiving Marshall Aid*:

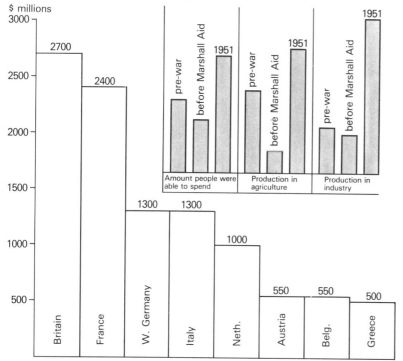

(D)

PEEP UNDER THE IRON CURTAIN

Questions

1   What did Churchill mean by the iron curtain? What lay behind it? (**A**)
2   Who is Joe in the cartoon? (**D**)
3   Name the figure peeping under the wall. (**D**)
4   What did the cigar-smoking figure call this wall? (**D**)
5   Why do you think a 'No Admittance' sign was placed on the wall? (**D**)
6   How did control of eastern Europe help the Russians protect themselves against an attack from the West? (**B**)
7   What evidence is there to show that Marshall Aid
    a)   gave people more money to spend
    b)   helped agriculture and industry recover in the countries which received the American help? (**C**)
8   Talking point: Winston Churchill called the Marshall Plan 'the most unselfish act in history' What do you think he meant? Do you agree?

The Berlin blockade and NATO

In 1945 Germany was divided into four zones, occupied by Britain, France, Russia and the USA. Berlin, though deep inside the Russian zone, was also divided into four zones.

In 1948 it was clear that the Russians were determined to keep East Germany under their control when they cut off all road, rail and canal links through East Germany to West Berlin. It appeared as though they were trying to force the Western powers out of Berlin.

To break the blockade, vital supplies were airlifted into West Berlin. Finally 11 months and 200 000 flights later, the Russians gave in. In May 1949 the blockade was lifted. Soon afterwards the Western powers amalgamated their zones to form the Federal Republic of Germany (West Germany).

While the Berlin crisis was brewing, another bombshell hit the West. In March 1948, Jan Masaryk, the last non-communist in the Czech government, was found dead in mysterious circumstances. Eastern Europe was now totally under Russian control.

Berlin, and then the Czech crisis, pushed the Americans into setting up an anti-communist military alliance – the North Atlantic Treaty Organisation (NATO). In April 1949 the 11 European nations plus the USA signed the treaty. If one member was attacked then the others would come to its help.

For Russia this was just another example of American aggression. In 1955 Russia set up its own communist military alliance, the Warsaw Pact.

(B) *Three views on why the Russians blockaded Berlin*:
'The Berlin Blockade was a major Moscow bid . . . to take over Europe.'
(L. FISCHER, *This is Our World*, 1956)

'When Berlin falls, Western Germany will be next. If we mean to hold Germany against Communism, we must not budge.'
(General LUCIUS CLAY, US Commander in Berlin)

'The Berlin Blockade was a move to test our capacity and will to resist. This action and their previous attempts to take over Greece and Turkey were part of a Russian plan to probe for soft spots in the Western Allies' positions all around their own perimeter.'
(President TRUMAN of the USA)

(A) *The Berlin airlift 28 June 1948 – 11 May 1949*

	USAF	RAF	CIVIL
Flights to Berlin and back	131 918	49 733	13 897
Miles flown	69 257 475	18 205 284	4 866 093
Tonnes flown in	1 101 405	255 526	79 470

(Compiled from various sources by author)

(C) *When the Russians sealed off Berlin, the Western powers had three options:*

Option	Advantages	Drawbacks
1 Ignore the Russians and drive through the blockade	• Show the Russians that the West would not bow to blackmail • At the time the Americans possessed the only atomic bombs	• Very high risk of war • Russian forces in Europe far outnumbered those of the Western allies
2 Pull out of Berlin	• Avoid any risk of war	• Loss of prestige for the Western powers • No one would trust the Americans in future to stand firm against communism
3 Supply West Berlin by air	• Less risk of war than 1 • Still show the rest of the world that the West was prepared to resist communism	• Enormously costly to supply 2 million Berliners by air • Risky operation – a daily minimum of 4000 tons of supplies was required

(D) (i) *Occupied Germany from 1945*
(ii) *Occupied Berlin*

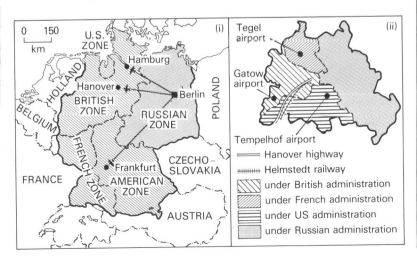

Questions

1 Carefully read the options open to the Western powers after the Russians blockaded Berlin. If you had been in a position of power at the time, which option would you have chosen? Explain your choice. (**C**)

2 Compare the extracts in (**B**). Who do they blame for the crisis? What reason does each one give for the blockade?

3 What sort of arguments might the Russians have put forward to refute the accusations made against them? (**B**)

4 Explain how Germany and Berlin were split up in 1945. (**D**)

5 Why did the Russian decision to cut off road, rail and canal links through East Germany create so many problems for the Western powers? (**D**) and (**T**)

6 Which air corridors were the Western powers able to use to break the blockade? (**D**)

7 How long did the airlift last? (**A**)

8 Talking point: The Berlin crisis marked the first time nuclear weapons were seriously considered to stop the Russians. Following the blockade American arms spending, which had been declining rapidly, increased. And for the first time in their history the Americans entered into a peacetime military alliance, NATO. Which of these results was likely to be the biggest barrier to a return to good relations between Russia and the USA?

Limited war in Korea

In the early 1950s the Cold War erupted in Asia. In 1949 China finally fell to Mao Tse-tung's communist forces after a long civil war. Chiang Kai-shek's American-backed forces were forced to flee to Taiwan (Formosa). To go with Europe's 'iron curtain', there was now an Asian 'bamboo curtain'.

Korea

Then, in 1950 communist troops from North Korea invaded South Korea in a surprise attack. The American President Truman, fearing a communist takeover, sent American troops to help the South Koreans. He also asked the United Nations to set up an international police force in the area.

Eventually 16 nations sent troops to help in this way. Led by the American, General Macarthur, the UN forces drove the North Koreans back.

In late 1950, however, the Chinese supported the North Koreans in another attack on the UN forces. The risk of a Third World War was enormous.

President Truman therefore decided to settle for a safer policy of *containment*. Under this the Korean War was fought as a 'limited' war, within a limited area and with limited non-nuclear weapons.

Eventually, in 1953, a truce was declared. In the peace settlement that followed Korea was divided along the 38th parallel, as it had been before the war started. Both sides had lost 1½ million each in the fighting.

(A) *American attitudes toward Russia, 1950*

'As you hear and read about Russia these days, do you believe Russia is trying to build herself up to be *the* ruling power of the world, or do you think Russia is just building up protection against being attacked in another war?'

	January 1950	November 1950 (after Korea)
Ruling power	70%	81%
Protection	18	9
Don't know	12	10

(Quoted in J.E. MUELLER, *Wars, Presidents and Public Opinion*)

(B) *(i) First phase of the Korean war, 1950*   *(ii) Second phase of the war, 1951*

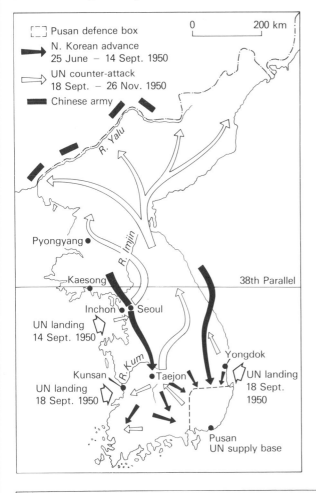

Legend:
- ⌐⌐ Pusan defence box
- N. Korean advance 25 June – 14 Sept. 1950
- ⇨ UN counter-attack 18 Sept. – 26 Nov. 1950
- Chinese army

0   200 km

R. Yalu

Pyongyang
R. Imjin
Kaesong
38th Parallel
Inchon ● ● Seoul
UN landing 14 Sept. 1950
Yongdok
Kunsan   R. Kum   ● Taejon   UN landing 18 Sept. 1950
UN landing 18 Sept. 1950
Pusan UN supply base

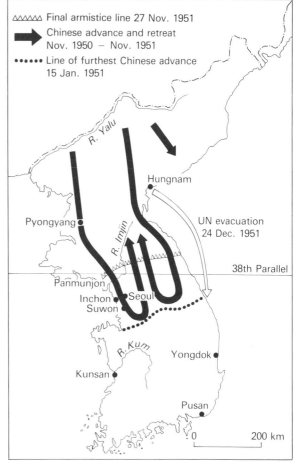

Legend:
- ᴧᴧᴧᴧ Final armistice line 27 Nov. 1951
- ➡ Chinese advance and retreat Nov. 1950 – Nov. 1951
- ●●●●● Line of furthest Chinese advance 15 Jan. 1951

R. Yalu
Hungnam
Pyongyang
R. Imjin
UN evacuation 24 Dec. 1951
38th Parallel
Panmunjon
Inchon ● ● Seoul
Suwon
R. Kum
Yongdok ●
Kunsan ●
Pusan ●
0   200 km

Questions

1   What parts of South Korea did the communists control by September 1950? (**B**)
2   Where did the UN invasion forces land in September 1950? What progress had they made by November 1950? (**B**)
3   The UN forces were sent to Korea solely to protect the South Koreans from aggression from the North. Why was it no longer possible to claim this when the UN forces invaded North Korea? (**B**)
4   Why do you think the Chinese felt threatened by the UN counter-attack into North Korea? (**B**) and (**T**)
5   When the Chinese invaded Korea, how far back did they manage to push the UN forces before they, in turn, were forced to retreat? (**B**)
6   When a final armistice line was agreed to in November 1953, how much territory had changed hands as a result of the war? (**B**)
7   What did most Americans feel about Russia in January 1950 (i.e., before the outbreak of the Korean war)? What change in attitude did the Korean war cause? (**A**)

Communist revolution in South East Asia

The end of colonialism

When the Western powers returned to South East Asia after the Second World War to reclaim their colonies, they met considerable opposition. The locals were no longer willing to accept foreign rule. Instead they wanted their independence.

In Malaya the British had to fight a long guerilla war with the communists. Even though the communists never had the support of most Malays, it still took 50 000 troops, a promise of independence and twelve long years, to crush the uprising.

The United States granted independence to the Philippines in 1946. Some American advisers however stayed to help crush some communist rebels, called the Huks.

The First Indo-Chinese War 1946–54

In 1945 the French returned to reclaim Indo-China, an area which included Laos, Cambodia and Vietnam. In Vietnam they found that the North was controlled by local communists led by Ho Chi Minh. Ho's Vietminh forces, as they were called, managed to fight off the French attack using hit and run guerilla warfare tactics. With Chinese help and the support of 80 percent of the population, they gradually wore down the French. In May 1954 the French forces were trapped at Dien Bien Phu and suffered a humiliating defeat.

In the peace settlement, known as the Geneva Agreement, Vietnam was divided into two parts – North and South. The North was ruled by Ho Chi Minh's communists. The South was ruled by an American-backed anti-communist government.

In 1954 the South-East Asian Treaty Organisation (SEATO) was formed by the USA, France, the UK, New Zealand, Thailand, Pakistan and the Philippines, to protect Asia from communism.

(A) *A Vietminh poster captured by French forces in Indo-China in 1945*

(B) *The containment of communism in South East Asia 1946–60*

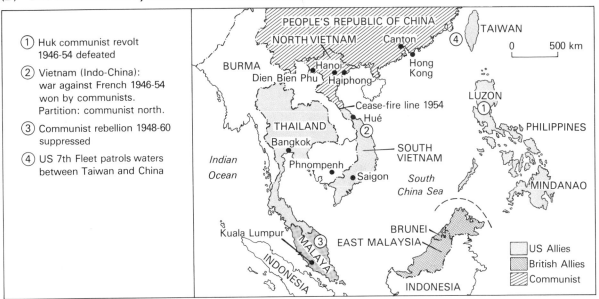

① Huk communist revolt 1946-54 defeated

② Vietnam (Indo-China): war against French 1946-54 won by communists. Partition: communist north.

③ Communist rebellion 1948-60 suppressed

④ US 7th Fleet patrols waters between Taiwan and China

(C) *In his memoirs, President Eisenhower explained what experts thought would have happened if elections had been held in South Vietnam in 1956:*

'... possibly 80 per cent of the population would have voted for the Communist Ho Chi Minh.'

(DWIGHT D. EISENHOWER, *Mandate for Change, 1953–56*, 1963)

(D) *A US Defence Department study on Vietnam described Ho Chi Minh's work:*

'... Ho was the only Vietnamese wartime leader with a national following, and he assured himself wider [support] among the Vietnamese people when in August–September, 1945, he overthrew the Japanese ... established the Democratic Republic of Vietnam, and staged receptions for incoming allied occupation forces.... For a few weeks in September, 1945, Vietnam was – for the first and only time in its modern history – free of foreign domination, and united from north to south under Ho Chi Minh....'

(Quoted in H. ZINN, *A People's History of the United States*)

Questions

1. In which parts of South East Asia were there communist uprisings following the Second World War? (**B**)
2. How did the Americans protect Taiwan from attack from communist China? (**B**)
3. Give three reasons why Ho Chi Minh was so popular among the Vietnamese people. (**D**) and (**T**)
4. Who does the soldier standing upright and the flag represent in the poster? (**A**)
5. Who does the soldier and the flag on the ground represent? (**A**)
6. What point is the poster making? (**A**)
7. Why did the Americans stop nationwide elections in South Vietnam from taking place in 1956? (**C**)
8. In 1941 the USA and Britain signed the Atlantic Charter. In it they promised to 'respect the right of all peoples to choose the form of government under which they live.'

   Did the Americans break this promise by encouraging the South Vietnamese not to hold the elections of 1956? Did they break the promise by continuing to support an unpopular South Vietnamese government with money and arms? Can an action such as this ever be justified by a government who claims to be defending the free world? Was there anything else the Americans could have done to stop the spread of communism in South East Asia?

Khrushchev and the East

Changing attitudes

When Stalin died in 1953 Russia's attitude to the West and her satellite states softened. The USSR was no longer militarily inferior to the USA. The new leaders also argued that a softer approach might win Russia more loyalty from its satellite states.

The East European countries were therefore given more freedom to run their own economies and armed forces. East European communists who had opposed Soviet rule were released from prison.

Destalinisation

In 1956 Khrushchev, in a speech to Twentieth Party Congress, openly attacked Stalin for his mistakes and crimes. When the news reached the satellites, unrest began to spread as people began to demand more freedom from Russian rule.

In Poland there were strikes, riots and demonstrations against Russian rule. To quieten the discontent, the Polish communist party appointed Wladislaw Gomulka to head the government. Gomulka had earlier been jailed by the Russians for setting up an independent communist party. The question now was whether Khrushchev would allow Gomulka to stay on. Eventually Khrushchev agreed so long as Gomulka kept Poland within the communist bloc.

In Hungary a full scale revolution led by Imre Nagy took place. Nagy promised to hold free elections and ordered Russian troops out of Hungary. This was too much for Khrushchev. Russian troops and tanks moved into Budapest and crushed the uprising. Nagy was arrested and a Soviet-backed government was installed.

(A) *During the Hungarian revolution crowds gathered to burn Soviet posters and propaganda*

B) *The Hungarians had simple methods of fighting the Soviet tanks. The Molotov cocktail was their basic anti-tank weapon:* [Russian] tanks were lured into cul-de-sacs [by the Hungarians] and then surrounded. Liquid soap was poured onto roads, so that tank tracks could not grip. Bales of silk were unrolled on the roadway and covered with oil, which sent tanks sliding hopelessly.

Freedom-fighters built dummy mines out of bricks covered with planks and rubbish; an even simpler method was to leave upturned soup plates in the road.... One road was blocked to tanks for two days by rows of upturned soup plates which were taken for anti-tank mines. Another trick was to suspend saucepans full of water from cables across the roads, which the Russians took for some sort of aerial mine....

Russian tactics were basically simple – to employ the maximum firepower against any target. If it was suspected that a sniper was hiding in a building, tank guns destroyed the building. In the last stages of the battle the Russians relied on indiscriminate terror to end resistance. Queues of housewives were shot down by machine guns; aircraft and artillery levelled buildings. When the last 30 defenders of the Kilian Barracks surrendered they were shot down as they emerged.'

(M. ORR, 'Hungary in Revolt', in *War in Peace*, 1981)

Questions

1 Whose poster is being burnt in (**A**)?
2 How did Noel Barber find Budapest on 26 October, 1956? (**C**)
3 What evidence was there that the Hungarians had put up fierce opposition to the Russian tanks? (**C**)
4 How did the Russians try to break the spirit of the revolutionaries? (**C**)
5 What evidence is there that the Hungarian revolutionaries were ill-equipped to fight a Russian invasion? (**B**)
6 What make-shift devices did the Hungarians use to halt the Russian tanks? (**B**)
7 What tactics did the Russians use to smash opposition in the cities? (**B**)
8 Talking point: Many Hungarians expected American help. Radio Free Europe, an American financed radio station in Germany, urged the Hungarians to rebel. During the revolution Dulles, the US Secretary of State, made a speech in which he congratulated the Hungarians on the way they were prepared to challenge the Red Army.

  Was it right of the Americans to encourage the Hungarians to rebel when they were not in fact prepared to give them help? Should the Americans have helped the Hungarians?

(C) *Noel Barber, Daily Mail reporter, reached Budapest on Friday 26 October 1956, three days after the first outbreaks of trouble:*

'As I moved deeper into the city, every street was smashed. Hardly a stretch of tramcar rails was left intact.... Hundreds of yards of paving stones had been torn up, the streets were littered with burnt-out cars. Even before I reached the Duna Hotel, I counted the carcasses of at least forty Soviet tanks. ... at the corner of Stalin Avenue ... two monster Russian T-54 tanks lumbered past, dragging bodies behind them, a warning to all Hungarians of what happened to the fighters....'

(Quoted in D. PRYCE-JONES, *The Hungarian Revolution*, 1969)

Khrushchev and the West

In the West 1955 marked a 'thaw' in the Cold War. The Russian, French, American and British leaders even agreed to meet at the first full-scale 'Summit Conference' for ten years. Although no one was prepared to disarm they all agreed that atomic war would be a disaster.

Peaceful co-existence

The following year Khrushchev called for peaceful co-existence between East and West. He wanted capitalist and communist countries to live side by side peacefully.

Despite the thaw, the gap between Russia and America remained huge. In America President Eisenhower and his foreign secretary, John Foster Dulles, claimed they were willing to 'go to the brink of war' to stop communism. Yet much of this talk was bluff. When Russian troops smashed the Hungarian revolt in 1956 the Americans did nothing. The risk of a nuclear war was too great.

Suez crisis

Because of the key position of the Middle East and its huge oil reserves, both the East and West were interested in that area. So in 1956 when the Egyptian leader Abdul Nasser *nationalised*, or took over the internationally-owned Suez Canal, there was a major crisis.

Britain and France were furious because the Canal carried all Western Europe's oil from the Persian Gulf. With the support of Israel they attacked Egypt. But although the attack was a military success, it quickly turned into a diplomatic disaster.

The Americans split with Britain and France and joined with the Russians in a UN demand for a ceasefire. Britain and France were then forced to withdraw and the West's influence in the Middle East fell to an all-time low. Russia's support for Egypt, on the other hand, gave her a valuable foothold in the region.

Worried by this, America began to give economic and military aid to any state threatened by communism. This policy was called the Eisenhower Doctrine.

A) *In 1956 Khrushchev surprised the West by declaring*:
The principle of peaceful co-existence is gaining ever wider international recognition.... And this is natural, for in present conditions there is no other way out. Indeed there are only two ways: either peaceful co-existence or the most destructive war in history. There is no third way.'

(Quoted in D. HEATER, *The Cold War*)

(B) *The balance of terror*:

	United States	Soviet Union
1945–8	American monopoly of nuclear weapons; United States could strike into heart of USSR by using bombers based on borders of Soviet Union	To counter the American threat large Soviet armies were kept in satellite countries to threaten Western Europe
1947	670 000 men under arms	2.8 million men under arms
1949	Stockpile 100+ atomic weapons	First Soviet atomic weapons test
1952	First H-bomb exploded	
1953	1000+ atomic and hydrogen weapons	First Soviet H-bomb exploded; 100–200 nuclear weapons; (bombers incapable of reaching USA)
1955	1300+ bombers capable of delivering nuclear weapons to USSR	350+ bombers capable of delivering nuclear weapons to USA

(C) *The effect of the Suez crisis on the Cold War*:

'The Suez incident was a bonus for the Soviet Union and little short of disaster for the West. It distracted world opinion from Hungary for a while.
... it seriously damaged Anglo-French and Western prestige in the Middle East.... Egypt and Syria turned increasingly to the Soviet Union for the arms and aid they needed, which the West was reluctant to supply. Suez gave the USSR a foothold in the Middle East.'

(C. BROWN AND P. MOONEY, *Cold War to Détente*, 1976)

Questions

1 What does Khrushchev mean by peaceful co-existence? Why do you think his speech was welcomed by people all round the world? (**A**)

2 Why does he think there was 'no other way out'? (**A**)

3 Give two reasons why the Americans enjoyed such a great lead in the arms race with Russia until the 1950s. (**B**)

4 How did the Russians try to cushion themselves against the advantages the Americans enjoyed until the mid 1950s? (**B**)

5 List three ways in which the Suez crisis benefited the Soviet Union. (**C**)

6 Talking point: Politicians on both sides of the Cold War, talk about the principle of deterrence. They say advanced nuclear weapons are necessary to preserve peace. Having the best weapons deters other nations from making war.

Sputnik and the Berlin Wall

On 4 August 1957 Americans were stunned to learn that the Russians had put into space the first man-made satellite – Sputnik 1. If the Russians were able to do this then they could also hit America with a nuclear warhead.

Khrushchev used this threat to push for more concessions from the West. In 1958 he delivered his Berlin Ultimatum, to make Berlin a demilitarised city. But the West refused to budge. If they withdrew their troops then Berlin would be absorbed into East Germany. Finally, after a lot of talk, the Russians backed down.

In 1959 Khrushchev visited the United States and talked with Eisenhower. The visit was so successful that the two leaders agreed to hold another summit meeting to be held in Paris the next year.

Two weeks before the Paris Summit started, the Russians shot down an American U-2 spy-plane over the USSR. Khrushchev asked Eisenhower to apologise for this, but Eisenhower refused. Khrushchev then stormed out and the meeting broke up.

The Berlin Wall

In 1961 Khrushchev failed to talk America's new President, John F. Kennedy, into evacuating Berlin.

In the meantime the position for the Russians in East Berlin was becoming desperate. East German skilled workers were fleeing to West Berlin in droves, seriously weakening the East German economy.

On 13 August 1961 the East Germans suddenly began building a wall across the city to divide the East from the West. At first it was roughly built of concrete slabs and rolls of barbed wire. Even so, people could not cross from one side to the other because the East German troops guarding the wall threatened to shoot. Families were split up and friends separated as the wall cut off contact between those living on either side.

Few East Berliners successfully escaped over the wall to the West. Many did not make it. Shrines on the Western side of the wall mark where they fell.

A) *The Berlin Wall today*

(B) *The U–2 affair and the Paris Summit – Time line*

1956   American U–2 spy flights begin over Russia
1960
May 1   American U–2 spy-plane is shot down over Russian airspace.
May 5   Khrushchev announces that an American plane has been shot down while flying over the USSR. (Khrushchev does not mention that the pilot Gary Powers is alive and well and so are his secret photographs.)
            At once the USA announces that a weather reconnaissance had strayed off course, probably because the pilot had blacked out.
May 7   Khrushchev says the pilot Gary Powers had been shot down 1300 miles inside Russia and Powers has admitted spying.
            In reply the USA admits the plane was indeed a spy-plane and had been grounded.
May 15   On the day before the Paris Summit is to begin, Khrushchev insists that the USA must apologise for the U–2 flights, cancel them and punish those responsible.
            Eisenhower announces that U–2 flights have been cancelled but finds other conditions unacceptable.
May 16   At the Summit meeting in Paris, Khrushchev attacks Americans and leaves Paris in a fury. The Summit is over before it has begun.

(C) *East German refugees crossing via West Berlin or across the West German border:*

1949	129 245
1950	197 788
1951	165 648
1952	182 393
1953	331 390
1954	184 198
1955	252 870
1956	279 189
1957	261 622
1958	204 092
1959	143 917
1960	199 188
1961	207 026
1962	21 356
1963	42 632
1964	41 876

- The Berlin Wall was built in August 1961
- The total East German population in 1949 was 17 500 000
- Between 1949 and 30 June 1961, a total of 2 600 000 refugees left East Germany via West Berlin or across the West German border

---

Questions

1 What obstacles would an East German have to overcome to escape to West Berlin today? (**A**)
2 What was   a) the lowest number and   b) the highest number of East German refugees to cross into West Germany between 1949 and 1961? (**C**)
3 Approximately what percentage of the 1949 population left East Germany between 1949 and 1961? (**C**)
4 The East German government claimed the wall was built to stop Western spies and saboteurs from crossing into the East. Do you agree? If not why do you think the wall was built? (**T**)
5 How were the Americans made to look ridiculous in the U–2 affair? (**B**)
6 Who do you think was responsible for the break up of the Paris Summit? Explain. (**B**) and (**T**)

The Cuban missile crisis

Until the mid 1950s Cuba was a poor sugar-producing island state ruled by a right-wing dictatorship. Much of Cuba's land and industry was American-owned. In fact the whole country was closely tied to the United States.

In 1959 a young left-wing lawyer, Fidel Castro, seized power. In an early move to destroy America's stranglehold over the economy he *nationalised* all the American-owned sugar plantations and mills. When the United States hit back by cutting off Cuban sugar imports, Castro turned to Russia for trade and aid.

Bay of Pigs

In early 1961, soon after taking office, President Kennedy approved a plan to invade Cuba and overthrow Castro. In April, a small army of anti-Castro refugees were landed at the Bay of Pigs. The attack was a total failure: the invaders were killed or captured on the beaches.

The missile crisis

On 14 October 1962 an American high-flying U–2 took photos of Russian nuclear missile sites on Cuba. President Kennedy was horrified. Cuba was only 90 miles from Florida. Virtually every major American city was a possible target.

Kennedy demanded that Russia remove the missiles from Cuba. To stop any more being shipped to Cuba, Kennedy ordered the US navy to place Cuba under a naval blockade or 'quarantine'. All Russian ships heading for Cuba were to be turned back. At the same time America's armed forces were placed on full alert.

Everyone now waited with bated breath to see what the Russians would do. What would happen when the Russian ships which were on their way to Cuba reached the blockade? To everyone's relief the ships slowed down, stopped and then turned back. A short time later Khrushchev agreed to withdraw the missiles. In return the United States promised never to invade Cuba.

A) *The Cuban missile crisis 1962: Soviet weaponry on Cuba*

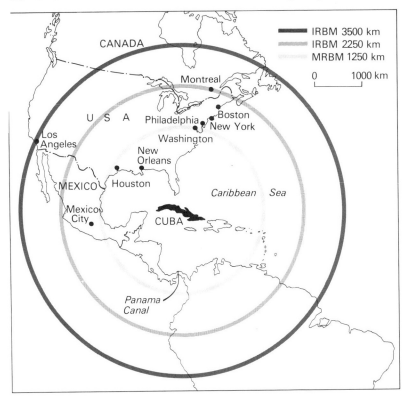

- 12 IRBMs: Intermediate range ballistic missiles with a range of over 4000 kilometres (2500 miles)
- 40 MRBMs: Medium range ballistic missiles with a range of over 1600 kilometres (1000 miles)
- 140 SAMs: Surface to Air Missiles
- 40 Jet Bombers
- 42 Mig–21 fighters
- 20 000 Russian personnel

(B) *To the brink and back*

On hearing that there were missile bases on Cuba, President Kennedy called a meeting of the Executive Committee of the National Security Council to advise him on what action to take. The options which this group discussed are set out below.

Option

(1) Do nothing. Let the Russians keep their bases on Cuba.

(2) Bring diplomatic pressures and warnings to bear on the Soviets.

(3) Negotiate directly with Castro.

(4) Place a naval blockade around Cuba.

(5) Stage an airstrike against the missile bases.

(6) Invade Cuba, seize the missile bases in a surprise landing.

Questions

1 What major American cities were in range of the Soviet a) MRBMs b) IRBMs? (**A**)

2 What was the purpose of the American quarantine? (**A**) and (**T**)

3 Kennedy called the Russian missiles offensive weapons. Khrushchev called them defensive weapons. Which do you think they were? Explain.

4 List a) the advantages and b) the drawbacks of each of the options Kennedy had to consider. (**B**)

5 List the options Kennedy faced. Which, in your opinion, involved a) a high risk of nuclear war b) a medium risk of nuclear war and c) a low risk of nuclear war? (**B**)

6 If you had been Kennedy, which of the options would you have taken? Say why. (**B**)

7 Who was to blame for the Cuban missile crisis? Was it the Russians or the Americans? Explain. (**A**) and (**T**)

8 Who deserves the credit for avoiding a nuclear war? Give reasons.

9 Who won the Cuban missile crisis? Was it Kennedy? Was it Khrushchev, or was it a draw? Explain.

10 Talking point: 'They talk about who won and who lost. Human reason won. Mankind won.' (Khrushchev on the Cuban missile crisis) What did Khrushchev mean? Do you agree with him? How can a crisis like the Cuban affair be avoided?

Improved relations and the Czech crisis

The Cuban missile crisis was a turning point in the Cold War. A nuclear war had only just been avoided. Ever since then both sides have made great efforts to avoid another direct confrontation.

To reduce the chances of an accidental war arising because of poor communication, a 'hotline' or telephone link was set up in 1963 between Moscow and Washington. In the same year a partial test ban treaty was signed by the USSR, the USA and the UK. The three powers agreed to ban all nuclear tests, except those carried out underground. Over 100 countries have since signed the treaty.

The Middle East

The hotline soon proved its use, in the 1967 Arab–Israeli War. In the build up beforehand, Russia had supplied arms to the Arabs while the USA armed the Israelis. Yet when the war broke out Russia and the USA used the hotline to stop the war escalating into another 'Cuban missile crisis'.

Both great powers kept in close contact again in 1974 when a fourth Arab–Israeli war erupted. This time the two superpowers used their influence to force the Arabs and Israelis to make peace.

But, although the Cold War had seemed to thaw in the mid-sixties the underlying fear and distrust remained.

Czechoslovakia

In 1968 the West was rocked when Russian and other Warsaw Pact troops invaded Czechoslovakia. The invasion ended a plan by the Czechoslovakian government under Alexander Dubcek to give Czechs more freedom. Dubcek wanted to give communism 'a human face' by giving Czechs the right to write and speak their minds. Czechs, under his reforms, would even be free to criticise the communist party.

This was just too much for the Russians. If the reforms spread, then the whole of Eastern Europe would be endangered. During the invasion Dubcek was arrested. Czechoslovakia returned to Russia's brand of communism.

(A) *Launching a nuclear attack from the United States*

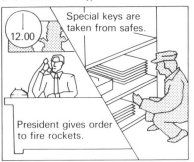

12.00 — Special keys are taken from safes.

President gives order to fire rockets.

12.01 — Keys inserted in missile computers.

Computers now in complete charge of rockets.

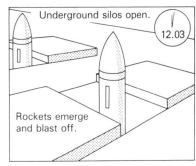

Underground silos open. 12.03

Rockets emerge and blast off.

(B) *Distribution of nuclear forces between the Soviet Union and the United States in 1970*

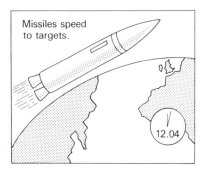

Missiles speed to targets.

12.04

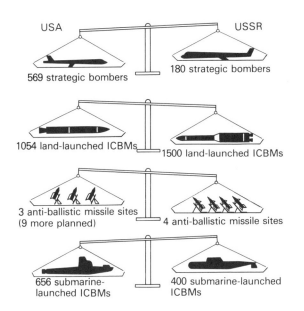

USA — USSR

569 strategic bombers — 180 strategic bombers

1054 land-launched ICBMs — 1500 land-launched ICBMs

3 anti-ballistic missile sites (9 more planned) — 4 anti-ballistic missile sites

656 submarine-launched ICBMs — 400 submarine-launched ICBMs

Questions

1 According to the diagram, describe how the president of the USA would launch a nuclear attack. (**A**)
2 How does the diagram highlight the usefulness of having a hotline linking the USA and Russia? (**A**) and (**T**)
3 Explain why Russia invaded Czechoslovakia in August 1968. (**T**)
4 Imagine you are a Czechoslovakian, write a letter describing how you feel about the Russian invasion, to a friend in America.
5 According to the diagram (**B**) which of the following best describes the state of the nuclear arms race in 1970:
   a) Russia was well ahead
   b) the USA was well ahead
   c) both sides were roughly equal.
   Explain your choice.
6 Talking point: 'We will learn to live together like brothers or we will perish like fools' (Martin Luther King). Discuss.

The Vietnam War 1954–75

At the Geneva Peace Settlement of 1954, Vietnam was split into two parts – the North ruled by Ho Chi Minh's communists and the South under a right-wing government backed by the Americans.

American aid

American money, arms and other aid were pumped into South Vietnam as part of a plan to contain the communists. But much of the aid ended up in the pockets of corrupt politicians. Very little was seen in the countryside by the peasants who made up the vast majority of the population. In fact many peasants supported local communist guerillas called the Vietcong.

As more and more ordinary Vietnamese turned to the communists, the Americans became more deeply involved. Under President Kennedy, the number of American troops and advisers had increased to 15 500 by 1963. But still the Vietcong, supplied by North Vietnam, were winning.

Escalation

Under President Johnson the number of Americans in Vietnam *escalated* or increased dramatically. In 1965 there were 60 000. Three years later there were 500 000. Some of America's allies, South Korea, Thailand, Australia and New Zealand, also sent small numbers of troops. To cut off the flow of arms to the Vietcong, the US airforce constantly bombed Hanoi and other parts of North Vietnam.

Nevertheless the attacks on the South continued to increase. With aid from Russia and China, the Vietcong had enough strength to carry on for years. In the United States too, there were massive anti-war protests. So in May 1968 President Johnson started peace talks and then President Nixon started to gradually withdraw American troops. Finally in 1973 a cease-fire was signed and the remaining US soldiers returned home.

Without American support, the South Vietnamese had little chance. By 1975 South Vietnam, Laos and Cambodia had been overrun by communist forces.

(A) *The bombing*

'By the end of the Vietnam war seven million tons of bombs had been dropped on Vietnam, more than twice the total bombs dropped on Europe and Asia in World War II – almost one 500 pound bomb for every human being in Vietnam. It was estimated there were 20 million bomb craters in the country.'

(H. ZINN, *A People's History of the United States*, 1980)

(B) *Burned by a misdirected firebomb, children flee down a road in South Vietnam, 1972*

(C) *Changes in American public support for the Vietnam war*

'In August 1965, 61 percent of the population thought the American involvement in Vietnam was not wrong.
By May 1971 it was exactly reversed; 61 percent thought ... involvement was wrong.'

(H. ZINN, *A People's History of the United States*, 1980)

(D) *US Forces committed to South Vietnam 1962–72*

1962	9000
1963	15 000
1964	16 000
1965	60 000
1966	268 000
1967	449 000
1968	535 000
1969	539 000
1970	415 000
1971	239 000
1972	47 000

(*War in Peace*, 1981)

(E) *Vietnam war dead*

United States	50 000
South Vietnam (troops and civilians)	400 000
North Vietnamese and Vietcong	900 000

Questions

1 In what year did the number of US forces in Vietnam suddenly increase? (**D**)

2 In what year did the number of American troops in Vietnam reach its peak? What caused the number of troops to drop after 1968? (**D**) and (**T**)

3 How many people died in Vietnam? Which side suffered the heaviest losses? (**E**)

4 What impressions do these figures leave you of the bombing of Vietnam? (**A**)

5 Thousands of pictures were shot of the horrors of the Vietnam war, yet (**B**) is a picture which has remained in many people's minds. Can you suggest why?

6 Describe and try to explain the change in American support for the Vietnam war between 1965 and 1971? (**C**)

7 How would this change have made it difficult for American presidents to continue with the war?

8 Talking point: The Vietnam war has been called America's single biggest post-war mistake. It has been called 'the wrong war, in the wrong place, at the wrong time'. Do you agree? What does Vietnam tell us about the limits of what a superpower can do?

The Sino–Soviet split

Following the Chinese communist takeover in 1949, Russia and China became friends. In 1950 they signed a treaty of friendship and, over the next few years, Russia helped China rebuild her shattered economy.

The split

But when Khrushchev succeeded Stalin in 1956 the relationship soured. Mao despised Khrushchev and his policy of peaceful co-existence with the West. Mao, it seemed, still wanted a violent revolution to overthrow capitalism.

The rift widened further in 1959 when the Soviets refused to supply the Chinese with the nuclear weapons secrets they had earlier promised. Soon afterwards Russia cut all aid to China.

Since then the Sino–Soviet split has continued to widen. When China attacked India in 1962, Russia sided with India. In the Indo–Pakistan war of 1965, Russia backed India while China sided with Pakistan. Border clashes erupted in 1962 and 1969. To make matters even more tense, the Chinese exploded their first atomic bomb in 1964 and their first hydrogen bomb in 1967.

Sino–American détente

As the Sino–Soviet gap widened, the gulf between the Chinese and the Americans began to close. In China's eyes the United States was not such a threat – especially since its defeat in Vietnam.

For the Americans the Sino–Soviet split was a piece of good luck. No longer was there a single united communist bloc to face up to. In fact it was now in America's interests to become friends with the Chinese. So in 1971 the United States allowed China to be admitted to the United Nations. In 1972 President Nixon became the first American president to visit Red China. Following this, trade and travel restrictions were relaxed. In 1979 full diplomatic relations between the United States and China were established.

The Strength of the Giants

	Size	Industry	Wealth	Population	Military strength	Total	Ranking
USA	7						
USSR	17						
CHINA	7						

(A) *The strength of the giants (1974)*

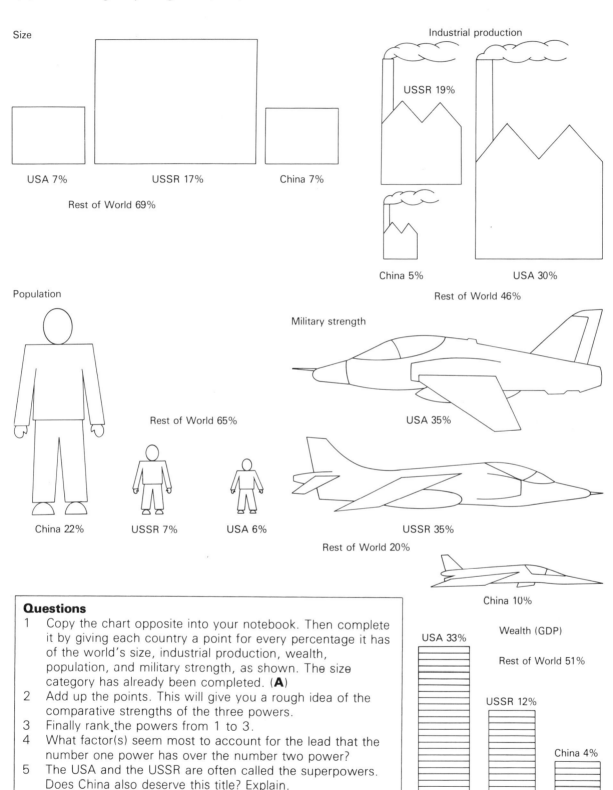

Size

USA 7%   USSR 17%   China 7%

Rest of World 69%

Industrial production

USSR 19%

China 5%   USA 30%

Rest of World 46%

Population

Rest of World 65%

China 22%   USSR 7%   USA 6%

Military strength

USA 35%

USSR 35%

Rest of World 20%

China 10%

Wealth (GDP)

USA 33%

Rest of World 51%

USSR 12%

China 4%

Questions

1   Copy the chart opposite into your notebook. Then complete it by giving each country a point for every percentage it has of the world's size, industrial production, wealth, population, and military strength, as shown. The size category has already been completed. (**A**)
2   Add up the points. This will give you a rough idea of the comparative strengths of the three powers.
3   Finally rank the powers from 1 to 3.
4   What factor(s) seem most to account for the lead that the number one power has over the number two power?
5   The USA and the USSR are often called the superpowers. Does China also deserve this title? Explain.

Détente and beyond

Soviet–American relations

For most of the 1970s, Soviet–American relations steadily improved. There were a number of reasons for this:

(1) *Arms*. The Russians and Americans were roughly equal in nuclear weapons. Both sides had enough nuclear weapons to destroy each other and the rest of the world many times over. It seemed commonsense to both sides to try to bring the arms race under control.

(2) *Complex world*. The world no longer divided neatly into two camps dominated by the Americans and Russians. China had split with the Russians. Japan had risen since the war to become the third largest industrial power. The Middle East countries with their oil wealth demanded a greater say in world affairs.

(3) *Limitations*. During this period the superpowers seemed to accept that there were limits to what even they could achieve. The Americans were defeated in Vietnam. Russia had to trade with the West to get enough food to feed its people.

The better relations between East and West led to limited agreements on nuclear weapons. In 1968 the superpowers and a number of other countries signed a Nuclear Non-Proliferation Treaty. Then in 1969, the Russians and Americans began a series of Strategic Arms Limitation Talks (SALT) to limit the output of nuclear weapons. In 1972 the second treaty, SALT II, was drawn up though it was still unsigned in 1981.

The end of détente

In the late 1970s American critics of détente began to accuse Russia of playing on America's goodwill in order to race ahead in the arms race. SALT II was therefore quietly shelved.

Relationships between Russia and America became even worse when Russia invaded Afghanistan in 1979. President Reagan's election in the following year showed that the Americans were in favour of his tougher policy towards Russia.

(A) *Effect of impact of a 10 megaton nuclear strike*

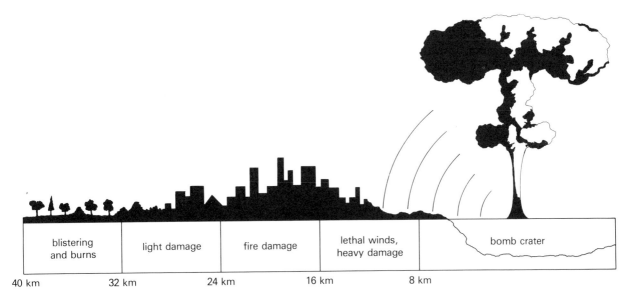

| blistering and burns | light damage | fire damage | lethal winds, heavy damage | bomb crater |

40 km   32 km   24 km   16 km   8 km

(B) *NATO and the Warsaw Pact*

	NATO	Warsaw Pact
Combat troops	1 170 000 of which 300 000 American	1 255 000 of which 715 000 Russian
Tanks	10 000	26 500
Aircraft	2848	5255
Nuclear warheads	7000	3500 (all in Soviet hands)

Questions

1. How many a) combat troops b) tanks c) aircraft d) nuclear warheads are there in NATO compared to the Warsaw Pact? (**B**)
2. Name in which areas a) both sides are roughly equal b) NATO is clearly superior c) the Warsaw Pact is clearly superior. (**B**)
3. What additional information would you need before you could calculate with any accuracy which side would be likely to win if a war broke out?
4. Some military experts say that in a conventional (non-nuclear) war, NATO forces would be quickly overrun because of lack of men and equipment and then they would be forced to use nuclear weapons. What evidence is there in the figures to support this theory?
5. Is this a good position for NATO to be in? What could be done to overcome this problem?
6. Using a local map and diagram (**A**), work out the effect a 10 megaton nuclear strike would have on your local area. Take your school as the centre of the blast.
7. Talking point: 'Better Red than Dead'. Do you agree?

Index

Acknowledgements

The author and publishers
wish to thank the following
who have kindly given
permission for the use of
copyright material:

Edward Arnold (Publishers)
Ltd for a table from *Years of
Change* by R. Wolfson;
Associated Book Publishers
Ltd for extracts from *A
History of the German
Republic* by A. Rosenburg;
*Mussolini and the Rise of
Italian Fascism* by R.N.L.
Absolom, and *The Cold War*
by I. Lister, published by
Methuen London Ltd; The
Balkin Agency on behalf of
Howard Zinn for extracts
from *A People's History of
the United States* © Howard
Zinn; J. M. Dent & Sons Ltd
for an extract from *The
Hundred Days to Hitler* by R.
Manvell and H. Frankel;
Fabian Society for an extract
from *Soviet Communism* by
S. and B. Webb; Granada
Publishing Ltd for extracts
from *The Russian Revolution*
by Lionel Kochan and *Stalin*
by H. Montgomery Hyde;
Guardian Newspapers Ltd for
an extract from the *Guardian*;
The Harvester Press Ltd for a
table from *China The People's
Republic* by J. Chesneaux;
A.M. Heath & Company Ltd
on behalf of Barbara Tuchman
for an extract from *August
1914*, published by Constable

& Co. Ltd; Heinemann Publishers (NZ) Ltd for a quote by historian Eric Goldman, reproduced in *The American Deal* by M. Bassett; David Higham Associates Ltd on behalf of A.J.P. Taylor for extracts from *How Wars Begin; The War Lords*; and *Revolutions and Revolutionaries*; Holt, Rinehart & Winston, CBS Publishing for part of table 18 from *Economic Systems in Action* by Alfred Oxenfelt and Vsevolod Holubnychy; Longman Group Ltd for extracts from *Notes on European History* by Teresa Lawrence, and *The Making of Russia* by Joan Hasler; Macmillan Publishing Co. Inc. for extracts from *Perspectives on the European Past* by G.A. Craig; *Past to Present: A World History*, Revised Edition, by S.H. Zebel and S. Schwartz, and *After the Crash* by John Rublowsky; Orbis Publishing Ltd for an extract from *War in Peace* by Michael Orr; Prentice-Hall, Inc., New Jersey, for an extract and data from *The Soviet Union* by Vadim Medish, © 1981; Random House, Inc. for the poem 'Merry-Go-Round' from *Selected Poems of Langston Hughes*; Martin Secker & Warburg Ltd for an extract from *The Great Fear* by David Caute; D. Mack Smith for an extract from *Italy* published by Michigan University Press; Stanford University Press for an extract from *The Bolshevik Revolution* by J. Bunyan and H.H. Fisher; Thames & Hudson Ltd for extracts from *The Soviet Achievement* by J.P. Nettl, and *The Chinese Revolution* by T. Mende; The University of Chicago Press Ltd for an extract from *The Perils of Prosperity* by W.E. Leuchtenberg; John Wiley & Sons, Inc. for extracts from *War Presidents and Public Opinion* by J. E. Mueller.

The author and publishers wish to acknowledge the following photograph sources:

Associated Newspapers Group p. 199; Associated Press pp. 147, 217; BBC Hulton Picture Library pp. 5, 35 bottom, 37 right, 43, 49, 59 left, 61 left & bottom right, 85, 89 top, 97 left, 105 bottom, 141, 161, 165, 175, 179, 207; Bilderdienst Suddeutscher Verlag pp. 47, 51; Bundesbildstelle Bonn p. 211; Camera Press pp. 167, 193; Cartoon by Sir David Low by permission of the Low Estate and the *Evening Standard* pp. 71, 77; *China Pictorial* pp. 186, 191 bottom; Christchurch Teacher College p. 113; Courtesy Falker Eusebio Arronatequi p. 80; Culver Pictures Inc p. 133 bottom; *Daily Mirror* p. 87 bottom; *Detroit News* p. 131; Franklin D. Roosevelt Lib/UPI p. 133 top; John Gittings p. 191 top; John Hillelson Agency pp. 154, 169; Historical Picture Service, Chicago pp. 127, 135; Imperial War Museum pp. 13, 19, 24, 25, 54, 57 left, 89 bottom; Institute of Contemporary History & Weiner Library pp. 57 right, 61 top right; Keystone Press Agency pp. 45, 59 right, 107 top left, 119, 177, 181; Library of Congress pp. 137, 145; London Express News and Features Service p. 53 left; Lords Gallery p. 35 top; Mansell Collection pp. 33, 39 left, 97 right, 99, 107 top right & bottom; MORO p. 37 left; Museum of the City of New York p. 129; Novosti Press Agency p. 95; Popperfoto pp. 41 left, 149, 159, 171, 185, 195; *Punch* pp. 15 left, 17, 21 left, 63, 79, 87 top; Institute of Social History, Amsterdam p. 65; William Sewell/Weidenfeld & Nicolson Archives p. 183; Ally Sloper's Half Holiday/Caligari p. 9; Snark International p. 204; Roger Viollet p. 173.

The publishers have made every effort to trace copyright holders, but if they have inadvertently overlooked any they will be pleased to make the necessary arrangements at the first opportunity.